# Preface

The European Community has formally committed itself to the aim of setting up a single market without frontiers by 1992. Because of its size, this common area of real economic and social unity—the most extensive in the world—will be a vital asset to us in our task of getting our industries back on their feet and making them competitive. It will provide new opportunities for each and every citizen of the Community and will be a main motor of European union.

Europe is a region of trade, but even more so of exchange between citizens. Freedom of movement is, in the highest sense, a matter of persons and ideas. It implies the right to exercise one's occupational or professional activity anywhere in Europe—for firms, professions and wage-earners alike.

This right has already become a reality; it must go further still. Such is the intention of the Single European Act which came into force on 1 July 1987 and which gives the Community the institutional resources for the setting up of a single market by 1992.

To achieve that objective it is essential that the Member States show political will. The Commission, on its part, is already well embarked upon the attainment of these new ambitions.

Jacques Delors
President of the Commission
of the European Communities

COMMISSION OF THE EUROPEAN COMMUNITIES

# A guide to working in a Europe without frontiers

by Jean-Claude Séché

Preface by Jacques Delo



DOCUMENT

# Notice

'A guide to working in a Europe without frontiers' is the first in a series of documents which set out to provide European citizens with comprehensive information on this subject. It is designed to contribute to public debate on European integration. Neither the Commission of the European Communities nor any person acting on its behalf is responsible for the use made of the information contained in the publication.

This series of documents will be updated and added to at regular intervals.

Further information can be obtained from the Commission of the European Communities, Division IX/E/3 – JECL 2/94, 200 rue de la Loi, B-1049 Brussels.

This publication is also available in:

ES ISBN 92-825-8063-6
DA ISBN 92-825-8064-4
DE ISBN 92-825-8065-2
GR ISBN 92-825-8066-0
FR ISBN 92-825-8068-7
IT ISBN 92-825-8069-5
NL ISBN 92-825-8070-9
PT ISBN 92-825-8071-7

Cataloguing data appear at the end of this publication.

The author would like to thank his colleagues in the Commission departments who helped draw up the guide. In particular he expresses his gratitude to Madame Juana Ruiz for producing the annexes and consolidating the instruments they contain.

Luxembourg: Office for Official Publications of the European Communities, 1988

ISBN 92-825-8067-9

Catalogue number: CB-PP-88-004-EN-C



*Printed in Belgium*

# Contents

# Introduction

You are a national of one of the Member States of the European Economic Community (Federal Republic of Germany, Belgium, Denmark, Spain, France, Greece, Ireland, Italy, Luxembourg, Netherlands, Portugal and the United Kingdom) and wish to exercise an activity in a Member State other than your own.

The aim of the guide is simply to familiarize you with relevant Community legislation and make the official instruments more accessible,[1] by giving you a picture of the present situation.

In a White Paper addressed to the European Council[2] the Commission spelled out the measures it considered necessary to set up an area without internal frontiers by 31 December 1992. In particular the Commission considers that Community citizens should be free to practise their occupation throughout the Community if they so wish without any formalities which could in the final analysis discourage them. Accordingly the Commission advocates the mutual recognition of diplomas without any prior harmonization of the conditions of access to occupations and their exercise.

## Your rights

The European Community is a Community governed by law where you enjoy rights as a national of a Member State. As a migrant, you are entitled to freedom of movement, one of the basic principles of the common market (Article 3(c) of the EEC Treaty) which is based on equal treatment with nationals of the host country. In other words you cannot be discriminated against on the grounds of nationality (Article 7 of the EEC Treaty). The host country must respect all the implications of this principle.

In return you are legitimately subject to the same obligations as nationals in the host country. You have a duty to prepare for this, mainly through some form of training. The Community is making a contribution, particularly through implementation of the European Community action scheme for the mobility of university students (Erasmus).

## How to exercise your rights

There are several ways open to you:

### National courts

There are no 'Community' courts in the Member States to ensure that Community law is observed by the national authorities. The Treaty left this task to the national courts which must in the case of conflict between national and Community law give precedence to the latter. You are therefore entitled to request the authorities in the Member State in which you are resident to apply Community law and in the case of refusal you may bring the matter before the competent national court as you would if it concerned the law of that country.

You can request the national court to submit to the Court of Justice of the European Communities matters concerning interpretation or the validity of Community law brought before it if a decision on this point is necessary before the court can rule (Article 177 of the EEC Treaty).

---

[1] See also Digest of texts concerning entry and residence, and the guide concerning rights and duties in respect of social security, published by the Office for Official Publications of the European Communities.

[2] See Annex 1bis.

The fact that the national courts are competent means that you cannot in normal circumstances bring a case directly to the Court of Justice. Nevertheless the Court makes sure that the Member States meet their obligations and watches over the action of other Community institutions to ensure it is in conformity with Community law (Council of Ministers and Commission) for cases can be brought before it by a national court or a Community institution depending on the situation.

### Commission of the European Communities

Without having a monopoly, it is the Commission's task to monitor application of Community legislation and to implement the necessary means to ensure that infringements of this law are penalized. Accordingly, it is vigilant as regards the identification, prevention and prosecution of infringements which may, if necessary, lead to an action before the Court of Justice.

You can usefully help the Commission in this task by bringing to its notice any cases of infringement of Community law that come to your attention by lodging a complaint to the Secretariat General of the Commission of the European Communities, 1049 Brussels, Belgium.

### European Parliament

The Community is encouraged to carry out its monitoring role by questions put by Members of the European Parliament. You may approach one of them and call his attention to a problem which he will submit to the Commission, the Council and possibly the national authorities concerned.

The European Parliament has also organized a system for the examination of petitions which can be sent to it at one of the following addresses:
(i) European Centre, Luxembourg;
(ii) 97/113 rue Belliard, 1040 Brussels;
(iii) Avenue de l'Europe, Strasbourg.

### National organizations

Since you are entitled to become established in a Member State other than your own and to be treated on an equal footing with nationals of that country, an effective method for safeguarding your rights is for you to approach nationals who are members of organizations (associations, trade unions, insurance funds, political parties, members of parliament and local representatives) who will assist you with any administrative and legal questions.

In some cases information services have been set up in the host country.[3] They may be able to assist you in your first steps. You can obtain the address from the Commission or national authorities.

## Living as a foreigner in the host country

Although European citizens have rights and obligations, their true European citizenship is not yet a fact. Although the Community seeks to establish equal treatment in the fullest sense between nationals of

[3] See p. 20.

Member States and persons in the host country, migrants are not yet on a fully equal footing with nationals. You may not be eligible for certain posts in the public service, your right of residence is not absolute, you are not usually entitled to vote in elections and your military obligations are determined by your country of origin.

Rules governing the nationality of physical persons are not within the competence of the Communities, but rest solely with the Member States, subject to any international agreements they may have concluded. Therefore, you would be well advised to take careful note of the position concerning your own nationality and that of your family in both the country of origin and the host country, and the choices left open to you. Some Member States accept dual nationality which eliminates all difficulties. Others do not—acquisition of the nationality of the host country would integrate you fully but the possible loss of the nationality of your country of origin would make it more difficult for you to reintegrate should you wish to return.

You should contact your consulate in the host country and if necessary an immigrants' association set up by your compatriots.

## Equal treatment and harmonization of legislation

The principle of equal treatment implies that you will be subject, like nationals of the host country, to the obligations laid down by the legislation of that country which in itself is not discriminatory.

However, observance of this obligation could nevertheless constitute an insurmountable obstacle. For example, if you are required to possess a diploma issued in the host country, you cannot meet this condition if for access to the same profession you hold a diploma issued in your country of origin. In the absence of recognized equivalence in the host country, you may be required to re-take an examination or even recommence your studies. It is to eliminate such non-discriminatory obstacles that the Community institutions seek to harmonize national legislation concerning access to and practice of the professions with a view to facilitating the exercise of freedom of movement in practice.

A description of the equal treatment arrangements from which you may benefit (I) is followed by the measures concerning the harmonization of legislation (II). In the Annex you will find the most significant pieces of Community legislation of interest to you.

# I. Equal treatment in the host country

Your freedom of movement in the Community covers the right to take up an occupational activity, the granting of social rights and benefits and the right of residence in the host country.

## A. Occupational activity

As a citizen of a Member State of the Community, you have the right to pursue an occupational activity in any Member State of the Community under the same conditions as nationals of the host country.

Except where expressly provided for in the Treaty, this principle covers all occupational activities, including those of a sporting or artistic nature where they are paid.

A distinction should, however, be made according to whether you are an employed person (Article 48 of the EEC Treaty) or a self-employed person (Articles 52 and 59 of the Treaty).

### *1. Employment*

Equal treatment in respect of freedom of movement for workers is an essential element of Community social legislation.

**Eligibility for employment**

If you are an employed person, there can be no discrimination against you on the grounds of your nationality from the point of view of eligibility for employment.[4] Regulation (EEC) No 1612/68 sets aside not only the requirement of a work permit, but also provisions or practices which:

(a) limit or restrict the advertising of vacancies in the press or through any other medium or subject it to conditions other than those applicable, in respect of the employment of nationals, to employers pursuing their activities in the territory of the host State;

(b) subject eligibility for employment to conditions of registration with employment offices or impede recruitment of individual workers, where persons who do not reside in the territory of that State are concerned;

(c) restrict by number or percentage the employment of foreign nationals in any undertaking, branch of activity or region, or at national level.

Member States do, however, have the right, if they wish, to reserve certain posts in the public service for their own nationals (Article 48(4)). Such posts are connected with the specific activities of the public service in so far as it is entrusted with the exercise of powers conferred by public law and with responsibility for safeguarding the general interests of the State. It is of little importance whether the person concerned has been taken on as a manual worker, a member of salaried staff or an official or whether his employment relationship is governed by public or private law. The nature of the activity is, however, the decisive factor:

(i) posts in the judiciary, police, armed forces or diplomatic service, as well as those of architects or supervisors in the administration, may be reserved for nationals;

(ii) you are, however, eligible for employment as a doctor, nurse or nursery nurse, for example, without discrimination on grounds of nationality;

(iii) some cases, such as teachers, have not yet been finally resolved.

[4] As regards Spain and Portugal, freedom of movement for workers will take effect only from 1993.

### Working conditions

Your terms of employment (professional qualifications, pay, conditions governing dismissal and trade union membership) are the same as those for nationals (Regulation (EEC) No 1612/68).

In particular, you have the right to vote for and be elected to bodies representing workers within the undertaking, although only nationals may be elected to administrative and managerial bodies.

## *2. Self-employed activities*

If you are either the head of an undertaking or if you have opted for a self-employed occupation (doctor, architect, consultant engineer, etc.) you may also pursue your activity in any Member State. You may do this on either a permanent (right of establishment) or temporary (provision of services) basis.

### Right of establishment (Article 52 of the EEC Treaty)

First, you may establish yourself permanently in the host country in order to pursue an economic activity

(i) either as a principal activity, by transferring your activity in its entirety or setting up and managing an undertaking in a country other than your own, which includes acquiring or taking control of an existing undertaking;

(ii) or as a secondary activity, by setting up an agency, branch or subsidiary (or, in the case of liberal professions, a second office); your company also has this right (Article 58 of the EEC Treaty) if its registered office is in a Member State, even if it is controlled by nationals of non-member countries, provided however that where its official registered office is in a non-member country its principal place of business is actually in the Community.

You have the right to take up and pursue activities as self-employed persons under the same conditions as nationals.

If nationals are unable to pursue a particular activity because it is prohibited (drug trafficking) or reserved for the State or a public undertaking holding a monopoly, then you are also not entitled to pursue such activity.

If, however, it is authorized, you are also entitled to pursue it, subject to any national regulations applicable to nationals in this area.

There is only one reservation set out in the Treaty concerning activities which in the host State are connected with the exercise of official authority (Article 55 of the EEC Treaty). The scope of this exception is, in fact, very limited: without being able to exclude nationals of other Member States from carrying on a profession, a Member State could, for example, in the case of a lawyer, reserve for its own nationals the ability to make up the complement of a court (where it sits with a number of judges) or, in the case of a notary, the ability to authenticate signatures on a document.

Subject to this reservation, your rights and obligations are the same: you cannot be required to produce a foreign traders' or professional licence; taxation,[5] social security contributions, real estate, intellectual property, right to invest,[6] to bring actions before national courts and to join professional organizations. However, you must also possess the professional qualification attested by a diploma, certificate or other evidence of formal qualification awarded by the host State or recognized as equivalent by that State.

---

[5] Subject to the application of any international agreements.

[6] For the transfer of funds, see p. 16.

**Freedom to provide services (Article 59 of the EEC Treaty)**

Secondly, you may pursue your economic activity in a State other than that in which you are permanently established, from your principal or secondary place of business in the Community.

This right is currently restricted only in the field of transport, for which the required Community directives (Article 61 of the EEC Treaty) have not yet established complete freedom to provide services.

Three situations may arise:

(i) you travel within the host country on a temporary basis to provide services: you visit a sick person on the other side of the frontier or you go there to have a machine repaired;

(ii) or, your patient may come to your surgery for a consultation, or your customer may come to you to have his machine repaired: in this case it is the person to whom the service is addressed who moves. In both these cases, the provision of services involves movement of persons;

(iii) in a third instance, however, there is no movement by either the person providing the service or the recipient: for example, you sell an insurance policy to an insured person living in a country other than that in which your company is established, perhaps to insure property situated in a third country.

With freedom to provide services, your legal situation is more complex than in the case of freedom of establishment. Your activity is governed by at least two sets of national regulations, those of the country in which you are established and those of one or more other countries involved: that of the recipient, that of the person providing services or, in the case of the insurance policy, the country where the insured property is located.

Compliance with the laws of the country in which you are established should normally be sufficient, provided they are comparable with those of the host country. However, the Court of Justice has largely acknowledged the obligation to observe the laws of the other country or countries involved as well, provided, of course, that there is no discrimination on grounds of nationality. For example, there is nothing to prevent a Member State which prohibits television advertising on its territory from extending such a ban to advertising originating from another Member State. Similarly, in the insurance sector, notwithstanding controls over undertakings in the country of establishment, prior control over all activities connected with the provision of services are justified on the grounds of the protection of consumers as policy holders and insured persons. It is for the State in which these services are provided to grant and withdraw the necessary authorization. Of course, these are constraints which hinder the effective exercise of freedom to provide services. Only coordination of laws at Community level is likely to overcome them.

## B. Social and political rights

Equal treatment allows you to enjoy rights and benefits of all kinds granted to nationals to the extent required for your integration in the host country. For this reason, you are granted a wider range of social rights than political rights.

### *1. Social rights*

**Social security**

In this area, you have the same rights and obligations as nationals. However, the differences between national systems is such that the Community was forced to draw up (Regulation (EEC) No 1408/71) a proper set of rules for the social protection of persons moving within the Community. Its aim is not to approximate the laws of the Member States, which therefore remain unchanged, still less to establish a unified Community social security system. It simply seeks to coordinate national schemes to facilitate the transfer from one national system to another and to regulate the consequences for one scheme of events which occurred under other schemes. The basic principles are as follows:

*(a) Applicable laws*

Apart from certain specific cases (seconded workers, international transport, commercial travellers) you are normally covered by the social security system of the country in which you pursue your activity. If you live in another country, certain benefits will, however, be granted to you by the country of residence (benefits in kind under sickness, maternity, unemployment insurance).

However, you cannot opt for a particular legislation, which has to be specified. Similarly, with the exception of old-age and, in some cases, invalidity pensions, you cannot draw benefits of the same kind concurrently in two or more countries.

*(b) Equal treatment*

You are subject to the legislation in force, for both contributions and benefits, as regards the eight traditional branches of social security (sickness/maternity, invalidity, old age, accidents at work, occupational disease, death, unemployment and family benefits).

*(c) Keeping rights which have been or are being acquired*

In going to work in a Community country, you do not lose the rights to which you would have been entitled in respect of insurance periods which you have completed in another country. The aggregation of insurance periods guarantees this.

First, it enables you, if necessary, to qualify for a right where this is conditional (old age and invalidity, unemployment) upon the completion of a qualifying period. The recognition of periods completed in one country enables you, if necessary, to satisfy this condition in another.

Second, aggregation may apply for the calculation of benefits, particularly of your pensions. The social security institution of each country under whose legislation you have been placed will determine the pension to which you would have been entitled if you had been insured in that country only and will pay you a proportion of this amount corresponding to the period that you have completed.[7]

*(d) Exporting of benefits*

Benefits due in one country are usually paid to you wherever you reside in the Community. Procedures for applying this principle, however, vary depending on the branches concerned.

Cash benefits in the case of sickness insurance may be exported but benefits in kind are provided in the country of residence as if you were insured there.

Unemployment benefits cannot be exported; in some conditions, however, an unemployed person may continue to draw benefit if he is authorized for up to a period of three months to travel to another Member State to seek employment there. The rule on exporting benefits is applied in full in the case of annuities and pensions (old age, invalidity, death, occupational disease and accidents at work).

Pensions not covered by Community law continue, however, to be paid in the country of which you are a national (war pensions) or in which you worked (public service retirement pensions).

---

[7] There are three countries in which you were insured: five years in country A, 10 years in country B and 15 in country C. You will receive 5/30 of pension A, 10/30 of pension B and 15/30 of pension C. Invalidity pensions will be calculated differently if you had been subject only to laws under which the amount of the pension does not vary according to the insurance period.

### Other social rights and benefits

As far as areas outside social security are concerned, you have a general right to equal treatment: e.g. reduced fares for large families, minimum subsistence income, guaranteed income for elderly people.

If you are an employee, you are entitled, on the same basis and under the same conditions as nationals, to training in vocational schools and rehabilitation or retraining centres, including measures enabling handicapped workers to regain their ability to work. Similarly, you are entitled to assistance from the public authorities in obtaining the accommodation you require and to be entered in the region in which you are employed on the lists of persons seeking accommodation, where such lists are kept.

If your children live in the host country they must be admitted to general education, apprenticeship schemes and vocational training under the same conditions as nationals. They have the same right to grants.

## *2. Civic and political rights*

### Civic rights

You are granted certain basic civic rights in so far as the exercise of such rights is connected with freedom of movement: the right to own property may be the essential condition for the pursuit of self-employed activities but it extends to employees as well (housing); freedom of conscience and the right to secrecy are inherent in the proper exercise of the medical or banking professions or the legal profession; freedom of opinion and expression is indissociable from the activities of the press; freedom of association allows a self-employed person to become a member of a professional order and an employee to exercise his union rights, including the right to strike.

### Right to vote

Freedom of movement does not, however, yet mean that you will be granted full political rights such as the right to vote. The European Parliament ruled in favour of granting the right to vote in local elections in the Member State of residence for nationals of Member States living in a Member State other than their own. In October 1986, the Commission presented it with a report to this effect.

In three Member States, however, you already have the right to vote. In Ireland, any person who has been ordinarily resident in the country for at least six months may take part in local elections; anyone may stand for elections in the local authority area in which they are resident. In Denmark, even the people who do not have Danish nationality are entitled to vote and stand in local elections if they have been resident in Denmark for three years. In the Netherlands, any foreign national who has been established there for at least five years may vote and stand in local elections. The United Kingdom is rather a special case: of EEC nationals, only the Irish have the right to vote and stand in local elections.

## C. Freedom of movement

The right to move freely within the territory of a Member State other than your own is essential to someone pursuing an occupational activity in that State.[8]

[8] See the compendium of texts and documents edited by the Publications Office.

## *1. Right of entry*

As a national of a Member State, you may travel to any other Community country for reasons not connected with an occupational activity and enter simply on presentation of your identity card or a valid passport. No other document or formality (visa) may be required.

Any of your children below the age of majority (18 in most Member States) also have this right but they may cross frontiers without their parents only with written authorization.

If you are travelling by car, you are no longer required to have your green insurance card.

If you are travelling for occupational reasons, you are entitled to transport professional equipment without paying taxes, in order to display it, present it or use it to carry out a specific project. To do so, however, you have to have a 'Community movement certificate' issued and authenticated by the authorities of the country in which you have your business address.[9]

If you wish to take an animal or a plant with you, you should obtain information beforehand, since the rules vary from one Community country to another.

## *2. Right of residence*

The right of residence for more than three months is still limited. It is granted if you are pursuing or have pursued (right to remain) an occupational activity in the host country or if you are receiving services. Some members of your family would also be covered, even if they are not nationals of a Member State: your spouse; your descendants and those of your spouse who are under the age of 21 or are dependants; dependent relatives in the ascending line of your spouse and yourself.

You will be issued with a residence permit, normally valid for five years, by the authorities of the place where you live.[10]

## *3. Right to remain*

When you have given up your occupational activities in a Member State, you will be able nevertheless to remain there permanently, as well as the members of your family. You will continue to be treated in the same way as nationals.

## *4. Respect for public policy in the host country*

You are of course subject to the same obligations as nationals in this connection. However, the host country could in addition take measures against you, under conditions laid down by Community law, including, in certain extreme cases, expulsion.

Your right to entry and residence could, first of all, be restricted on grounds of public health. However, the disease would have to be one included on a Community list and this reason could be invoked only on entry

---

[9] Council Regulation (EEC) No 3/84 of 19 December 1983 introducing arrangements for movement within the Community of goods sent from one Member State for temporary use in one or more other Member States (OJ L 2, 4.1.1984, p. 1).

[10] When you move house, removal of your personal property across the frontier will not be subject to the payment of taxes a second time (VAT or other taxes), under Council Directive of 28 March 1983 on tax exemptions applicable to permanent imports from a Member State of the personal property of individuals (OJ L 105, 23.4.1983, p. 64). Inquiries regarding the conditions of application of these exemptions should be made in the Member State of importation.
At the latest one year after the transfer of residence, you should submit an application to exchange your driving licence for a licence issued by the country in which you are newly resident.

onto national territory and could not be used as grounds for refusing to renew your residence permit or expelling you from the country.

Secondly, you could be accused of a violation of public policy only on the grounds of your individual conduct, and not for economic ends for example. In any event, such misconduct would have to be of a fairly serious nature for which the Member State would also take measures against its own nationals.

If this was the case, you would be covered by procedural rules aimed at ensuring that you were properly defended.

## D. The right to transfer funds

The Commission has recently presented to the Council proposals for the creation of a European financial area by 1992. In addition to freedom to carry on an occupational activity in another Member State, Community law already gives you the right to transfer the funds required for that purpose.

### *1. Current payments (Article 106 of the EEC Treaty)*

Any current payment relating to the exercise of freedom of movement of goods and persons is free of all restrictions. This allows you to transfer funds for various reasons: transport, press, publicity, insurance, business trips, etc. The same applies to the transfer of wages, salaries and pensions. Tourists, for their part, are entitled, as persons receiving services, to transfer all the necessary funds. Even where the State lays down limits, the currency allowance should be sufficient.[11]

### *2. Capital (Article 67 of the EEC Treaty)*

Unlike current payments, capital movements have been liberalized only to the extent laid down by a Council Directive,[12] while short-term investments and certain transactions in securities have not yet been liberalized, although some Member States have opted to go beyond their Community obligations in this respect.

However, liberalization of capital movements constitutes an extremely important corollary to the exercise of the other fundamental freedoms guaranteed under the EEC Treaty. In order to facilitate the right of establishment, restrictions have been lifted on direct investments,[13] which includes taking control of a company through the acquisition of shares and property investments.[13] Corresponding to the free movement of persons is the liberalization of capital movements of a personal nature (gifts and endowments, inheritance, transfers of capital to residents who are emigrating or to emigrants returning to their country of origin, etc.).[14] Finally, connected with the free movement of goods are the granting and repayment of loans linked to commercial transactions.

In the absence of complete liberalization of capital movements, Member States are still justified in exercising controls over transfers of funds.

---

[11] Portugal may continue to impose certain restrictions on transfers connected with tourism until 31 December 1990.

[12] Council Directive of 11 May 1960 (OJ 43, 12.7.1960), last amended by Directive 86/566 of 17 November 1986 (OJ L 332, 26.11.1986).

[13] In Spain, Greece and Portugal, certain restrictions still apply to these movements of capital. These countries were granted a period of grace; the last will expire on 31 December 1992.

[14] Greece, however, may subject these movements to prior authorization.

# II. Harmonization of legislation — Community directives

The ban on discrimination on grounds of nationality does not affect national systems, which can nevertheless constitute impediments to the free exercise of an occupation in another Member State. To promote that freedom, the Council of the European Communities has adopted directives based on Article 57 of the EEC Treaty concerning the mutual recognition of diplomas and containing provisions to facilitate in practice the right of establishment and freedom to provide services.[15]

A directive is a legal instrument which requires the Member States to bring their national laws into line with Community law within a specified time-limit (for example two years). Each Member State is free to select the appropriate legal means (law, decree, order, etc.) to achieve the desired end. Where the text is clear and specific, you can have recourse to it before the national courts: in case of conflict between the directive and a national measure, the directive prevails.

Directives are implemented in close liaison with the competent authorities of the Member States and, with regard to matters concerning training, with the assistance of advisory committees.[16]

## A. Recognition of diplomas (persons in paid employment and the self-employed)

Under Community directives adopted by the Council, the Member States recognize diplomas issued for the purposes of employment by the other Member States.

While these provisions apply both to persons in paid employment and to the self-employed, they do not concern all occupations. They contain arrangements which may vary depending on the occupation in question.[17]

When diplomas are recognized at Community level at the same time a minimum required standard of qualification is established and, for each occupation, recognition depends on the extent to which standards have been harmonized.

Accordingly, several situations may be encountered.

### *1. Recognition of diplomas based on harmonization of training conditions*

To exercise certain occupations in another country (doctors, nurses, dentists, veterinary surgeons, midwives and pharmacists), a diploma is recognized provided it was issued in accordance with the directives and has the same effect as diplomas issued by that Member State.

In this case, harmonization of training in the Member States pursuant to a Community directive was sufficient for the reciprocal recognition of the diplomas issued by the respective countries, and in some cases the person concerned has the choice, in the country where the diploma was obtained, of several types of training (e.g. midwives).

In the case of medical specialists, a diploma can be recognized only in the country or countries where such a specialization exists: for example, diplomas in general surgery or paediatrics are common to all Member States; this is not true in the case of infant psychiatry or geriatrics.

---

15 See Annexes.

16 See list in Annexes.

17 With respect to use of the title issued on completion of training, see section 'Right to a title', p. 20.

## *2. Recognition without harmonization of training conditions*

Architects' training is not coordinated by a directive. Your diploma will however be recognized in another Member State if it meets certain conditions, described in the directive, regarding the standard and duration of training.

## *3. Recognition of diplomas combined with work experience*

In some countries, access to the legal title of architect is subject to completion (in addition to obtaining a diploma) of a period of practical experience. In this case, a period of practical experience of equal duration carried out in another Member State is recognized.

## *4. Acquired rights*

Your diploma may also be recognized even if it does not correspond to the training conditions specified in the directives. However, such recognition refers only to diplomas awarded for training begun before the directives came into force. Production of a certificate certifying that you have carried out a certain activity for a duration specified in each directive is generally required.

## *5. Recognition of qualifications based on work experience*

In the case of some occupations, in crafts or business, special systems for the recognition of vocational qualifications are applied by means of a directive. [18]

To exercise your occupation in a Member State where access to the activity in question is subject to the possession of given occupational qualifications, it is sufficient to prove that you have practised the occupation in your country of origin or of provenance during a period laid down by the directive, even if in that country no diploma is required for this purpose.

## *6. Diplomas not recognized at Community level*

In the case of occupations not covered by a directive providing for the recognition of diplomas (for example, lawyers, accountants, consulting engineers, physiotherapists), you must obtain information from the competent authorities in the host country (for example by approaching the cultural attaché of your embassy) to find out the conditions for the recognition of your diploma. Even in the absence of an agreement between the two countries, you can request the host country to take account of qualifications acquired in another Member State and to assess whether or not they correspond to the qualifications they require.

In the case of refusal to recognize your diploma, the matter can be brought before a court to determine whether or not it is legal in the light of Community law, and you are entitled to be informed of the grounds for the decision.

[18] See the 'hairdressers' and 'insurance agents and brokers' Directives in Annexes 13 and 14. Similar directives were adopted in the following sectors: wholesale trade and intermediaries in commerce, industry and craft occupations, industry and the crafts, retail trade, personal services, food industries and manufacture of beverages, wholesale coal trade, toxic products, itinerant activities, insurance agents and brokers, various activities.

## *7. Proposal for the general recognition of diplomas*

The Commission has put forward a proposal covering these occupations recommending that the Council adopt a general system for the recognition of higher education diplomas awarded for occupations having a minimum training period of three years.[19]

In addition to the higher education diploma, in cases where your training is considered to be of a lower standard than that required for the award of the corresponding diploma in the host Member State you can be required to complete a period of practical work experience or an adaptation course.

# B. Measures to facilitate the exercise of an occupation

In the case of the liberal professions requiring professional qualifications, the coordination of legislation mainly concerns training conditions. However, specific provisions have been laid down to facilitate their right to exercise their profession in a Member State other than their country of origin or provenance.

On the other hand, other self-employed activities (insurance, banking, public works) require no qualifications. Access to the occupation and its exercise are covered by very detailed regulations in the Member States which it would be useful to harmonize by means of directives.

## *1. Liberal professions*

Apart from midwives, dental surgeons and pharmacists, who are covered by special Community arrangements (description of the tasks which they may perform), the directives harmonizing national legislation on the liberal professions cover only the coordination of training, as a prerequisite for the recognition of diplomas. On the other hand, the directive on commercial agents relates to the exercise of the occupation, with no coordination of training. The measures adopted by the directives are intended only for nationals of a Member State wishing to become established in another Member State or to provide services there.

### Measures to facilitate the right of establishment

*Character, reputation and access to the occupation, solvency*

If the host country requires proof of good character or good repute for access to the occupation, you show the document which you would have shown in your country of origin. If the latter does not require proof of this type, you must show an extract from the judicial record or an equivalent document issued by a competent authority in your country of origin.

If necessary, for the exercise of the profession of architect, you may similarly provide evidence that you have not previously been declared bankrupt or that you are covered by an insurance against the financial consequences of your professional liability.

---

[19] Proposal of 9 July 1985 (OJ C 143, 10.6.1987, p. 7); amended proposal of 13 May 1986 (OJ C 217, 28.8.1986, p. 11).

*Professional discipline while exercising the profession*

The host country is required to establish that you have not infringed the professional code when practising in your country of origin. To this end, the latter will forward the necessary information to the host country. The host country may not, however, suspend or refuse you the right of establishment unless the information thus forwarded refers to sanctions that would deny you the right to practise your activity in the country of origin.

*Taking the oath*

The wording of the oath may give rise to objections on your part of a philosophical, political or religious nature. In this case an appropriate and equivalent formulation should be proposed by the host country.

*Right to a title*

The directives draw a distinction between use of the professional title and of the training title:

(i) in the event of mutual recognition, you use the professional title of the host country;

(ii) in addition, you may use a training title acquired in your country of origin, in the language of that country.

*Information services*

The host Member State must allow persons taking advantage of the directives to be informed of legislation of concern to them (for example, in health and social matters) and, where appropriate, of the code of conduct of that country. To this end it may set up information services and require applicants for establishment to contact these services.

*Knowledge of languages*

Depending on the activity in question, adequate knowledge of the language of the host country (or of the region) may be regarded as a requirement under the code of conduct. However, a Member State may not in the case of a person holding a diploma issued in another Member State make the right to exercise an occupation subject to proof of knowledge of a particular language, and he may not be required to pass a language examination.

**Measures to facilitate freedom to provide services**

Certain facilities are available in the case of occupations covered by a Community directive. Some of the facilities are the same as those pertaining to the right of establishment: for instance, the right to use a title or the right to information services (however, the host country cannot oblige the person providing services to contact them), whereas other facilities are specific to the provision of services.

*Exemption from authorization, registration or membership; prior declaration*

In the case of the provision of services you are exempt from the requirement to obtain authorization, to register or to become a member of a professional body. The host country may however require temporary and automatic registration or *pro forma* membership of a professional body or registration.

On the other hand, the competent authorities of the host country may require you to make a prior declaration regarding the provision of services in cases where such provision would require a temporary stay in the country. In urgent cases this declaration can be made after the services have been provided.

*Legal profession*

Compared with the situation as regards the other liberal professions the coordination of legislation concerning the legal profession is unusual. In the absence of mutual recognition of diplomas (due to the diversity of national law) recognition concerns only the status of lawyer as recognized in the country of origin, the titles for which are listed in the directive.

While the other directives are aimed at facilitating the right of establishment and, where applicable, freedom to provide services, the 'Lawyers'' Directive solely concerns the provision of services. In this connection it draws a distinction between two types of lawyers' activities.

In the case of activities concerned with the administration of justice (representation and defence in court) you have to observe both the rules of the country to whose bar you belong and those of the host country.

On the other hand, with regard to extra-judicial activities (legal counselling), subject to certain reservations in the directive, only the rules of the country of origin must be observed.

## 2. *Insurance, banking, public works*

Directives have been adopted on sectors of particular importance for completing the common market.

### Insurance

Alignment of national rules was carried out to facilitate the right of establishment in the field of non-life insurance[20] and life insurance.[21]

In the country where your company sets up its head office the approval it must seek is subject to harmonized conditions (legal form, programme of activities).

Activities of agencies and branches (secondary establishment) in another Member State are facilitated: approval cannot be refused; certain financial guarantees (solvency margin) are calculated in respect of the head office for the Community as a whole. In future it will be possible for existing branches simultaneously providing life insurance and other classes of insurance to set up as secondary establishments in Member

[20] Council Directive 73/239 of 24 July 1973 relating to the business of direct insurance other than life assurance (OJ L 228, 16.8.1973, p. 3).

[21] Council Directive 79/267 of 5 March 1979 on life insurance (OJ L 63, 13.3.1979, p. 1), amended by the Act of Accession of Greece (OJ L 291, 19.11.1979, p. 90) and by the Act of Accession of Spain and Portugal (OJ L 302, 15.11.1985, p. 157 following the note). See also proposals for a directive relating to the compulsory winding-up of direct insurance undertakings (OJ C 71, 19.3.1987, p. 5) and the annual accounts and consolidated accounts of insurance undertakings (OJ C 131, 18.5.1987, p. 1). For insurance agents and brokers, see under heading 'Measures to facilitate the exercise of an occupation', p. 19.

States where this is banned, by setting up an agency or branch for non-life insurance and a subsidiary for life insurance.[22]

On the other hand, freedom to provide services (apart from re-insurance and co-insurance) has not yet come into effect in the absence of Council agreement on the proposals for a directive on the non-life insurance sector[23] presented by the Commission.

### Banking

The requisite co-ordination in this field is far from complete. An outline directive on the right of establishment has imposed certain conditions regarding the opening of a head office which include the existence of own resources.[24] But determination of the latter is still at the proposal stage.[25]

Directives have also been adopted on the supervision of banks on a consolidated basis[26] and on the annual accounts,[27] together with a recommendation on the monitoring and inspection of major risks.[28]

The Commission has submitted proposals to the Council on the reorganization and winding-up of banks,[29] mortgage credit[30] and the publication of annual accounting documents.[31]

The authorization required for the establishment of agencies or branches is automatically granted as in the case of insurance. It is made easier by the outline directive: establishment of the undertaking can no longer be refused on the grounds of its legal form; the bank is entitled to use the same name as that which it uses in the Member State where it has its head office.

Needless to say, setting up a European financial area means that freedom to provide services in banking would also be facilitated. For the most part, however, it is linked to greater liberalization of capital movements (Article 69 of the EEC Treaty).

### Public works contracts

Concluding a public works contract in a Member State other than that in which you are established is one form of the provision of services to which you are entitled by the Treaty (Article 59 of the EEC Treaty).

---

22 See also Council Directives 87/343 and 87/344 of 22 June 1987 concerning respectively credit insurance and suretyship insurance and legal expenses insurance (OJ L 185, 4.7.1987, p. 72 and p. 77).

23 Proposal for a second Council Directive on direct insurance other than life insurance and laying down provisions to facilitate the effective exercise of freedom to provide services (OJ C 32, 12.2.1976, p. 2); proposal for a Council Directive on the coordination of laws, regulations and administrative provisions relating to insurance contracts (OJ C 190, 28.7.1979, p. 2).

24 Council Directive 77/780 of 12 December 1977 relating to the taking up and pursuit of the business of credit institutions (OJ L 322, 17.12.1977, p. 30).

25 Proposal for a Council Directive concerning own resources of credit establishments (OJ C 241, 27.9.1986, p. 4).

26 Council Directive of 13 June 1983 on the supervision of credit institutions on a consolidated basis (OJ L 193, 18.7.1983, p. 18).

27 Council Directive of 8 December 1986 on the annual accounts and consolidated accounts of banks and other financial institutions (OJ L 372, 31.12.1986, p. 1).

28 Commission Recommendation 87/62 of 22 December 1986 on monitoring and controlling of large exposures of credit institutions (OJ L 33, 4.2.1987, p. 10).

29 Proposal for a Council Directive relating to the reorganization and the winding-up of credit institutions (OJ C 356, 31.12.1985, p. 55).

30 Proposal for a Council Directive on freedom of establishment and the free supply of services in the field of mortgage credit (OJ C 42, 14.2.1985, p. 4). Amended proposal (OJ C 161, 19.6.1987, p. 4).

31 Proposal for a Council Directive on the obligations of branches established in a Member State by credit institutions and financial institutions having their head office outside that Member State regarding the publication of annual accounting documents (OJ C 230, 11.9.1986, p. 4).

However, to give effect to this right, public supply contracts must no longer always be awarded to enterprises of the country. To this end, a directive has coordinated the procedures for the award of public works contracts,[32] but the present situation is not satisfactory. In 1986, the Commission submitted a proposal for an amendment to the Council with a view to extending the scope of the directive to achieve greater transparency of the market and bring about some degree of deregulation and simplification. Other proposals will be put before the Council with a view to genuinely opening up the market for public supply contracts in the Community by 1992.

As a national of a Member State, you already enjoy rights with respect to the exercise of your occupation in the Community, either as a result of the direct application of the Treaty or under Community directives. Make sure that your rights are observed.

However, this is not enough. Call for an extension of those rights to accelerate the creation of the large internal market and completion of a people's Europe in 1992, so that the European area will genuinely be without frontiers.

[32] Council Directive 71/305 of 26 July 1971 concerning the coordination of procedures for the award of public works contracts (OJ L 185, 16.8.1971, p. 5).
See also handbook on public works contracts in the Community (OJ C 358, 31.12.1987, p. 1).

[33] COM(86) 679 final.

# ANNEXES

# INSTRUMENTS CONCERNING THE EXERCISE OF AN OCCUPATION IN A MEMBER STATE OTHER THAN THE COUNTRY OF ORIGIN OR THE PLACE FROM WHICH THE WORKER COMES



N.B.: The text supplied here incorporate amendments published in the Official Journal up to 23 November 1987. In particular, articles of the EEC Treaty are given as amended by the Single European Act (SEA), which entered into force on 1 July 1987.

11. Transporters
11.1. Directive 74/561/EEC of 12 November 1974.
11.2. Directive 74/562/EEC of 12 November 1974.
11.3. Directive 77/796/EEC of 12 December 1977.
11.4. Directive 87/540/EEC of 9 November 1987.

12. Lawyers
Directive 77/249/EEC of 22 March 1977.

13. Insurance agents and brokers
13.1. Directive 77/92/EEC of 13 December 1976.
13.2. Commission communication ( evidence, statements, certificates).

14. Hairdressers
Directive 82/489/EEC of 19 July 1982.

15. Self-employed commercial agents
Directive 86/653/EEC of 18 December 1986.

– List of Judgments on the right of establishment and freedom to provide services.

– List of Directives on the recognition of qualifications based on work experience.

– List of Advisory Committees on training.

# 1. EEC-Treaty

*Article 3*

For the purposes set out in Article 2, the activities of the Community shall include, as provided in this Treaty and in accordance with the timetable set out therein

••••••

*(c)* the abolition, as between Member States, of obstacles to freedom of movement for persons, services and capital;

••••••

*Article 7*

Within the scope of application of this Treaty, and without prejudice to any special provisions contained therein, any discrimination on grounds of nationality shall be prohibited.

The Council may, on a proposal from the Commission and in cooperation with the European Parliament, adopt, by a qualified majority, rules designed to prohibit such discrimination. (*)

*Article 8a* (**)

The Community shall adopt measures with the aim of progressively establishing the internal market over a period expiring on 31 December 1992, in accordance with the provisions of this Article and of Articles 8b, 8c, 28, 57 (2), 59, 70 (1), 84, 99, 100a and 100b and without prejudice to the other provisions of this Treaty.

The internal market shall comprise an area without internal frontiers in which the free movement of goods, persons, services and capital is ensured in accordance with the provisions of this Treaty.

---

(*) Second paragraph as amended by Article 6 (2) of the SEA.

(**) Article added by Article 13 of the SEA.

## *CHAPTER 1*

## WORKERS

### *Article 48*

*1.* Freedom of movement for workers shall be secured within the Community by the end of the transitional period at the latest.

*2.* Such freedom of movement shall entail the abolition of any discrimination based on nationality between workers of the Member States as regards employment, remuneration and other conditions of work and employment.

*3.* It shall entail the right, subject to limitations justified on grounds of public policy, public security or public health:

*(a)* to accept offers of employment actually made;

*(b)* to move freely within the territory of Member States for this purpose;

*(c)* to stay in a Member State for the purpose of employment in accordance with the provisions governing the employment of nationals of that State laid down by law, regulation or administrative action;

*(d)* to remain in the territory of a Member State after having been employed in that State, subject to conditions which shall be embodied in implementing regulations to be drawn up by the Commission.

*4.* The provisions of this Article shall not apply to employment in the public service.

*Article 49*

As soon as this Treaty enters into force, the Council shall, acting by a qualified majority on a proposal from the Commission, in cooperation with the European Parliament and after consulting the Economic and Social Committee, issue directives or make regulations setting out the measures required to bring about, by progressive stages, freedom of movement for workers, as defined in Article 48, in particular:*

*(a)* by ensuring close cooperation between national employment services;

*(b)* by systematically and progressively abolishing those administrative procedures and practices and those qualifying periods in respect of eligibility for available employment, whether resulting from national legislation or from agreements previously concluded between Member States, the maintenance of which would form an obstacle to liberalization of the movement of workers;

*(c)* by systematically and progressively abolishing all such qualifying periods and other restrictions provided for either under national legislation or under agreements previously concluded between Member States as imposed on workers of other Member States conditions regarding the free choice of employment other than those imposed on workers of the State concerned;

*(d)* by setting up appropriate machinery to bring offers of employment into touch with applications for employment and to facilitate the achievement of a balance between supply and demand in the employment market in such a way as to avoid serious threats to the standard of living and level of employment in the various regions and industries.

*Article 51*

The Council shall, acting unanimously on a proposal from the Commission, adopt such measures in the field of social security as are necessary to provide freedom of movement for workers; to this end, it shall make arrangements to secure for migrant workers and their dependants:

*(a)* aggregation, for the purpose of acquiring and retaining the right to benefit and of calculating the amount of benefit, of all periods taken into account under the laws of the several countries;

*(b)* payment of benefits to persons resident in the territories of Member States.

* First sentence as amended by Article 6 (3) of the SEA.

*CHAPTER 2*

## RIGHT OF ESTABLISHMENT

*Article 52*

Within the framework of the provisions set out below, restrictions on the freedom of establishment of nationals of a Member State in the territory of another Member State shall be abolished by progressive stages in the course of the transitional period. Such progressive abolition shall also apply to restrictions on the setting up of agencies, branches or subsidiaries by nationals of any Member State established in the territory of any Member State.

Freedom of establishment shall include the right to take up and pursue activities as self-employed persons and to set up and manage undertakings, in particular companies or firms within the meaning of the second paragraph of Article 58, under the conditions laid down for its own nationals by the law of the country where such establishment is effected, subject to the provisions of the Chapter relating to capital.

*Article 54*

••••••

*2.* **In order to implement this general programme or, in the absence of such programme, in order to achieve a stage in attaining freedom of establishment as regards a particular activity, the Council shall, acting on a proposal from the Commission, in cooperation with the European Parliament and after consulting the Economic and Social Committee, issue directives, acting unanimously until the end of the first stage and by a qualified majority thereafter.***

*3.* The Council and the Commission shall carry out the duties devolving upon them under the preceding provisions, in particular:

••••••

*(g)* by coordinating to the necessary extent the safeguards which, for the protection of the interests of members and others, are required by Member States of companies or firms within the meaning of the second paragraph of Article 58 with a view to making such safeguards equivalent throughout the Community;

••••••

*Article 55*

The provisions of this Chapter shall not apply, so far as any given Member State is concerned, to activities which in that State are connected, even occasionally, with the exercise of official authority.

The Council may, acting by a qualified majority on a proposal from the Commission, rule that the provisions of this Chapter shall not apply to certain activities.

---

* Paragraph 2 as amended by Article 6 (4) of the SEA.

*Article 56*

*1.* The provisions of this Chapter and measures taken in pursuance thereof shall not prejudice the applicability of provisions laid down by law, regulation or administrative action providing for special treatment for foreign nationals on grounds of public policy, public security or public health.

*2.* Before the end of the transitional period, the Council shall, acting unanimously on a proposal from the Commission and after consulting the European Parliament, issue directives for the coordination of the aforementioned provisions laid down by law, regulation or administrative action. After the end of the second stage, however, the Council shall, acting by a qualified majority on a proposal from the Commission and in cooperation with the European Parliament, issue directives for the coordination of such provisions as, in each Member State, are a matter for regulation or administrative action.([1])

*Article 57*

*1.* In order to make it easier for persons to take up and pursue activities as self-employed persons, the Council shall, on a proposal from the Commission and in cooperation with the European Parliament, acting unanimously during the first stage and by a qualified majority thereafter, issue directives for the mutual recognition of diplomas, certificates and other evidence of formal qualifications.*

*2.* For the same purpose, the Council shall, before the end of the transitional period, acting on a proposal from the Commission and after consulting the European Parliament, issue directives for the coordination of the provisions laid down by law, regulation or administrative action in Member States concerning the taking up and pursuit of activities as self-employed persons. Unanimity shall be required for directives the implementation of which involves in at least one Member State amendment of the existing principles laid down by law governing the professions with respect to training and conditions of access for natural persons.** In other cases the Council shall act by a qualified majority, in cooperation with the European Parliament.***

••••••

*Article 58*

Companies or firms formed in accordance with the law of a Member State and having their registered office, central administration or principal place of business within the Community shall, for the purposes of this Chapter, be treated in the same way as natural persons who are nationals of Member States.

'Companies or firms' means companies or firms constituted under civil or commercial law, including cooperative societies, and other legal persons governed by public or private law, save for those which are non-profit-making.

([1]) Second sentence of paragraph 2 as amended by Article 6 (5) of the SEA.
* Paragraph 1 as amended by Article 6 (6) of the SEA.
** Second sentence of paragraph 2 as amended by Article 16 (2) of the SEA.
*** Third sentence of paragraph 2 as amended by Article 6 (7) of the SEA.

*CHAPTER 3*

## SERVICES

*Article 59*

Within the framework of the provisions set out below, restrictions on freedom to provide services within the Community shall be progressively abolished during the transitional period in respect of nationals of Member States who are established in a State of the Community other than that of the person for whom the services are intended.

The Council may, acting by a qualified majority on a proposal from the Commission, extend the provisions of the Chapter to nationals of a third country who provide services and who are established within the Community.*

*Article 60*

Services shall be considered to be 'services' within the meaning of this Treaty where they are normally provided for remuneration, in so far as they are not governed by the provisions relating to freedom of movement for goods, capital and persons.

'Services' shall in particular include:

*(a)* activities of an industrial character;

*(b)* activities of a commercial character;

*(c)* activities of craftsmen;

*(d)* activities of the professions.

Without prejudice to the provisions of the Chapter relating to the right of establishment, the person providing a service may, in order to do so, temporarily pursue his activity in the State where the service is provided, under the same conditions as are imposed by that State on its own nationals.

*Article 61*

*1.* Freedom to provide services in the field of transport shall be governed by the provisions of the Title relating to transport.

••••••

*Article 66*

The provisions of Articles 55 to 58 shall apply to the matters covered by this Chapter.

* Second paragraph as amended by Article 16 (3) of the SEA.

## DECLARATION BY THE GOVERNMENT OF THE FEDERAL REPUBLIC OF GERMANY

on

the definition of the expression 'German national'

At the time of signature of the Treaty establishing the European Economic Community and the Treaty establishing the European Atomic Energy Community, the Government of the Federal Republic of Germany makes the following declaration:

'All Germans as defined in the Basic Law for the Federal Republic of Germany shall be considered nationals of the Federal Republic of Germany.'

# COUNCIL

## NEW DECLARATION

**by the Government of the United Kingdom of Great Britain and Northern Ireland on the definition of the term 'nationals'**

In view of the entry into force of the British Nationality Act 1981, the Government of the United Kingdom of Great Britain and Northern Ireland makes the following Declaration which will replace, as from 1 January 1983, that made at the time of signature of the Treaty of Accession by the United Kingdom to the European Communities:

> 'As to the United Kingdom of Great Britain and Northern Ireland, the terms "nationals", "nationals of Member States" or "nationals of Member States and overseas countries and territories" wherever used in the Treaty establishing the European Economic Community, the Treaty establishing the European Atomic Energy Community or the Treaty establishing the European Coal and Steel Community or in any of the Community acts deriving from those Treaties, are to be understood to refer to:
>
> (a) British citizens;
>
> (b) persons who are British subjects by virtue of Part IV of the British Nationality Act 1981 and who have the right of abode in the United Kingdom and are therefore exempt from United Kingdom immigration control;
>
> (c) British Dependent Territories citizens who acquire their citizenship from a connection with Gibraltar.'

The reference in Article 6 of the third Protocol to the Act of Acession of 22 January 1972, on the Channel Islands and the Isle of Man, to 'any citizen of the United Kingdom and Colonies' is to be understood as referring to 'any British citizen'.

OJ No C 23, 28.1.1983, p.1.

# 1a. Extracts from the White Paper

# COMPLETING THE INTERNAL MARKET

**White Paper from the Commission to the European Council**

## INTRODUCTION

1. «Unifying this market (of 320 million) presupposes that Member States will agree on the abolition of barriers of all kinds, harmonisation of rules, approximation of legislation and tax structures, strengthening of monetary cooperation and the necessary flanking measures to encourage European firms to work together. It is a goal that is well within our reach provided we draw the lessons from the setbacks and delays of the past. The Commission will be asking the European Council to pledge itself to completion of a fully unified internal market by 1992 and to approve the necessary programme together with a realistic and binding timetable».

2. In such terms did the Commission define its task in the «Programme of the Commission for 1985» which was presented to the European Parliament on 6 March. On 29 and 30 March, the European Council in Brussels broadly endorsed this view and

   'laid particular emphasis on... action to achieve a single market by 1992 thereby creating a more favourable environment for stimulating enterprise, competition and trade; it called upon the Commission to draw up a detailed programme with a specific timetable before its next meeting».

3. This White Paper is designed to spell out the programme and timetable. Given the European Council's clear and repeated commitment to the completion of the common market, the Commission does not intend in this Paper to rehearse again the economic and political arguments that have so often led to that conclusion. Instead the Commission, which wholeheartedly shares the Council's commitment and objective, sets out here the essential and logical consequences of accepting that commitment, together with an action programme for achieving the objective.

4. The Treaty clearly envisaged from the outset the creation of a single integrated internal market free of restrictions on the movement of goods; the abolition of obstacles to the free movement of persons, services and capital; the institution of a system ensuring that competition in the common market is not distorted; the approximation of laws as required for the proper functioning of the common market; and the approximation of indirect taxation in the interest of the common market.

5. In the early days attention concentrated on the common customs tariff, which was established eighteen months ahead of the 12-year programme set out in the Treaty. It was a remarkable achievement – one that we can look back on with pride and one from which we can derive inspiration for the future. That task achieved, attention turned to indirect taxes. The high water mark was perhaps the adoption – unanimously by the Council – of the 6th VAT directive in 1977. But thereafter momentum was lost partly through the onset of the recession, partly through a lack of confidence and vision.

6. The recession brought another problem. The Treaty specifically required not simply the abolition of customs duties as between the Member States, but also the elimination of quantitative restrictions and of all measures having equivalent effect. Originally it was assumed that such «non-tariff barriers», as they are commonly called, were of limited importance compared with actual duties. But during the recession they multiplied as each Member State endeavoured to protect what it thought was its short term interests – not only against third countries but against fellow Member States as well. Member States also increasingly sought to protect national markets and industries through the use of public funds to aid and maintain non-viable companies. The provision in the EEC Treaty that restrictions on the freedom to provide services should «be progressively abolished during the transitional period» not only failed to be implemented during the transitional period, but over important areas failed to be implemented at all. Disgracefully, that remains the case.

7. But the mood has begun to change, and the commitment to be rediscovered: gradually at first, but now with increasing tempo. The Heads of State and Governments at the European Council meeting in Copenhagen in 1982 pledged themselves to the completion of the internal market as a high priority. The pledge was repeated at Fontainebleau in June 1984; at Dublin in December of that year; and, most recently, in Brussels, in March 1985. The time for talk has now passed. The time for action has come. That is what this White Paper is about.

8. The case for the completion of the internal market has been argued elsewhere: and, as the communiqués at successive European Councils have indicated, it has been accepted by the Heads of State and Governments of the Member States. But it is worth recalling that the objective of completing the internal market has three aspects:

- First, the welding together of the ten, soon to be twelve, individual markets of the Member States into one single market of 320 million people;
- Second, ensuring that this single market is also an expanding market – not static but growing;
- Third, to this end, ensuring that the market is flexible so that resources, both of people and materials, and of capital and investment, flow into the areas of greatest economic advantage.

9. Whilst, therefore, the discussion in this Paper will be directed primarily to the first of these objectives there will be a need to keep the other two objectives constantly in mind and to ensure that the measures taken contribute to those ends.

10. For convenience the measures that need to be taken have been classified in this Paper under three headings:

- Part one: the removal of physical barriers
- Part two: the removal of technical barriers
- Part three: the removal of fiscal barriers.

11. The most obvious example of the first category are customs posts at frontiers. Indeed most of our citizens would regard the frontier posts as the most visible example of the continued division of the Community and their removal as the clearest sign of the integration of the Community into a single market. Yet they continue to exist mainly because of the technical and fiscal divisions between Member States. Once we have removed those barriers, and found alternative ways of dealing with other relevant problems such as public security, immigration and drug controls, the reasons for the existence of the physical barriers will have been eliminated.

12. The reason for getting rid entirely of physical and other controls between Member States is not one of theology or appearance, but the hard practical fact that the maintenance of any internal frontier controls will perpetuate the costs and disadvantages of a divided market; the more the need for such controls diminishes – short of total elimination – the more disproportionate become the costs, expenses and disadvantages of maintaining the frontiers and a divided market.

13. While the elimination of physical barriers provides benefits for traders, particularly through the disappearance of formalities and of frontier delays, it is through the elimination of technical barriers that the Community will give the large market its economic and industrial dimension by enabling industries to make economies of scale and therefore to become more competitive. An example of this second category – technical barriers – are the different standards for individual products adopted in different Member States for health or safety reasons, or for environmental or consumer protection. Here the Commission has recently launched a major new initiative which has been welcomed and endorsed by the Council. The barriers to the freedom to provide services could perhaps be regarded as a separate category; but these barriers are analogous to the technical barriers which obstruct the free movement of goods, and they are probably best regarded as part of the same category. There is an additional merit in such an approach since the traditional dichotomy between «goods» and «services» has fostered an attitude in which «services» are somehow regarded as inferior and relegated to the bottom of the queue. Technical barriers are technical barriers whether they apply to goods or services and all should be treated on an equal footing. The general thrust of the Commission's approach in this area will be to move away from the concept of harmonisation towards that of mutual recognition and equivalence. But there will be a continuing role for the approximation of Member States' laws and regulations, as laid down in Article 100 of the Treaty. Clearly, action under this Article would be quicker and more effective if the Council were to agree not to allow the unanimity requirement to obstruct progress where it could otherwise be made.

14. The removal of fiscal barriers may well be contentious and this despite the fact that the goals laid down in the Treaty are quite explicit and that important steps have already been taken along the road of approximation. This being so, the reasons why approximation of fiscal legislation is an essential and integral element in any programme for completing the internal market are explained in detail in Part Three of this Paper. Approximation of indirect taxation will raise severe problems for some Member States. It may, therefore, be necessary to provide for derogations.

15. We recognise that many of the changes we propose will present considerable difficulties for Member States and time will be needed for the necessary adjustments to be made. The benefits to an integrated Community economy of the large, expanding and flexible market are so great that they should not be denied to its citizens because of difficulties faced by individual Member States. These difficulties must be recognised, to some degree they must be accommodated, but they should not be allowed permanently to frustrate the achievement of the greater progress, the greater prosperity and the higher level of employment that economic integration can bring to the Community.

16. Last year, the Commission submitted a Consolidation Programme[1] identifying a series of proposals to be adopted by the Council in 1984 and 1985. This White Paper pursues this effort in a wider perspective and with a view to completing the Internal Market by 1992. It therefore comprises the essential items of last year's paper without expressly repeating the Consolidation Programme which still remains valid.

17. This White Paper is not intended to cover every possible issue which affects the integration of the economies of the Member States of the Community. It focusses on the Internal Market and the measures which are directly necessary to achieve a single integrated market embracing the 320m people of the enlarged Community. There are many other matters – all of them important in their own way – which bear upon economic integration, indirectly affect the achievement of the Internal Market and are the subject of other Community policies.

18. For example, it is a fact that in order to facilitate the key role which the internal market can play in the policy for the recovery of industrial structures, the suspension of internal borders must be accompanied by actions which strengthen research and the technological base of the Community's industry. Such actions will allow firms to benefit from the size of the single market. It is within this context that the present work of strengthening the Community's technological base should be seen.

19. Similarly, the strengthening of coordination of economic policies and the EMS will be essential factors in the integration of national markets. However, any action taken to ensure the free movement of factors of production must necessarily be accompanied by increased surveillance by the Commission in the field of competition rules to ensure that firms and Member States adhere to these rules. In particular, a strong and coherent competition policy must ensure that the partitioning of the internal market is not permitted to occur as a result of protectionist state aids or restrictive practices by firms. Moreover the commercial identity of the Community must be consolidated so that our trading partners will not be given the benefit of a wider market without themselves making similar concessions.

20. There are many other areas of Community policy that interact with the Internal market in that they both affect its workings and will benefit from the stimulus that will be provided by its completion. This is particularly true of transport, social, environment and consumer protection policy. As far as social aspects are concerned, the Commission will pursue the dialogue with governments and social partners to ensure that the opportunities afforded by completion of the Internal Market will be accompanied by appropriate measures aimed at fulfilling the Community's employment and social security objectives.

21. The Commission is firmly convinced that the completion of the Internal Market will provide an indispensable base for increasing the prosperity of the Community as a whole. The Commission is, however, conscious that there may be risks that, by increasing the possibilities for human, material and financial services to move without obstacle to the areas of greatest economic advantage, existing discrepancies between regions could be exacerbated and therefore the objective of convergence jeopardized. This means that full and imaginative use will need to be made of the resources available through the structural funds. The importance of the funds will therefore be enhanced.

22. Although this White Paper will touch on these matters where they have a direct bearing on the working of the Internal Market, it will not attempt to cover them in full and in detail as they represent considerable areas of study in their own right and merit separate and fuller consideration elsewhere. The existence of these problems does not mean that the frontiers and other frontier controls should not be abolished. On the contrary the task we face is to find solutions to the problems on the basis that the frontiers will have been abolished.

23. A detailed timetable for implementing the Commission's proposed programme of measures for the removal of physical, technical and fiscal barriers is to be found in the Annex to this Paper.

[1] COM(84) 305 final of 13 June 1984.

## PART ONE: THE REMOVAL OF PHYSICAL BARRIERS

.....

### III. CONTROL OF INDIVIDUALS

47. The formalities affecting individual travellers are a constant and concrete reminder to the ordinary citizen that the construction of a real European Community is far from complete.

48. Even though these controls are often no more than spot checks, they are seen as the outward sign of an arbitrary administrative power over individuals and as an affront to the principle of freedom of movement within a single Community.

49. This prompted the Fontainebleau European Council to give the Adonnino Committee the task of examining the measures to be taken to bring about «the abolition of all police and customs formalities for people crossing intra-Community borders». The Committee thought this aspect to be so important that it presented an interim report in March of this year.

50. The formalities in question are, in normal circumstances, of two different kinds: police checks relating to the identity of the person concerned and the safety of personal effects being carried; and tax checks relating to personal effects being carried. We concentrate here on the police checks. The removal of fiscal barriers and controls is covered in Part Three.

51. The Commission's efforts and initiatives in this area have been aimed at making checks at internal frontiers more flexible, as they cannot be abolished altogether until, in line with the concerns expressed by the European Council, adequate safeguards are introduced against terrorism and drugs.

52. Agreement has already been reached on the Commission's proposal for a common passport testifying to the individual's position as a citizen of a Member State. As an additional step towards abolition of physical controls the Commission has proposed the introduction of a means of self-identification which would enable the authorities to see at a glance that the individual is entitled to free passage – the Green Disc. This proposal is at present before the Council and should be adopted forthwith.

53. As noted in the introduction to this Part, police checks at internal frontiers are bound up with the legitimate concerns of the political authorities in the fight against terrorism, drugs and crime. Consequently, they can only be abolished as part of a legislative and administrative process whereby they are transferred to the strengthened external frontiers of the Community and cooperation between the relevant national authorities is further enhanced.

54. The Commission will at an early stage seek a commitment from the Member States that no new or more stringent controls or formalities affecting individuals are introduced at internal frontiers. The Commission will as a next step be proposing measures to eliminate completely by 1988 checks on leaving one Member State when entering another. This type of check has already been virtually abolished in practice at internal frontier crossings by road. This step would entail administrative cooperation between the police authorities and the information transmission networks to enable the police in the country of entry to carry out checks an behalf of the police in the country of departure. A system of this kind would provide continuing protection in the combat against terrorism. Moreover, such a system would not preclude security – as opposed to identity – checks being carried out in airports.

55. By 1992, the Commission wishes to arrive at the stage whereby checks on entry are also abolished for Community citizens arriving from another Community country. To this end, directives will be proposed concerning:

- The approximation of arms legislation; the absence of checks must not provide an incentive to buy arms in countries with less strict legislation. A proposal will be made in 1985 with the target of approval in 1988 at the latest;

- The approximation of drugs legislation: proposals will be made in 1987, for adoption in 1989;

- Non-Community citizens: the abolition of checks at internal frontiers will make it much easier for nationals of non-Community countries to move from Member State to another. As a first step, the

Commission will propose in 1988 at the latest coordination of the rules on residence, entry and access to employment, applicable to nationals of non-Community countries. In this regard problems may arise over the question of the change of residence of non-Community citizens between the Member States, and these will need to be looked at. Measures will be proposed also in 1988 at the latest on the right of asylum and the position of refugees. Decisions will be needed on these matters by 1990 at the latest;

- Visa policy: the freedom of movement for non-Community nationals, which visas provide, may undermine the agreements which Member States have with non-member countries. It will therefore be necessary to go further than the existing collaboration in the context of political cooperation and develop a Community policy on visas. This would need to strike the right balance between national foreign policy prerogatives and preserving the effectiveness of existing bilateral agreements. The requisite proposals should be made in 1988 for adoption by 1990. There will also be a need to fix common rules concerning extradition policy. The necessary proposal, to be made in 1989, should be adopted by 1991.

56. The adoption of these measures by the Council, accompanied by a redeployment of resources to strengthen controls at the external frontiers, and enhanced cooperation between police and other relevant agencies within the Member States, should enable police checks at internal frontiers to be eliminated by 1992.

## PART TWO: THE REMOVAL OF TECHNICAL BARRIERS

.....

### III. FREE MOVEMENT FOR LABOUR AND THE PROFESSIONS: A NEW INITIATIVE IN FAVOUR OF COMMUNITY CITIZENS

88. The Commission considers it crucial that the obstacles which still exist within the Community to free movement for the self-employed and employees be removed by 1992. It considers that Community citizens should be free to engage in their professions throughout the Community, if they so wish, without the obligation to adhere to formalities which, in the final analysis, could serve to discourage such movement.

89. In the case of employees, it should be noted that such free movement is almost entirely complete and the rulings of the Court of Justice restrict the right of public authorities in Member States to reserve posts for nationals. Certain problems still exist, however, and the Commission intends to make the necessary proposals which will eliminate the last obstacles standing in the way of the free movement and residence of migrant Community workers. Furthermore the Commission will take measures in order to remove cumbersome administrative procedures relating to residence permits. The Commission has already submitted a proposal concerning the taxation of these workers and their families. The main problem in this case is the taxation of wage-earners who reside in one Member State and earn their income in another (this affects mainly frontier workers).

90. The Commission will also make further efforts to bring about the adoption and swift implementation of its proposal concerning the comparability of vocational training qualifications aimed at ensuring that vocational proficiency certificates are more easily comparable. In practical terms, this objective should be achieved by 1988 so that the second phase can be launched before 1990. This second phase would involve the introduction of an European «vocational training card», serving as proof that the holder has been awarded a specific qualification.

91. In the field of rights of establishment for the self-employed, little progress has been made, the main reason being the complexities involved in the endeavour to harmonize professional qualifications. However these endeavours have resulted in a considerable degree of freedom of movement for those engaged in the health sector. The European Council, owing to the hold-ups previously experienced in this sphere, indicated its desire to promote measures that would offer tangible improvements in the everyday life of Community citizens. In particular, during the meeting in Fontainebleau it called for the creation of a general system for the mutual recognition of university degrees. In line with the same philosophy, the Commission believes that there should be mutual recognition of apprenticeship courses.

92. The Adonnino Committee submitted a preliminary report in March this year which contains some guidelines on this subject, and the Commission has been requested to put them into concrete form.

93. For this reason, with the aim of removing obstacles to the right of establishment, the Commission – which approved the conclusions of the Adonnino report – will submit to the Council a draft framework Directive on a general system of recognition in the course of this year. The main elements in this system will be: the principle of mutual trust between the Member States; the principle of the comparability of university studies between the Member States; the mutual recognition of degrees and diplomas without prior harmonization of the conditions for access to and the exercise of professions; and the extension of the general system to salary earners. Lastly, any difference, notably as regards training, between the Member States would be compensated by professional experience.

94. Finally, measures to ensure the free movement of individuals must not be restricted to the workforce only. Consequently, the Commission intends to increase its support for cooperation programmes between further education establishments in different Member States with a view to promoting the mobility of students, facilitating the academic recognition of degrees and thus diplomas, and helping young people, in whose hands the future of the Community's economy lies, to think in European terms. At the end of this year, it will make new proposals on this subject, notably concerning a Community scholarship scheme of grants for students wishing to pursue part of their studies or the acquisition of relevant professional experience in another Member State.

## IV. A COMMON MARKET FOR SERVICES

95. In the Commission's view, it is no exaggeration to see the establishment of a common market in services as one of the main preconditions for a return to economic prosperity. Trade in services is as important for an economy as trade in goods. The diversity of activities which can be classed as «services» and the fact that the providers of services seem unaware of their common interests in the sector are two of the reasons why their role and importance have been undervalued for so long. Another reason has been the fact that, in the past, many services were provided by industry itself whereas now there is a trend to create specialist companies or at least specialist units for service activities. Despite the provisions of Articles 59 and 62 of the Treaty, progress on the freedom to provide services across internal frontiers has been much slower than the progress achieved on free movement of goods. This is particularly regrettable, since in recent years specialisation and the rapid development of new types of services has done much to demonstrate the potential for growth and job creation in the service sector as a whole.

96. Two examples should suffice to illustrate this potential, and to point out the risk that the Community might lose ground to its main trading competitors if it fails to take sufficiently far-reaching action.

97. First, in 1982 market services and non-market services already accounted for 57% of the value added to the Community economy while industry's contribution has dropped to less than 26%. Secondly, a comparison of employment prospects in the different sectors between 1973 and 1982 reveals that there has been a steady decline in employment in industry, which became even more rapid after 1979/1980. By contrast, over the same period, more than 5 million jobs were created in the Community's market services sector. This figure, while impressive in absolute terms, looks less so relative to the equivalent figures for the USA (13.4 million) and even Japan (6.7 million). Another cause for concern is that in the Community, unlike in our main competitors, this trend has tailed off since 1980 as a result of the recession.

98. Although freedom to provide services in the Community has been directly applicable since the end of the transitional period as the Court of Justice recognized in the Van Binsbergen judgement, firms and individuals have not yet succeeded in taking full advantage of this freedom.

99. For these reasons, the Commission considers that swift action should be taken to open up the whole market for services. This applies both to the new service areas such as information marketing and audiovisual services; and to the so-called traditional (but rapidly evolving) services such as transport, banking and insurance which, if properly mobilised, can play a key supporting role for industry and commerce.

### «Traditional» Services

100. Of prime importance – because the Community has been depriving itself of the potential benefits for far too long – is the need to open up the cross-border market in the traditional services, notably banking and insurance and transport. The Commission would emphasize here that proposals necessary to open up these two sectors have already been made but still await Council's decision. The Council should, therefore, take the appropriate decisions as indicated in the timetable to be completed by 1990.

### Financial services

101. The liberalisation of financial services, linked to that of capital movements, will represent a major step towards Community financial integration and the widening of the Internal Market.

102. The accent is now put increasingly on the free circulation of «financial products», made ever easier by developments of technology. Some comparison can be made between the approach followed by the Commission after the «Cassis de Dijon» judgements with regard to industrial and agricultural products and what now has to be done for insurance policies, home-ownership savings contracts, consumer credit, participation in collective investment schemes, etc. The Commission considers that it should be possible to facilitate the exchange of such «financial products» at a Community level, using a minimal coordination of rules (especially on such matters as authorisation, financial supervision and reorganisation, winding up, etc) as the basis for mutual recognition by Member States of what each does to safeguard the interests of the public.

103. Such harmonisation, particularly as regards the supervision of ongoing activities, should be guided by the principle of «home country control». This means attributing the primary task of supervising the financial institution to the competent authorities of

its Member State of origin, to which would have to be communicated all information necessary for supervision. The authorities of the Member State which is the destination of the service, whilst not deprived of all power, would have a complementary role. There would have to be a minimum harmonisation of surveillance standards, though the need to reach agreement on this must not be allowed further to delay the necessary and overdue decisions.

104. The implementation of these principles in the field of credit institutions (especially banks) is being pursued actively, in particular on the following lines:

- the standards of financial stability which credit institutions must live up to and the management principles which they must apply (concerning, for instance, their own funds, the solvency and liquidity ratios, the monitoring of large exposures) are being thoroughly coordinated;

- the rules contained in the fourth and seventh company law Directives on annual accounts and consolidated accounting are being adapted to the sector of credit institutions;

- furthermore, the conditions which must be fulfilled by institutions seeking access to the markets as well as the measures to be taken at Community level when it comes to reorganising or winding up an institution in case of crisis are being coordinated;

- to name a more specific area, the Commission is working towards the mutual recognition of the financial techniques used by mortgage credit institutions and of the rules applying to the supervision of such institutions.

105. As regards insurance undertakings, directives adopted in 1973 (non-life) and 1979 (life) to facilitate the exercise of the right of establishment already coordinate rules and practices for the supervision of insurers and particularly of their financial stability. Moreover, close cooperation between supervisory authorities has been in existence for a long time. The ground is thus prepared for freedom of services across frontiers, which should therefore not present insurmountable problems, especially since the Directive of 11 May 1960 liberates capital movements with regard to premiums and payments in respect of all forms of insurance. It must nevertheless be noted that a Directive intended to facilitate the exercise of freedom of services in non-life insurance by spelling out the part to be played by the various supervisory authorities in cross-frontier operations has not yet been adopted by the Council. It will furthermore be necessary in the near future to examine closely those aspects of freedom of services which are peculiar to life assurance.

106. In the securities sector, the coordination of rules applicable to undertakings for collective investment in transferable securities (UCITS) is aimed at providing equivalent safeguards for investors in respect of the units issued by UCITS, irrespective of the Member State in which the UCITS is situated. Once approved by the authorities in its home Member State, a UCITS will be able freely to market its units throughout the Community, without permitting additional controls to be introduced. Thus this directive would be an example of the principle of «home country control». Mutual recognition will be made possible by the coordination of the safeguards offered by the financial product in question.

107. Apart from the UCITS proposal, other work still remains to be done to ensure that securities markets operate satisfactorily and in the best interests of investors. Work currently in hand to create a European securities market system, based on Community stock exchanges, is also relevant to the creation of an internal market. This work is designed to break down barriers between stock exchanges and to create a Community-wide trading system for securities of international interest. The aim is to link stock exchanges electronically, so that their members can execute orders on the stock exchange market offering the best conditions to their clients. Such an interlinking would substantially increase the depth and liquidity of Community stock exchange markets, and would permit them to compete more effectively not only with stock exchanges outside the Community but also with unofficial and unsupervised markets within it.

**Transport**

108. The right to provide transport services freely throughout the Community is an important part of the Common Transport Policy set out in the Treaty. It should be noted that transport represents more than 7% of the Community's g.d.p., and that the development of a free market in this sector would have considerable economic consequences for industry and trade. The recent decision of the Court in the case brought by the European Parliament against the Council for failure to act in the field of the common transport policy (Case 13/83) highlights the necessity of making rapid progress in this area.

109. In addition to the measures already mentioned in the context of the elimination of frontier checks in road haulage traffic, the completion of the internal market requires the following actions in the transport sector:

- for the transport of goods by road between Member States, the phasing out of quantitative restrictions (quotas) and the establishment of conditions under which non-resident carriers may operate transport services in another Member State (cabotage) will be completed by 1988 at the latest.
- for the transport of passengers by road, freedom to provide services will be introduced by 1989.
- for the international transport of goods by inland waterway, freedom to provide services where this is not yet the case will be introduced. Where necessary, conditions will be established under which non-resident carriers may operate inland navigation services in another Member State (cabotage). Both measures should come into effect by 1989.
- the freedom to provide sea transport services between Member States shall be established by the end of 1986 at the latest, though with the possibility of a limited period for phasing out certain types of restrictions.
- in the air transport sector, it is necessary to provide by 1987 for greater freedom in air transport services between Member States. This will involve in particular changing the system for the setting and approval of tariffs, and limiting the rights of Governments to restrict capacity and access to the market.

110. Implementation of common policy measures in the transport sector by the dates mentioned above will require decisions by the Council by December 1985 (air fares and some aspects of maritime transport); by June 1986 (remaining aspects in the aviation and maritime sectors); and by December 1986 (road haulage, inland waterways, coach services).

111. If the Council fails to make progress towards the adoption of proposed Regulations concerning the application of competition rules to air and to sea transport, the Commission intends to take Decisions recording existing infringements and authorising Member States to take measures as determined by the Commission according to Article 89 of the EEC Treaty.

112. All these measures form only part of the common transport policy which extends to other measures (e.g. state aid policy, improvement of railway financing, harmonization in the road sector, infrastructure planning and investment) which are not of direct relevance to the internal market but which are an essential element of this policy.

**New technologies and Services**

113. The development of new technologies has led to the creation and development of new cross-border services which are playing an increasingly important role in the economy. However, these services can develop their full potential only when they serve a large, unobstructed market. This applies equally to audiovisual services, information and data processing services and to computerized marketing and distribution services.

114. In addition, the Commission would stress that a market free of obstacles at Community level necessitates the installation of appropriate telecommunication networks with common standards.

115. In the field of audiovisual services, the objective for the Community should be to seek to establish a single Community-wide broadcasting area. Broadcasting is an important part of the communications industry which is expected to develop very rapidly into a key sector of the Community economy and will have a decisive impact on the future competitiveness of Community industries in the internal market.

116. In accordance with the Treaty objective of creating a common market for services, all those who provide and relay broadcast services and who receive them should be able, if they wish, to do so on a Community-wide basis. This freedom goes hand in hand with the right of freedom of information regardless of frontiers.

117. As a result of the development of broadcasting within essentially national frameworks, legal obstacles, actual and potential, lie in the path of those seeking to develop broadcasting activities across the borders of Member States. These obstacles consist mainly of different limitations on the extent to which broadcast programmes may contain advertising; as well as of the rights of owners of copyright and related rights to authorise retransmission by cable of broadcasts for each Member State separately. On the basis of the Commission's Green Paper, adopted

in May 1984, on the establishment of the common market for broadcasting, especially by satellite and cable, a number of measures are necessary to realise a single Community-wide broadcasting area. As a first step towards this objective, the Commission will submit appropriate proposals in 1985. The Council should take a decision before 1987.

118. The information market is also undergoing far reaching changes as a result of the application of new information technologies. These changes are mainly due to:

- the almost exponential growth of the amount of information available;
- the growing speed with which new information becomes obsolete;
- the strong tendency of information to flow across borders; and
- the application of new information technologies.

119. Information itself and information services are becoming more and more widely traded and valuable commodities, and in many respects primary resources for industry and commerce. The opening of the market for it is therefore of increasing importance. Moreover, the functioning of markets for other commodities depends upon the transmission and availability of information. As a commodity, however, it has unique and difficult properties.

120. The information market has been supported by a series of programmes decided by the Council on 27 July 1981 and 27 November 1984. The current one is due for mid-term evaluation in the course of this year. But a satisfactory internal market requires more. It requires, as the European Council has recognized, a common policy and strategy within which a transparent regulation and transparent conditions can be built. The Commission has issued a general discussion paper on this subject and intends to follow it up with appropriate proposals and guidelines in the period 1985-1987.

121. The European marketing and distribution system will also undergo a thorough technological transformation. Home videotex will permit the ordering of products direct from the manufacturer, thus revolutionizing traditional distribution channels, while ensuring greater market transparency. These new technologies, which will bring in their wake a need for adequate consumer protection, could lead to increased commercial activity within the Community, particularly in the mail-order sector.

122. Electronic banking too will promote information and commercial transactions. The new payment cards (memory cards, on-line cards) will tend to replace existing cheques and credit cards. Although an agreement already exists on the compatibility of videotex equipment in the Community, there is no similar agreement for the production of the new cards.

123. The Commission intends to make proposals to help define common technical features of the machines used to produce the new payment cards, so that they can be identical throughout the Community. It will also seek to encourage, in conformity with Community competition rules, the conclusion of agreements at European level between banks, traders, producers and consumers on the compatibility of systems, networks linkage, user rules and/or rates of commission.

# DECLARATIONS BY THE EUROPEAN COUNCIL RELATING TO THE INTERNAL MARKET

«The European Council... instructs the Council:

- to decide, before the end of March 1983, on the priority measures proposed by the Commission to reinforce the internal market».

Copenhagen, 3/4 December 1982.

«It asks the Council and the Member States to put in hand without delay a study of the measures which could be taken to bring about in the near future...

- the abolition of all police and customs formalities for people crossing intra-Community frontiers...».

Fontainebleau, 25/26 June 1984.

«The European Council... agreed that the Council, in its appropriate formations:

- ... should take steps to complete the Internal Market, including implementation of European standards».

Dublin, 3/4 December 1984.

«... the European Council laid particular emphasis on the following... fields of action:

a) action to achieve a single large market by 1992 thereby creating a more favourable environment for stimulating enterprise, competition and trade; it called upon the Commission to draw up a detailed programme with a specific timetable before its next meeting».

Brussels, 29/30 March 1985.

# 2. Employees

Official Journal of the European Communities No L 257/ 19.10.68

# REGULATION (EEC) No 1612/68 OF THE COUNCIL

of 15 October 1968

on freedom of movement for workers within the Community (*)

THE COUNCIL OF THE EUROPEAN COMMUNITIES,

Having regard to the Treaty establishing the European Economic Community, and in particular Article 49 thereof;

Having regard to the proposal from the Commission;

Having regard to the Opinion of the European Parliament[1];

Having regard to the Opinion of the Economic and Social Committee[2];

Whereas freedom of movement for workers should be secured within the Community by the end of the transitional period at the latest; whereas the attainment of this objective entails the abolition of any discrimination based on nationality between workers of the Member States as regards employment, remuneration and other conditions of work and employment, as well as the right of such workers to move freely within the Community in order to pursue activities as employed persons subject to any limitations justified on grounds of public policy, public security or public health;

Whereas by reason in particular of the early establishment of the customs union and in order to ensure the simultaneous completion of the principal foundations of the Community, provisions should be adopted to enable the objectives laid down in Articles 48 and 49 of the Treaty in the field of freedom of movement to be achieved and to perfect measures adopted successively under Regulation No 15[3] on the first steps for attainment of freedom of movement and under Council Regulation No 38/54/EEC[4] of 25 March 1964 on freedom of movement for workers within the Community;

Whereas freedom of movement constitutes a fundamental right of workers and their families; whereas mobility of labour within the Community must be one of the means by which the worker is guaranteed the possibility of improving his living and working conditions and promoting his social advancement, while helping to satisfy the requirements of the economies of the Member States; whereas the right of all workers in the Member States to pursue the activity of their choice within the Community should be affirmed;

Whereas such right must be enjoyed without discrimination by permanent, seasonal and frontier workers and by those who pursue their activities for the purpose of providing services;

Whereas the right of freedom of movement, in order that it may be exercised, by objective standards, in freedom and dignity, requires that equality of treatment shall be ensured in fact and in law in respect of all matters relating to the actual pursuit of activities as employed persons and to eligibility for housing, and also that obstacles to the mobility of workers shall be eliminated, in particular as regards the worker's right to be joined by his family and the conditions for the integration of that family into the host country;

Whereas the principle of non-discrimination between Community workers entails that all nationals of Member States have the same priority as regards employment as is enjoyed by national workers;

Whereas it is necessary to strengthen the machinery for vacancy clearance, in particular by developing direct co-operation between the central employment services and also between the regional services, as well as by increasing and co-ordinating the exchange of information in order to ensure in a general way a clearer picture of the labour market; whereas workers wishing to move should also be regularly informed of living and working conditions; whereas, furthermore, measures should be provided for the case where a Member State undergoes or foresees disturbances on its labour market which may seriously threaten the standard of living and level of employment in a region or an industry; whereas for

---

[1] OJ No 268, 6.11.1967, p. 9.
[2] OJ No 298, 7.12.1967, p. 10.
[3] OJ No 57, 26.8.1961, p. 1073/61.
[4] OJ No 62, 17.4.1964, p. 965/64.

(*) Text as amended by Regulation EEC No 312/76 of the Counsil of 9.2.1976, OJ No L 39 of 14.2.1976.

this purpose the exchange of information, aimed at discouraging workers from moving to such a region or industry, constitutes the method to be applied in the first place but, where necessary, it should be possible to strengthen the results of such exchange of information by temporarily suspending the above-mentioned machinery, any such decision to be taken at Community level;

Whereas close links exist between freedom of movement for workers, employment and vocational training, particularly where the latter aims at putting workers in a position to take up offers of employment from other regions of the Community; whereas such links make it necessary that the problems arising in this connection should no longer be studied in isolation but viewed as inter-dependent, account also being taken of the problems of employment at the regional level; and whereas it is therefore necessary to direct the efforts of Member States toward co-ordinating their employment policies at Community level;

Whereas the Council, by its Decision of 15 October 1968[1] made Articles 48 and 49 of the Treaty and also the measures taken in implementation thereof applicable to the French overseas departments;

HAS ADOPTED THIS REGULATION:

## *PART I*

## EMPLOYMENT AND WORKERS' FAMILIES

### TITLE I

### Eligibility for employment

*Article 1*

1. Any national of a Member State, shall, irrespective of his place of residence, have the right to take up an activity as an employed person, and to pursue such activity, within the territory of another Member State in accordance with the provisions laid down by law, regulation or administrative action governing the employment of nationals of that State.

2. He shall, in particular, have the right to take up available employment in the territory of another Member State with the same priority as nationals of that State.

*Article 2*

Any national of a Member State and any employer pursuing an activity in the territory of a Member State may exchange their applications for and offers of employment, and may conclude and perform contracts of employment in accordance with the provisions in force laid down by law, regulation or administrative action, without any discrimination resulting therefrom.

*Article 3*

1. Under this Regulation, provisions laid down by law, regulation or administrative action or administrative practices of a Member State shall not apply:

— where they limit application for and offers of employment, or the right of foreign nationals to take up and pursue employment or subject these to conditions not applicable in respect of their own nationals; or

— where, though applicable irrespective of nationality, their exclusive or principal aim or effect is to keep nationals of other Member States away from the employment offered.

This provision shall not apply to conditions relating to linguistic knowledge required by reason of the nature of the post to be filled.

2. There shall be included in particular among the provisions or practices of a Member State referred to in the first subparagraph of paragraph 1 those which:

(a) prescribe a special recruitment procedure for foreign nationals;

(b) limit or restrict the advertising of vacancies in the press or through any other medium or subject it to conditions other than those applicable in respect of employers pursuing their activities in the territory of that Member State;

(c) subject eligibility for employment to conditions of registration with employment offices or impede recruitment of individual workers, where persons who do not reside in the territory of that State are concerned.

*Article 4*

1. Provisions laid down by law, regulation or administrative action of the Member States which restrict by number or percentage the employment of foreign nationals in any undertaking, branch of activity or region, or at a national level, shall not apply to nationals of the other Member States.

[1] OJ No L 257, 19.10.1968, p. 1.

2. When in a Member State the granting of any benefit to undertakings is subject to a minimum percentage of national workers being employed, nationals of the other Member States shall be counted as national workers, subject to the provisions of the Council Directive of 15 October 1963. (1)

*Article 5*

A national of a Member State who seeks employment in the territory of another Member State shall receive the same assistance there as that afforded by the employment offices in that State to their own nationals seeking employment.

*Article 6*

1. The engagement and recruitment of a national of one Member State for a post in another Member State shall not depend on medical, vocational or other criteria which are discriminatory on grounds of nationality by comparison with those applied to nationals of the other Member State who wish to pursue the same activity.

2. Nevertheless, a national who holds an offer in his name from an employer in a Member State other than that of which he is a national may have to undergo a vocational test, if the employer expressly requests this when making his offer of employment.

TITLE II

**Employment and equality of treatment**

*Article 7*

1. A worker who is a national of a Member State may not, in the territory of another Member State, be treated differently from national workers by reason of his nationality in respect of any conditions of employment and work, in particular as regards remuneration, dismissal, and should he become unemployed, reinstatement or re-employment;

2. He shall enjoy the same social and tax advantages as national workers.

3. He shall also, by virtue of the same right and under the same conditions as national workers, have access to training in vocational schools and retraining centres.

4. Any clause of a collective or individual agreement or of any other collective regulation concerning eligibility for employment, employment, remuneration and other conditions of work or dismissal shall be null and void in so far as it lays down or authorises discriminatory conditions in respect of workers who are nationals of the other Member States.

*Article 8*

1. A worker who is a national of a Member State and who is employed in the territory of another Member State shall enjoy equality of treatment as regards membership of trade unions and the exercise of rights attaching thereto, including the right to vote and to be eligible for the administration or management posts of a trade union; he may be excluded from taking part in the management of bodies governed by public law and from holding an office governed by public law. Furthermore, he shall have the right of eligibility for workers' representative bodies in the undertaking. The provisions of this Article shall not affect laws or regulations in certain Member States which grant more extensive rights to workers coming from the other Member States. (*)

2. (**)

*Article 9*

1. A worker who is a national of a Member State and who is employed in the territory of another Member State shall enjoy all the rights and benefits accorded to national workers in matters of housing, including ownership of the housing he needs.

2. Such worker may, with the same right as nationals, put his name down on the housing lists in the region in which he is employed, where such lists exist; he shall enjoy the resultant benefits and priorities.

If his family has remained in the country whence he came, they shall be considered for this purpose as residing in the said region, where national workers benefit from a similar presumption.

TITLE III

**Workers' families**

*Article 10*

1. The following shall, irrespective of their nationality, have the right to install themselves with a

(1) OJ No 159, 2.11 1963, p. 2661/63.

(*) Paragraph as amended by Regulation EEC No 312/76, Article 1, paragraph 1.
(**) Paragraph as deleted by Regulation EEC No 312/76, Article 1, paragraph 2.

worker who is a national of one Member State and who is employed in the territory of another Member State:

(a) his spouse and their descendants who are under the age of 21 years or are dependants;

(b) dependent relatives in the ascending line of the worker and his spouse.

2. Member States shall facilitate the admission of any member of the family not coming within the provisions of paragraph 1 if dependent on the worker referred to above or living under his roof in the country whence he comes.

3. For the purposes of paragraphs 1 and 2, the worker must have available for his family housing considered as normal for national workers in the region where he is employed; this provision, however must not give rise to discrimination between national workers and workers from the other Member States.

*Article 11*

Where a national of a Member State is pursuing an activity as an employed or self-employed person in the territory of another Member State, his spouse and those of the children who are under the age of 21 years or dependent on him shall have the right to take up any activity as an employed person throughout the territory of that same State, even if they are not nationals of any Member State.

*Article 12*

The children of a national of a Member State who is or has been employed in the territory of another Member State shall be admitted to that State's general educational, apprenticeship and vocational training courses under the same conditions as the nationals of that State, if such children are residing in its territory.

Member States shall encourage all efforts to enable such children to attend these courses under the best possible conditions.

# 3. Doctors

Official Journal of the European Communities No L 167/30. 6. 75

II

*(Acts whose publication is not obligatory)*

# COUNCIL

## COUNCIL DIRECTIVE

**of 16 June 1975**

**concerning the mutual recognition of diplomas, certificates and other evidence of formal qualifications in medicine, including measures to facilitate the effective exercise of the right of establishment and freedom to provide services** (*)

(75/362/EEC)

THE COUNCIL OF THE EUROPEAN COMMUNITIES,

Having regard to the Treaty establishing the European Economic Community, and in particular Articles 49, 57, 66 and 235 thereof;

Having regard to the proposal from the Commission;

Having regard to the Opinion of the European Parliament (1);

Having regard to the Opinion of the Economic and Social Committee (2);

Whereas, pursuant to the Treaty, all discriminatory treatment based on nationality with regard to establishment and provision of services is prohibited as from the end of the transitional period; whereas the principle of such treatment based on nationality applies in particular to the grant of any authorization required to practise as a doctor and also to the registration with or membership of professional organizations or bodies;

Whereas it nevertheless seems desirable that certain provisions be introduced to facilitate the effective exercise of the right of establishment and freedom to provide services in respect of the activities of doctors;

Whereas, pursuant to the Treaty, the Member States are required not to grant any form of aid likely to distort the conditions of establishment;

Whereas Article 57 (1) of the Treaty provides that directives be issued for mutual recognition of diplomas, certificates and other evidence of formal qualifications; whereas the aim of this Directive is the recognition of diplomas, certificates and other evidence of formal qualifications whereby activities in the field of medicine can be taken up and pursued and the recognition of diplomas, certificates and other evidence of formal qualifications in respect of specialists;

Whereas, with regard to the training of the specialist, mutual recognition of training qualifications is advisable where these qualifications, while not being a condition of access to take up the activities of a specialist, nonetheless entitle him to use a specialist title;

Whereas, in view of the differences between the Member States, regarding the number of medical specialties and the type or the length of training courses for such specialties, certain coordinating provisions intended to enable Member States to proceed with the mutual recognition of diplomas, certificates and other evidence of formal qualifications should be laid down; whereas such coordination has been effected by Council Directive No 75/363/EEC (3) of 16 June 1975 concerning the coordination of provisions laid down by law, regulation or administrative action in respect of the activities of doctors;

Whereas the coordination referred to above was not intended to harmonize all the provisions of the Member States on the training of specialists and it is nevertheless appropriate to proceed with the mutual recognition of diplomas, certificates and other evidence of formal qualifications as a specialist

(*) Text as amended by:
- the Act of Accession for Greece (Official Journal of the European Communities No L 291, 19.11.1979, p.90);
- Directive 82/76/EEC of 26 February 1982 (Official Journal of the European Communities No L 43, 15.2.1982, p.21);
- Act of Accession for Spain and Portugal (Official Journal of the European Communities No L 302, 15.11.1985, p.158).

(1) OJ No C 101, 4. 8. 1970, p. 19.
(2) OJ No C 36, 28. 3. 1970, p. 17.
(3) OJ No L 167, 30.6.1975, p.14.

which are not common to all the Member States, without however excluding the possibility of subsequent harmonization in this field; whereas it was considered in this connection that recognition of diplomas, certificates and other evidence of formal qualifications as a specialist must be restricted to those Member States where such specialization is known;

Whereas, with regard to the possession of a formal certificate of training, since a directive on the mutual recognition of diplomas does not necessarily imply equivalence in the training covered by such diplomas, the use of such qualifications should be authorized only in the language of the Member State of origin or of the Member State from which the foreign national comes;

Whereas, to facilitate the application of this Directive by the national authorities, Member States may prescribe that, in addition to formal certificates of training, the person who satisfies the conditions of training required by this Directive must provide a certificate from the competent authorities of his country of origin or of the country from which he comes stating that these certificates of training are those covered by the Directive;

Whereas this Directive does not affect the provisions laid down by law, regulation or administrative action in the Member States, which prohibit companies or firms from practising medicine or impose on them certain conditions for such practice;

Whereas, in the case of the provision of services, the requirement of registration with or membership of professional organizations or bodies, since it is related to the fixed and permanent nature of the activity pursued in the host country, would undoubtedly constitute an obstacle to the person wishing to provide the service, by reason of the temporary nature of his activity; whereas this requirement should therefore be abolished; whereas however, in this event, control over professional discipline, which is the responsibility of these professional organizations or bodies, should be guaranteed; whereas, to this end, it should be provided, subject to the application of Article 62 of the Treaty, that the person concerned may be required to submit to the competent authority of the host Member State particulars relating to the provision of services;

Whereas, with regard to the requirements relating to good character and good repute, a distinction should be drawn between the requirements to be satisfied on first taking up the profession and those to be satisfied to practice it;

Whereas, as far as the activities of employed doctors are concerned, Council Regulation (EEC) No 1612/68 [1] of 15 October 1968 on freedom of movement for workers within the Community, lays down no specific provisions relating to good character or good repute, professional discipline or use of title for the professions covered; whereas, depending on the individual Member State, such rules are or may be applicable both to employed and self-employed persons; whereas the activities of doctors are subject in all Member States to possession of a diploma, certificate or other evidence of formal qualification in medicine; whereas such activities are pursued by both employed and self-employed persons, or by the same persons in both capacities in the course of their professional career; whereas, in order to encourage as far as possible the free movement of those professional persons within the Community, it therefore appears necessary to extend this Directive to employed doctors,

HAS ADOPTED THIS DIRECTIVE:

## CHAPTER I

## SCOPE

### *Article 1*

This Directive shall apply to the activities of doctors.

## CHAPTER II

## DIPLOMAS, CERTIFICATES AND OTHER EVIDENCE OF FORMAL QUALIFICATIONS IN MEDICINE

### *Article 2*

Each Member State shall recognize the diplomas, certificates and other evidence of formal qualifications awarded to nationals of Member States by the other Member States in accordance with Article 1 of Directive No 75/363/EEC and which are listed in Article 3, by giving such qualifications, as far as the right to take up and pursue the self-employed activities of a doctor is concerned, the same effect in its territory as those which the Member State itself awards.

### *Article 3*

The diplomas, certificates and other evidence of formal qualifications referred to in Article 2 are as follows:

[1] OJ No L 257, 19. 10. 1968, p. 2.

(a) *in Germany:*

1. 'Zeugnis über die ärztliche Staatsprüfung' (the State examination certificate in medicine) awarded by the competent authorities and the 'Zeugnis über die Vorbereitungszeit als Medizinalassistent' (certificate stating that the preparatory period as medical assistant has been completed) in so far as German law still requires such a period to complete medical training;

2. the certificates from the competent authorities of the Federal Republic of Germany stating that the diplomas awarded after 8 May 1945 by the competent authorities of the German Democratic Republic are recognized as equivalent to those listed in point 1 above;

(b) *in Belgium:*

'diplôme légal de docteur en médecine, chirurgie et accouchements/Wettelijk diploma van doctor in de genees-, heel- en verloskunde' (diploma of doctor of medicine, surgery and obstetrics required by law) awarded by the university faculties of medicine, the Central Examining Board or the State University Education Examining Board;

(c) *in Denmark:*

'bevis for bestået lægevidenskabelig embedseksamen' (diploma of doctor of medicine required by law) awarded by a university faculty of medicine and 'dokumentation for gennemført praktisk uddannelse' (certificate of practical training issued by the competent authorities of the health service);

(d) *in France:*

1. 'diplôme d'État de docteur en médecine' (State diploma of doctor of medicine) awarded by the university faculties of medicine, the university joint faculties of medicine and pharmacy, or by the universities;

2. 'diplôme d'université de docteur en médecine' (university diploma of doctor of medicine) where that diploma certifies completion of the same training course as that laid down for the State diploma of doctor of medicine;

(e) *in Ireland:*

a primary qualification granted in Ireland after passing a qualifying examination held by a competent examining body and a certificate of experience granted by that body which give entitlement to registration as a fully registered medical practitioner;

(f) *in Italy:*

'diploma di abilitazione all'esercizio della medicina e chirurgia' (diploma conferring the right to practise medicine and surgery) awarded by the State Examining Commission;

(g) *in Luxembourg:* (*)

'diplôme d'État de docteur en médecine, chirurgie et accouchements' (State diploma of doctor of medicine, surgery and obstetrics) awarded by the State Examining Board, and endorsed by the Minister of Education, and 'certificat de stage' (certificate of practical training) endorsed by the Minister for Public Health;

(h) *in the Netherlands:*

'universitair getuigschrift van arts' (university certificate of doctor);

(i) *in the United Kingdom:*

a primary qualification granted in the United Kingdom after passing a qualifying examination held by a competent examining body and a certificate of experience granted by that body which give entitlement to registration as a fully registered medical practitioner;

(j) in Greece: (**)

πτυχίο ἰατρικῆς Σχολῆς (degree awarded by the Faculty of Medicine) awarded by a University Faculty of Medicine, and πιστοποιητικό πρακτικῆς ἀσκήσεωσ (certificate of practical training) issued by the Ministry for Social Services;

(*) Text as amended by Directive 82/76/EEC.
(**) Text as amended by the Act of Accession for Greece.

(k) *in Spain:* (*)

"Título de Licenciado en Medicina y Cirurgía" (university degree in medicine and surgery) awarded by the Ministry of Education and Science;

(l) *in Portugal:* (*)

"Carta de curso de licenciatura em medicina" (diploma confirming the completion of medical studies), awarded by a university, and the "Diploma comprovativo da conclusão do internato geral" (diploma confirming the completion of general internship), awarded by the competent authorities of the Ministry of Health.

CHAPTER III

## DIPLOMAS, CERTIFICATES AND OTHER EVIDENCE OF FORMAL QUALIFICATIONS IN SPECIALIZED MEDICINE COMMON TO ALL MEMBER STATES

### *Article 4*

Each Member State shall recognize the diplomas, certificates and other evidence of formal qualifications in specialized medicine awarded to nationals of Member States by the other Member States in accordance with Articles 2, 3, 4 and 8 of Directive No 75/363/EEC and which are listed in Article 5, by giving such qualifications the same effect in its territory as those which the Member State itself awards.

### *Article 5*

1. The diplomas, certificates and other evidence of formal qualifications referred to in Article 4 shall be those which, having been awarded by the competent authorities or bodies listed in paragraph 2, correspond, for the purpose of the specialized training concerned, to the qualifications recognized in the various Member States and listed in paragraph 3.

2. The diplomas, certificates and other evidence of formal qualifications awarded by the competent authorities or bodies referred to in paragraph 1 are as follows:

*in Germany:*

'die von den Landesärztekammern erteilte fachärztliche Anerkennung' (recognized certificate of medical specialist, issued by the Chamber of Physicians of the 'Land' concerned);

*in Belgium:*

'le titre d'agrégation en qualité de médecin spécialiste/erkenningstitel van specialist' (formal evidence of having qualified as a medical specialist) issued by the Minister for Public Health;

*in Denmark:*

'bevis for tilladelse til at betegne sig som speciallæge' (certificate concerning the title of specialist) issued by the competent authorities of the health service;

*in France:*

— 'le certificat d'études spéciales de médecine' (certificate of specialized studies in medicine) issued by a university faculty of medicine, university joint faculties of medicine and pharmacy or by universities;

— certificates of qualified medical specialist, drawn up by the Council of the Ordre des médecins;

— 'le certificat d'études spéciales de médecine' (certificate of specialized studies in medicine) issued by a university faculty of medicine, university joint faculties of medicine and pharmacy or equivalent certificates drawn up under a decree of the Minister for Education;

*in Ireland:*

certificate of specialist doctor issued by the competent authority recognized for this purpose by the Minister for Health;

*in Italy:*

'diploma di medico specialista, rilasciati dal rettore di una universita' (diploma of specialized doctor, granted by a Rector of a University);

*in Luxembourg:*

'certificat de médecin spécialiste' (certificate of specialist doctor) issued by the Minister for Public Health on the advice of the medical college;

(*) Text as amended by the Act of Accession for Spain and Portugal.

*in the Netherlands:*

'het door de Specialisten-Registratiecommissie (SRC) afgegeven getuigschrift van erkenning en inschrijving in het Specialistenregister' (certificate of recognition and registration in the Register of Specialists, issued by the Commission for the Registration of Specialists (CRS) );

*in the United Kingdom:*

certificate of completion of specialist training issued by the competent authority recognized for this purpose;

in Greece: (*)

τίτλος ιατρικής ειδικότητος (certificate of specialization in medicine) issued by the Minitry for Social Services;

*in Spain:* (**)

"Título de Especialista" (professional qualification of specialist) awarded by the Ministry of Education and Science;

*in Portugal:* (**)

"Grau de Assistente" (assistant grade), awarded by the competent authorities of the Ministry of Health, or "Título de Especialista" (professional qualification of specialist) awarded by the professional association for medical practitioners.

3. The titles currently used in the Member States which correspond to the specialized training courses in question are as follows:

— *anaesthetics:*

| | |
|---|---|
| Germany: | Anästhesiologie(***) |
| Belgium: | anesthésiologie/anesthesiologie(***) |
| Denmark: | anæstesiologi |
| France: | anesthésie-réanimation |
| Ireland: | anaesthetics |
| Italy: | anestesia e rianimazione |
| Luxembourg: | anesthésie-réanimation |
| Netherlands: | anesthesie |
| United Kingdom: | anaesthetics |
| Greece: | αναισθησιολογία (*) |
| Spain: | anestesiología y reanimación (**) |
| Portugal: | anestesiologia; (**) |

— *general surgery:*

| | |
|---|---|
| Germany: | Chirurgie |
| Belgium: | chirurgie/heelkunde |
| Denmark: | kirurgi eller kirurgiske sygdomme |
| France: | chirurgie générale |
| Ireland: | general surgery |
| Italy: | chirurgia generale |
| Luxembourg: | chirurgie générale |
| Netherlands: | heelkunde |
| United Kingdom: | general surgery |
| Greece: | χειρουργική (*) |
| Spain: | cirugía general (**) |
| Portugal: | cirurgia geral; (**) |

— *neurological surgery:*

| | |
|---|---|
| Germany: | Neurochirurgie |
| Belgium: | neurochirurgie/neurochirurgie |
| Denmark: | neurokirurgi eller kirurgiske nervesygdomme |
| France: | neurochirurgie |
| Ireland: | neurological surgery |
| Italy: | neurochirurgia |
| Luxembourg: | neurochirurgie |
| Netherlands: | neurochirurgie |
| United Kingdom: | neurological surgery |
| Greece: | νευροχειρουργική (*) |
| Spain: | neurocirugía (**) |
| Portugal: | neurocirurgia; (**) |

— *obstetrics and gynaecology:*

| | |
|---|---|
| Germany: | Frauenheilkunde und Geburtshilfe |
| Belgium: | gynécologie-obstétrique/ gynecologie- verloskunde (***) |
| Denmark: | gynækologi og obstetrik eller kvindesygdomme og fødselshjælp |
| France: | gynécologie-obstétrique (***) |
| Ireland: | obstetrics and gynaecology |
| Italy: | obtetricia e ginecologia |
| Luxembourg: | gynécologie-obstetrique |
| Netherlands: | verloskunde en gynaecologie |
| United Kingdom: | obstetrics and gynaecology |
| Greece: | μαιευτική — γυναικολογία (*) |
| Spain: | obstetricia y ginecología (**) |
| Portugal: | ginecologia e obstetrícia; (**) |

(*) Text as amended by the Act of Accession for Greece.
(**) Text as amended by the Act of Accession for Spain and Portugal.
(***) Text as amended by Directive 82/76/EEC.

— *general (internal) medicine:*

| | |
|---|---|
| Germany: | Innere Medizin |
| Belgium: | médicine interne/inwendgie geneeskunde |
| Denmark: | intern medicin eller medicinske sygdomme |
| France: | médecine interne |
| Ireland: | general (internal) medicine |
| Italy: | medicina interna |
| Luxembourg: | maladies internes |
| Netherlands: | inwendige geneeskunde |
| United Kingdom: | general medicine |
| Greece: | παθολογία (*) |
| Spain: | medicina interna (**) |
| Portugal: | medicina interna; (**) |

— *ophthalmology:*

| | |
|---|---|
| Germany: | Augenheilkunde |
| Belgium: | ophtalmologie/ophtalmologie |
| Denmark: | oftalmologi eller øjensygdomme |
| France: | ophtalmologie |
| Ireland: | ophthalmology |
| Italy: | oculistica |
| Luxembourg: | ophtalmologie |
| Netherlands: | oogheelkunde |
| United Kingdom: | ophthalmology |
| Greece: | όφθαλμολογία (*) |
| Spain: | oftalmología (**) |
| Portugal: | oftalmologia; (**) |

— *oto rhino laryngology:*

| | |
|---|---|
| Germany: | Hals-Nasen-Ohrenheilkunde (***) |
| Belgium: | oto-rhino-laryngologie/ otorhino- laryngologie (***) |
| Denmark: | oto-rhino-laryngologi eller øre-næse-halssygdomme |
| France: | oto-rhino-laryngologie |
| Ireland: | otolaryngology |
| Italy: | otorinolaringoiatria |
| Luxembourg: | oto-rhino-laryngologie |
| Netherlands: | keel-, neus-, en oorheelkunde |
| United Kingdom: | otolaryngology |
| Greece: | ώτορινολαρυγγολογία (*) |
| Spain: | otorrinolaringología (**) |
| Portugal: | otorrinolaringologia; (**) |

— *paediatrics:*

| | |
|---|---|
| Germany: | Kinderheilkunde |
| Belgium: | pédiatrie/kindergeneeskunde (***) |
| Denmark: | pædiatri eller børnesygdomme |
| France: | pédiatrie |
| Ireland: | paediatrics |
| Italy: | pediatria |
| Luxembourg: | pediatrie |
| Netherlands: | kindergeneeskunde |
| United Kingdom: | paediatrics |
| Greece: | παιδιατρική (*) |
| Spain: | pediatría y sus áreas específicas (**) |
| Portugal: | pediatria; (**) |

— *respiratory medicine:*

| | |
|---|---|
| Germany: | Lungen- und Bronchialheilkunde |
| Belgium: | pneumologie/pneumologie |
| Denmark: | medicinske lungesygdomme |
| France: | pneumo-phtisiologie |
| Ireland: | respiratory medicine |
| Italy: | tisiologia e malattie dell'apparato respiratorio |
| Luxembourg: | pneumo-phtisiologie |
| Netherlands: | ziekten der luchtwegen |
| United Kingdom: | respiratory medicine |
| Greece: | φυματιολογία — πνευμονολογία (*) |
| Spain: | neumología (**) |
| Portugal: | pneumologia; (**) |

— *urology:*

| | |
|---|---|
| Germany: | Urologie |
| Belgium: | urologie/urologie |
| Denmark: | urologi eller urinvejenes kirurgiske sygdomme |
| France: | urologie |
| Ireland: | urology |
| Italy: | urologia |
| Luxembourg: | urologie |
| Netherlands: | urologie |
| United Kingdom: | urology |
| Greece: | οὐρολογία (*) |
| Spain: | urología (**) |
| Portugal: | urologia; (**) |

(*) Text as amended by the Act of Accession for Greece.
(**) Text as amended by the Act of Accession for Spain and Portugal.
(***) Text as amended by Directive 82/76/EEC.

— *orthopaedics:*

| | |
|---|---|
| Germany: | Orthopädie |
| Belgium: | orthopédie/orthopedie |
| Denmark: | ortopædisk kirurgi |
| France: | orthopédie |
| Ireland: | orthopaedic surgery |
| Italy: | ortopedia e traumatologia |
| Luxembourg: | orthopédie |
| Netherlands: | orthopedie |
| United Kingdom: | orthopaedic surgery |
| Greece: | ορθοπεδική (*) |
| Spain: | traumatoligía y cirugía ortopédica (**) |
| Portugal: | ortopedia. (**) |

CHAPTER IV

DIPLOMAS, CERTIFICATES AND OTHER EVIDENCE OF FORMAL QUALIFICATIONS IN SPECIALIZED MEDICINE PECULIAR TO TWO OR MORE MEMBER STATES

*Article 6*

Each Member State with provisions on this matter laid down by law, regulation or administrative action shall recognize the diplomas, certificates and other evidence of formal qualifications in specialized medicine awarded to nationals of Member States by other Member States in accordance with Articles 2, 3, 5 and 8 of Directive No 75/363/EEC and which are listed in Article 7, by giving such qualifications the same effect in its territory as those which the Member State itself awards.

*Article 7*

1. The diplomas, certificates and other evidence of formal qualifications referred to in Article 6 shall be those which, having been awarded by the competent authorities or bodies listed in Article 5 (2), correspond for the purposes of the specialized training in question to the designations listed in paragraph 2 of this Article in respect of those Member States which give such training.

2. The designations currently used in the Member States which correspond to the specialist training courses in question are as follows:

*clinical biology:*

| | |
|---|---|
| Belgium: | biologie clinique/klinische biologie |
| France: | biologie médicale |
| Italy: | patologia diagnostica di laboratorio |
| Spain: | análisis clínicos (**) |
| Portugal: | patologia clinica; (**) |

*biological haematology:*

| | |
|---|---|
| Denmark: | klinisk blodtypeserologi |
| Luxembourg: | hématologie biologique |
| Spain: | hematologia y hemoterapia (**) |
| Portugal: | hematologia clínica; (**) |

*microbiology — bacteriology:*

| | |
|---|---|
| Denmark: | klinisk mikrobiologi |
| Ireland: | microbiology |
| Italy: | microbiologia |
| Luxembourg: | microbiologie |
| Netherlands: | medische microbiologie (***) |
| United Kingdom: | medical microbiology |
| Germany: | Mikrobiologie und Infektionsepidemiologie (***) |
| Greece: | μικροβιολογία (*) |
| Spain: | microbiología y parasitología; (**) |

*pathological anatomy:*

| | |
|---|---|
| Germany: | Pathologie (***) |
| Denmark: | patalogisk anatomi og histologi eller vævsundersøgelse |
| France: | anatomie pathologique |
| Ireland: | morbid anatomy and histopathology |
| Italy: | anatomia patologica |
| Luxembourg: | anatomie pathologique |
| Netherlands: | pathologische anatomie |
| United Kingdom: | morbid anatomy and histopathology |
| Greece: | παθολογική ἀνατομία (*) |
| Spain: | anatomía patológica (**) |
| Portugal: | anatomia patologica; (**) |

*biological chemistry:*

| | |
|---|---|
| Denmark: | klinisk kemi |
| Ireland: | chemical pathology |
| Luxembourg: | chimie biologique (***) |
| Netherlands: | klinische chemie |
| United Kingdom: | chemical pathology |
| Spain: | bioquímica clínica; (**) |

(*) Text as amended by the Act of Accession for Greece.
(**) Text as amended by the Act of Accession for Spain and Portugal.
(***) Text as amended by Directive 82/76/EEC.

*immunology:*

| | |
|---|---|
| Ireland: | clinical immunology |
| United Kingdom: | immunology |
| Spain: | immunología; (*) |

*plastic surgery:*

| | |
|---|---|
| Belgium: | chirurgie plastique/ plastische heelkunde |
| Denmark: | plastikkirurgi |
| France: | chirurgie plastique et reconstructive |
| Ireland: | plastic surgery |
| Italy: | chirurgia plastica |
| Luxembourg: | chirurgie plastique |
| Netherlands: | plastishe chirurgie |
| United Kingdom: | plastic surgery |
| Greece: | πλαστική χειρουργική (**) |
| Spain: | cirugía plástica y reparadora (*) |
| Portugal: | cirurgia plastica; (*) |

*thoracic surgery:*

| | |
|---|---|
| Belgium: | chirurgie thoracique/heelkunde op de thorax |
| Denmark: | thoraxkirurgi eller brysthulens kirurgiske sygdomme |
| France: | chirurgie thoracique |
| Ireland: | thoracic surgery |
| Italy: | chirurgia toracica |
| Luxembourg: | chirurgie thoracique |
| Netherlands: | cardio-pulmonale chirurgie |
| United Kingdom: | thoracic surgery |
| Greece: | χειρουργική θώρακος (**) |
| Spain: | cirugía torácica (*) |
| Portugal: | circurgia torácica; (*) |

*paediatric surgery:*

| | |
|---|---|
| Ireland: | paediatric surgery |
| Italy: | chirurgia pediatrica |
| Luxembourg: | chirurgie pédiatrique(***) |
| United Kingdom: | paediatric surgery |
| Greece: | χειρουργική παίδων (**) |
| Spain: | cirugía pediátrica (*) |
| Portugal: | cirurgia pediátrica; (*) |

*vascular surgery:*

| | |
|---|---|
| Belgium: | chirurgie des vaisseaux/ bloedvatenheelkunde |
| Italy: | cardio-angio chirurgia |
| Luxembourg: | chirurgie cardio-vasculaire |
| Spain: | angiología y cirugía vascular (*) |
| Portugal: | cirurgia vascular; (*) |

*cardiology:*

| | |
|---|---|
| Belgium: | cardiologie/cardiologie |
| Denmark: | cardiologi eller hjerte — og kredsløbssygdomme |
| France: | cardiologie et médecine des affections vasculaires |
| Ireland: | cardiology |
| Italy: | cardiologia |
| Luxembourg: | cardiologie et angiologie |
| Netherlands: | cardiologie |
| United Kingdom: | cardio-vascular disease |
| Greece: | καρδιολογία (**) |
| Spain: | cardiología (*) |
| Portugal: | cardiologia; (*) |

*gastro-enterology:*

| | |
|---|---|
| Belgium: | gastro-entérologie/ gastro-enterologie |
| Denmark: | medicinsk gastroenterologi eller medicinske mave-tarmsygdomme |
| France: | maladies de l'appareil digestif |
| Ireland: | gastroenterology |
| Italy: | malattie dell'apparato digerente della nutrizione e del ricambio |
| Luxembourg: | gastro-entérologie et maladies de la nutrition |
| Netherlands: | maag- en darmziekten |
| United Kingdom: | gastroenterology |
| Greece: | γαστρεντερολογία (**) |
| Spain: | aparato digestivo(*) |
| Portugal: | gastro-enterologia; (*) |

*rheumatology:*

| | |
|---|---|
| Belgium: | rhumatologie/reumatologie |
| France: | rhumatologie |
| Ireland: | rheumatology |
| Italy: | reumatologia |
| Luxembourg: | rhumatologie |
| Netherlands: | reumatologie |
| United Kingdom: | rheumatology |
| Greece: | ρευματολογία (**) |
| Spain: | reumatología (*) |
| Portugal: | reumatologia; (*) |

*general haematology:*

| | |
|---|---|
| Ireland: | haematology |
| Italy: | ematologia |
| Luxembourg: | hématologie |
| United Kingdom: | haematology |
| Greece: | αίματολογία (**) |
| Spain: | hematología y hemoterapia (*) |
| Portugal: | imunohemoterapia; (*) |

(*) Text as amended by the Act of Accession for Spain and Portugal.
(**) Text as amended by the Act of Accession for Greece.
(***) Text as amended by Directive 82/76/EEC.

*endocrinology:*

| | |
|---|---|
| Ireland: | endocrinology and diabetes mellitus |
| Italy: | endocrinologia |
| Luxembourg: | endocrinologie |
| United Kingdom: | endocrinology and diabetes mellitus |
| Greece: | ἐνδοκρινολογία (*) |
| Spain: | endocrinología y nutricion (**) |
| Portugal: | endocrinologia-nutriçao; (**) |

*physiotherapy:*

| | |
|---|---|
| Belgium: | médecine physique/ fysische geneeskunde (***) |
| Denmark: | fysiurgi og rehabilitering |
| France: | rééducation et réadaptation fonctionnelles |
| Italy: | fisioterapia |
| Netherlands: | revalidatie |
| Luxembourg: | rééducation et réadaptation fonctionnelles (***) |
| Greece: | φυσική ἰατρική ἀποκατάσταση (*) |
| Spain: | rehabilitación (**) |
| Portugal: | fisiatria; (**) |

*stomatology:*

| | |
|---|---|
| France: | stomatologie |
| Italy: | odontostomatologia |
| Luxembourg: | stomatologie |
| Spain: | estomatología (**) |
| Portugal: | estomatologia; (**) |

*neurology:*

| | |
|---|---|
| Germany: | Neurologie |
| Denmark: | neuromedicin eller mediciniske nervesygdomme |
| France: | neurologie |
| Ireland: | neurology |
| Italy: | neurologia |
| Luxembourg: | neurologie |
| Netherlands: | neurologie |
| United Kingdom: | neurology |
| Greece: | Νευρολογία (***) |
| Spain: | neurologia (**) |
| Portugal: | neurologia; (**) |

*psychiatry:*

| | |
|---|---|
| Germany: | Psychiatrie |
| Denmark: | psykiatri |
| France: | psychiatrie |
| Ireland: | psychiatry |
| Italy: | psichiatria |
| Luxembourg: | psychiatrie |
| Netherlands: | psychiatrie |
| United Kingdom: | psychiatry |
| Greece: | Ψυχιατρική (***) |
| Spain: | psiquiatria (**) |
| Portugal: | psiquiatria; (**) |

*neuro-psychiatry:*

| | |
|---|---|
| Germany: | Nervenheilkunde (Neurologie und Psychiatrie) (***) |
| Belgium: | neuro-psychiatrie/ neuropsychiatrie |
| France: | neuro-psychiatrie |
| Italy: | neuropsichiatria |
| Luxembourg: | neuro-psychiatrie |
| Netherlands: | zenuw- en zielsziekten |
| Greece: | νευρολογία — ψυχιατρική; (*) |

*dermato-venereology:*

| | |
|---|---|
| Germany: | Dermatologie und Venerologie |
| Belgium: | dermato-vénéréologie/ dermato-venereologie |
| Denmark: | dermato-venerologi eller hud- og kønssygdomme |
| France: | dermato-vénéréologie |
| Italy: | dermatologia e venerologia |
| Luxembourg: | dermato-vénéréologie |
| Netherlands: | huid- en geslachtsziekten |
| Greece: | δερματολογία — ἀφροδισιολογία (*) |
| Spain: | dermatologia médico-quirurgica y venereologia (**) |
| Portugal: | dermatovenereologia; (**) |

*dermatology:*

| | |
|---|---|
| Ireland: | dermatology |
| United Kingdom: | dermatology; |

*venereology:*

| | |
|---|---|
| Ireland: | venereology |
| United Kingdom: | venereology; |

(*) Text as amended by the Act of Accession for Greece.
(**) Text as amended by the Act of Accession for Spain and Portugal.
(***) Text as amended by Directive 82/76/EEC.

*radiology:*

| | |
|---|---|
| Germany: | Radiologie |
| France: | radiologie |
| Italy: | radiologia |
| Luxembourg: | électro-radiologie |
| Netherlands: | radiologie |
| Greece: | ἀκτινολογία — ραδιολογία (*) |
| Spain: | electroradiologia (**) |
| Portugal: | radiologia; (**) |

*diagnostic radiology:*

| | |
|---|---|
| Belgium: | radiodiagnostic/röntgendiagnose (***) |
| Denmark: | diagnostisk radiologi eller røntgenundersøgelse |
| France: | radio-diagnostic |
| Ireland: | diagnostic radiology |
| Netherlands: | radiodiagnostiek |
| United Kingdom: | diagnostic radiology |
| Greece: | Ακτινοδιαγνωστική (*) |
| Luxembourg: | radiodiagnostic (***) |
| Spain: | radiodiagnostico (**) |
| Portugal: | radiodiagnostico; (**) |

*radiotherapy:*

| | |
|---|---|
| Belgium: | radio- et radiumthérapie/radio- en radiumtherapie (***) |
| Denmark: | terapeutisk radiologi eller strålebehandling |
| France: | radio-thérapie |
| Ireland: | radiotherapy |
| Netherlands: | radiotherapie |
| United Kingdom: | radiotherapy |
| Greece: | ἀκτινοθεραπευτική (*) |
| Spain: | oncologia radioterapica (**) |
| Portugal: | radioterapia (**) |
| Luxembourg: | radiothérapie; (***) |

*tropical medicine:*

| | |
|---|---|
| Belgium: | médicine tropicale/tropische geneeskunde |
| Denmark: | tropemedicin |
| Ireland: | tropical medicine |
| Italy: | medicina tropicale |
| United Kingdom: | tropical medicine |
| Portugal: | medicina tropical; (**) |

*child psychiatry:*

| | |
|---|---|
| Germany: | Kinder- und Jugendpsychiatrie |
| Denmark: | børnepsykiatri |
| France: | pédo-psychiatrie |
| Italy: | neuropsichiatria infantile |
| Luxembourg: | psychiatrie infantile (***) |
| United Kingdom: | child and adolescent psychiatry (***) |
| Greece: | παιδοψυχιατρική (*) |
| Portugal: | pedopsiquiatria; (**) |

*geriatrics:*

| | |
|---|---|
| Ireland: | geriatrics |
| United Kingdom: | geriatrics |
| Spain: | geriatría; (**) |

*renal diseases:*

| | |
|---|---|
| Denmark: | nefrologi eller medicinske nyresygdomme |
| Ireland: | nephrology |
| Italy: | nefrologia |
| United Kingdom: | renal diseases |
| Greece: | νεφρολογία (*) |
| Spain: | nefrologia (**) |
| Portugal: | nefrologia; (**) |

*communicable diseases:*

| | |
|---|---|
| Ireland: | communicable diseases |
| Italy: | malattie infettive |
| United Kingdom: | communicable diseases; |

*community medicine:*

| | |
|---|---|
| Ireland: | community medicine |
| United Kingdom: | community medicine; |

*pharmacology:*

| | |
|---|---|
| Germany: | Pharmakologie |
| Ireland: | clinical pharmacology and therapeutics |
| United Kingdom: | clinical pharmacology and therapeutics |
| Spain: | farmacología clínica; (**) |

*occupational medicine:*

| | |
|---|---|
| Ireland: | occupational medicine |
| United Kingdom: | occupational medicine; |

(*) Text as amended by the Act of Accession for Greece.
(**) Text as amended by the Act of Accession for Spain and Portugal.
(***) Text as amended by Directive 82/76/EEC.

*allergology:*

| | |
|---|---|
| Italy: | allergologia ed immunologia clinica |
| Netherlands: | allergologie |
| Greece: | αλλεργιολογία (*) |
| Spain: | alergología (**) |
| Portugal: | imuno-alergologia; (**) |

*gastro-enterological surgery:*

| | |
|---|---|
| Belgium: | chirurgie abdominale/heelkunde op het abdomen |
| Denmark: | kirurgisk gastroenterologi eller kirurgiske mave-tarmsygdomme |
| Italy: | chirurgia dell'apparato digerente |
| Spain: | cirugía del aparato digestivo. (**) |

*Article 8*

1. Nationals of Member States wishing to acquire one of the diplomas, certificates or other evidence of formal qualifications of specialist doctors not referred to in Articles 4 and 6, or which, although referred to in Article 6, are not awarded in the Member State of origin or the Member State from which the foreign national comes, may be required by a host Member State to fulfil the conditions of training laid down in respect of the specialty by its own law, regulation or administrative action.

2. The host Member State shall, however, take into account, in whole or in part, the training periods completed by the nationals referred to in paragraph 1 and attested by the award of a diploma, certificate or other evidence of formal training by the competent authorities of the Member State of origin or the Member State from which the foreign national comes provided such training periods correspond to those required in the host Member State for the specialized training in question.

3. The competent authorities or bodies of the host Member State, having verified the content and duration of the specialist training of the person concerned on the basis of the diplomas, certificates and other evidence of formal qualifications submitted, shall inform him of the period of additional training required and of the fields to be covered by it.

CHAPTER V

EXISTING CIRCUMSTANCES

*Article 9*

1. In the case of nationals of Member States whose diplomas, certificates and other evidence of formal qualifications in medicine do not satisfy all the minimum training requirements laid down in Article 1 Directive No 75/363/EEC, each Member State shall recognize, as being sufficient proof, the diplomas, certificates and other evidence of formal qualifications in medicine awarded by those Member States before the implementation of Directive No 75/363/EEC, accompanied by a certificate stating that those nationals have effectively and lawfully been engaged in the activities in question for at least three consecutive years during the five years prior to the date of issue of the certificate.

2. In the case of nationals of Member States whose diplomas, certificates and other evidence of formal qualifications in specialized medicine do not satisfy the minimum training requirements under Articles 2, 3, 4 and 5 of Directive No 75/363/EEC, each Member State shall recognize, as sufficient proof, the diplomas, certificates and other evidence of formal qualifications in specialized medicine awarded by the Member States before the implementation of Directive No 75/363/EEC. The Member State may, however, require that such diplomas, certificates and other evidence of formal qualifications be accompanied by a certificate issued by the competent authorities or bodies of the Member State of origin or of the Member State from which the foreign national comes, stating that he has been engaged in the activity in question as a specialist for a period equal to twice the difference between the length of specialized training of the Member State of origin or of the Member State from which the foreign national comes and the minimum training period referred to in Directive No 75/363/EEC where these periods are not equal to the minimum training periods laid down in Articles 4 and 5 of Directive No 75/363/EEC.

However, if, before the present Directive is implemented, the host Member State required a minimum training period less than the one at issue referred to in Articles 4 and 5 of Directive No 75/363/EEC, the difference mentioned in the first subparagraph can only be determined by reference to the minimum training period laid down by that State. (***)

(*) Text as amended by the Act of Accession for Greece.
(**) Text as amended by the Act of Accession for Spain and Portugal.
(***) Article 9(1) and (2) was supplemented by Directive 81/1057/EEC (see point 7).

3. In the case of nationals of the Member States whose diplomas, certificates and other evidence of formal qualifications in specialized medicine do not conform with the qualifications or designations set out in Articles 5 and 7, each Member State shall recognize the diplomas, certificates and other evidence of formal qualifications awarded by those Member States, together with a certificate of equivalence signed by the competent authorities or bodies, as sufficient proof.

4. Member States which, before notification of this Directive, have repealed the provisions laid down by law, regulation or administrative action on the awarding of diplomas, the drawing up of certificates and other evidence of formal qualifications in neuropsychiatry, dermato-venereology or radiology and have, before notification of this Directive, taken measures on behalf of their own nationals to regularize existing circumstances, shall accord the right to benefit from such measures to nationals of the Member States, in so far as their diplomas, certificates and other evidence of formal qualifications in neuropsychiatry, dermato-venereology or radiology fulfil the conditions laid down in this matter either in Articles 2 and 5 of Directive No 75/363/EEC or in paragraph 2 of this Article.

## CHAPTER VI

## USE OF ACADEMIC TITLE

### *Article 10*

1. Without prejudice to Article 18, host Member States shall ensure that the nationals of Member States who fulfil the conditions laid down in Articles 2, 4, 6 and 9 have the right to use the lawful academic title or, where appropriate, the abbreviation thereof, of their Member State of origin or of the Member State from which they come, in the languages of that State. Host Member States may require this title to be followed by the name and location of the establishment or examining board which awarded it.

2. If the academic title used in the Member State of origin, or in the Member State from which a foreign national comes, can be confused in the host Member State with a title requiring in that State additional training which the person concerned has not undergone, the host Member State may require such a person to use the title employed in the Member State of origin or the Member State from which he comes in suitable wording to be drawn up by the host Member State.

## CHAPTER VII

## PROVISIONS TO FACILITATE THE EFFECTIVE EXERCISE OF THE RIGHT OF ESTABLISHMENT AND FREEDOM TO PROVIDE SERVICES IN RESPECT OF THE ACTIVITIES OF DOCTORS

### A. Provisions specifically relating to the right of establishment

### *Article 11*

1. A host Member State which requires of its nationals proof of good character or good repute when they take up for the first time any activity referred to in Article 1 shall accept as sufficient evidence, in respect of nationals of other Member States, a certificate issued by a competent authority in the Member State of origin or in the Member State from which the foreign national comes, attesting that the requirements of the Member State as to good character or good repute for taking up the activity in question have been met.

2. Where the Member State of origin or the Member State from which the foreign national comes does not require proof of good character or good repute of persons wishing to take up the activity in question for the first time, the host Member State may require of nationals of the Member State of origin or of the Member State from which the foreign national comes an extract from the 'judicial record' or, failing this, an equivalent document issued by a competent authority in the Member State of origin or the Member State from which the foreign national comes.

3. If the host Member State has detailed knowledge of a serious matter which has occurred, prior to the establishment of the person concerned in that State, outside its territory and which is likely to affect the taking up within its territory of the activity concerned, it may inform the Member State of origin or the Member State from which the foreign national comes.

The Member State of origin or the Member State from which the foreign national comes shall verify the accuracy of the facts. Its authorities shall decide on the nature and extent of the investigation to be made and shall inform the host Member State of any consequential action which they take with regard to the certificates or documents they have issued.

Member States shall ensure the confidentiality of the information which is forwarded. (*)

*Article 12*

1. Where, in a host Member State, provisions laid down by law, regulation or administrative action are in force laying down requirements as to good character or good repute including provisions for disciplinary action in respect of serious professional misconduct or conviction of criminal offences and relating to the pursuit of any of the activities referred to in Article 1, the Member State of origin or the Member State from which the foreign national comes shall forward to the host Member State all necessary information regarding measures or disciplinary action of a professional or administrative nature taken in respect of the person concerned or criminal penalties imposed on him when pursuing his profession in the Member State of origin or in the Member State from which he came.

2. If the host Member State has detailed knowledge of a serious matter which has occurred, prior to the establishment of the person concerned in that State, outside its territory and which is likely to affect the pursuit within its territory of the activity concerned, it may inform the Member State of origin or the Member State from which the foreign national comes.

The Member State of origin or the Member State from which the foreign national comes shall verify the accuracy of the facts. Its authorities shall decide on the nature and extent of the investigation to be made and shall inform the host Member State of any consequential action which they take with regard to the information which they have forwarded in accordance with paragraph 1.(*)

3. Member States shall ensure the confidentiality of the information which is forwarded.

*Article 13*

Where a host Member State requires of its own nationals wishing to take up or pursue any activity referred to in Article 1, a certificate of physical or mental health, that State shall accept as sufficient evidence thereof the presentation of the document required in the Member State of origin or the Member State from which the foreign national comes.

Where the Member State of origin or the Member State from which the foreign national comes does not impose any requirements of this nature on those wishing to take up or pursue the activity in question, the host Member State shall accept from such national a certificate issued by a competent authority in that State corresponding to the certificates issued in the host Member State.

*Article 14*

Documents issued in accordance with Articles 11, 12 and 13 may not be presented more than three months after their date of issue.

*Article 15*

1. The procedure for authorizing the person concerned to take up any activity referred to in Article 1, pursuant to Articles 11, 12 and 13, must be completed as soon as possible and not later than three months after presentation of all the documents relating to such person, without prejudice to delays resulting from any appeal that may be made upon the termination of this procedure.

2. In the cases referred to in Article 11 (3) and Article 12 (2), a request for re-examination shall suspend the period laid down in paragraph 1.

The Member State consulted shall give its reply within a period of three months.

On receipt of the reply or at the end of the period the host Member State shall continue with the procedure referred to in paragraph 1.

*Article 15a*

Where a host Member State requires its own nationals wishing to take up or pursue one of the activities referred to in Article 1 to take an oath or make a solemn declaration and where the form of such an oath or declaration cannot be used by nationals of other Member States, that Member State shall ensure that an appropriate and equivalent form of oath or declaration is offered to the person concerned. (**)

(*) Paragraph as amended by Directive 82/76/EEC.
(**) Article added by Directive 82/76/EEC.

## B. Special provisions relating to the provision of services

*Article 16*

1. Where a Member State requires of its own nationals wishing to take up or pursue any activity referred to in Article 1, an authorization or membership of, or registration with, a professional organization or body, that Member State shall in the case of the provision of services exempt the nationals of Member States from that requirement.

The person concerned shall provide services with the same rights and obligations as the nationals of the host Member State; in particular he shall be subject to the rules of conduct of a professional or administrative nature which apply in that Member State.

For this purpose and in addition to the declaration provided for in paragraph 2 relating to the services to be provided, Member States may, so as to permit the implementation of the provisions relating to professional conduct in force in their territory, require either automatic temporary registration or *pro forma* membership of a professional organization or body or, as an alternative, registration, provided that such registration or membership does not delay or in any way complicate the provision of services or impose any additional costs on the person providing the services. (*)

Where a host Member State adopts a measure pursuant to the second subparagraph or becomes aware of facts which run counter to these provisions, it shall forthwith inform the Member State where the person concerned is established.

2. The host Member State may require the person concerned to make a prior declaration to the competent authorities concerning the provision of his services where they involve a temporary stay in its territory.

In urgent cases this declaration may be made as soon as possible after the services have been provided.

3. Pursuant to paragraphs 1 and 2, the host Member State may require the person concerned to supply one or more documents containing the following particulars:

— the declaration referred to in paragraph 2;

— a certificate stating that the person concerned is lawfully pursuing the activities in question in the Member State where he is established;

— a certificate that the person concerned holds one or other of the diplomas, certificates or other evidence of formal qualification appropriate for the provision of the services in question and referred to in this Directive.

4. The document or documents specified in paragraph 3 may not be produced more than 12 months after their date of issue.

5. Where a Member State temporarily or permanently deprives, in whole or in part, the right of one of its nationals or of a national of another Member State established in its territory to pursue one of the activities referred to in Article 1, it shall, as appropriate, ensure the temporary or permanent withdrawal of the certificate referred to in the second indent of paragraph 3.

*Article 17*

Where registration with a public social security body is required in a host Member State for the settlement with insurance bodies of accounts relating to services rendered to persons insured under social security schemes, that Member State shall exempt nationals of Member States established in another Member State from this requirement, in cases of provision of services entailing travel on the part of the person concerned.

However, the persons concerned shall supply information to this body in advance, or, in urgent cases, subsequently, concerning the services provided.

## C. Provisions common to the right of establishment and freedom to provide services

*Article 18*

Where in a host Member State the use of the professional title relating to one of the activities

(*) Subparagraph added by Directive82/76/EEC.

referred to in Article 1 is subject to rules, nationals of other Member States who fulfil the conditions laid down in Article 2 and Article 9 (1) shall use the professional title of the host Member State which, in that State, corresponds to those conditions of qualification and shall use the abbreviated title.

The first subparagraph shall also apply to the use of professional titles of specialist doctors by those who fulfil the conditions laid down in Articles 4 and 6 and Article 9 (2) (3) and (4).

(*)

*Article 20*

1. Member States shall take the necessary measures to enable the persons concerned to obtain information on the health and social security laws and, where applicable, on the professional ethics of the host Member State.

For this purpose Member States may set up information centres from which such persons may obtain the necessary information. In the case of establishment, the host Member States may require the beneficiaries to contact these centres.

2. Member States may set up the centres referred to in paragraph 1 within the competent authorities and bodies which they must designate within the period laid down in Article 25 (1).

3. Member States shall see to it that, where appropriate, the persons concerned acquire, in their interest and in that of their patients, the linguistic knowledge necessary to the exercise of their profession in the host country.

CHAPTER VIII

FINAL PROVISIONS

*Article 21*

Member States which require their own nationals to complete a preparatory training period in order to become eligible for appointment as a doctor of a social security scheme may impose the same requirement on nationals of the other Member States for a period of five years following notification of this Directive. The training period may not, however, exceed six months.

*Article 22*

In the event of justified doubts, the host Member State may require of the competent authorities of another Member State confirmation of the authenticity of the diplomas, certificates and other evidence of formal qualifications issued in that other Member State and referred to in Chapters II to V, and also confirmation of the fact that the person concerned has fulfilled all the training requirements laid down in Directive No 75/363/EEC.

*Article 23*

Within the time limit laid down in Article 25 (1), Member States shall designate the authorities and bodies competent to issue or receive the diplomas, certificates and other evidence of formal qualifications as well as the documents and information referred to in this Directive and shall forthwith inform the other Member States and the Commission thereof.

*Article 24*

This Directive shall also apply to the nationals of Member States who, in accordance with Regulation (EEC) No 1612/68, are pursuing or will pursue as employed persons one of the activities referred to in Article 1.

*Article 25*

1. Member States shall bring into force the measures necessary to comply with this Directive within 18 months of its notification and shall forthwith inform the Commission thereof.

2. Member States shall communicate to the Commission the texts of the main provisions of national law which they adopt in the field covered by this Directive.

(*) Article 19 repealed by Directive 82/76/EEC.

*Article 26*

Where a Member State encounters major difficulties in certain fields, when applying this Directive, the Commission shall examine these difficulties in conjunction with that State and shall request the opinion of the Committee of Senior Officials on Public Health set up by Decision No 75/365/ EEC (1).

When necessary, the Commission shall submit appropriate proposals to the Council.

*Article 27*

This Directive is addressed to the Member States.

Done at Luxembourg, 16 June 1975.

*For the Council*

*The President*

R. RYAN

(1) OJ No L 167, 30.6.1975, p.19.

Official Journal of the European Communities No L 167/ 30. 6. 75

# COUNCIL DIRECTIVE

## of 16 June 1975

## concerning the coordination of provisions laid down by law, regulation or administrative action in respect of activities of doctors (*)

(75/363/EEC)

THE COUNCIL OF THE EUROPEAN COMMUNITIES,

Having regard to the Treaty establishing the European Economic Community, and in particular Articles 49, 57, 66 and 235 thereof;

Having regard to the proposal from the Commission;

Having regard to the Opinion of the European Parliament [1];

Having regard to the Opinion of the Economic and Social Committee [2];

Whereas with a view to achieving the mutual recognition of diplomas, certificates and other evidence of formal qualifications in medicine, laid down by Directive No 75/362/EEC [3] of 16 June 1975 concerning the mutual recognition of diplomas, certificates and other evidence of formal qualifications in medicine, including measures to facilitate the effective exercise of the right of establishment and freedom to provide services, the comparable nature of training courses in the Member States enables coordination in this field to be confined to the requirement that minimum standards be observed, which then leaves the Member States freedom of organization as regards teaching;

Whereas with a view to mutual recognition of diplomas, certificates and other evidence of formal qualifications in specialized medicine and in order to put all members of the profession who are nationals of the Member States on an equal footing within the Community, some coordination of the requirements for training in specialized medicine seems necessary; whereas certain minimum criteria should be laid down for this purpose concerning the right to take up specialized training, the minimum training period, the method by which such training is given and the place where it is to be carried out, as well as the supervision to which it should be subject; whereas these criteria only concern the specialities common to all the Member States or to two or more Member States;

Whereas the coordination of the conditions for the pursuit of these activities, as envisaged by this Directive, does not exclude any subsequent coordination;

Whereas the coordination envisaged by this Directive covers the professional training of doctors; whereas, as far as training is concerned, most Member States do not at present distinguish between doctors who pursue their activities as employed persons and those who are self-employed; whereas for this reason and in order to encourage as far as possible the free movement of professional persons within the Community, it appears necessary to extend the application of this Directive to employed doctors,

HAS ADOPTED THIS DIRECTIVE:

### *Article 1*

1. The Member States shall require persons wishing to take up and pursue a medical profession to hold a diploma, certificate or other evidence of formal qualifications in medicine referred to in Article 3 of Directive No 75/362/EEC which guarantees that during his complete training period the person concerned has acquired:

(a) adequate knowledge of the sciences on which medicine is based and a good understanding of the scientific methods including the principles of measuring biological functions, the evaluation of scientifically established facts and the analysis of data;

(b) sufficient understanding of the structure, functions and behaviour of healthy and sick persons, as well as relations between the state of health and the physical and social surroundings of the human being;

(c) adequate knowledge of clinical disciplines and practices, providing him with a coherent picture of mental and physical diseases, of medicine from the points of view of prophylaxis, diagnosis and therapy and of human reproduction;

(d) suitable clinical experience in hospitals under appropriate supervision.

2. A complete period of medical training of this kind shall comprise at least a six-year course or 5 500

[1] OJ No C 101, 4. 8. 1970, p. 19.
[2] OJ No C 36, 28. 3. 1970, p. 19.
[3] OJ No L 167, 30.6.1975, p.1.

(*) Text as amended by Directive 82/76/EEC (OJ No L 43, 15.2.1982, p.21).

hours of theoretical and practical instruction given in a university or under the supervision of a university.

3. In order to be accepted for this training, the candidate must have a diploma or a certificate which entitles him to be admitted to the universities of a Member State for the course of study concerned.

4. In the case of persons who started their training before 1 January 1972, the training referred to in paragraph 2 may include six months' full-time practical training at university level under the supervision of the competent authorities.

5. Nothing in this Directive shall prejudice any facility which may be granted in accordance with their own rules by Member States in respect of their own territory to authorize holders of diplomas, certificates or other evidence of formal qualifications which have not been obtained in a Member State to take up and pursue the activities of a doctor.

*Article 2*

1. Member States shall ensure that the training leading to a diploma, certificate or other evidence of formal qualifications in specialized medicine, meets the following requirements at least:

(a) it shall entail the successful completion of six years' study within the framework of the training course referred to in Article 1;

(b) it shall comprise theoretical and practical instruction;

(c) it shall be a full-time course supervised by the competent authorities or bodies pursuant to point 1 of the Annex hereto; (*) (**)

(d) it shall be in a university centre, in a teaching hospital or, where appropriate, in a health establishment approved for this purpose by the competent authorities or bodies;

(e) it shall involve the personal participation of the doctor training to be a specialist in the activity and in the responsibilities of the establishments concerned.

2. Member States shall make the award of a diploma, certificate or other evidence of formal qualifications in specialized medicine subject to the possession of one of the diplomas, certificates or other evidence of formal qualifications in medicine referred to in Article 1.

3. Within the time limit laid down in Article 7, Member States shall designate the authorities or bodies competent to issue the diplomas, certificates or other evidence of formal qualifications referred to in paragraph 1.

*Article 3*

1. Without prejudice to the principle of full-time training as set out in Article 2 (1) (c), and until such time as the Council takes decisions in accordance with paragraph 3, Member States may permit part-time specialist training, under conditions approved by the competent national authorities, when training on a full-time basis would not be practicable for well-founded individual reasons.

2. Part-time training shall be given in accordance with point 2 of the Annex hereto and at a standard qualitatively equivalent to full-time training. This standard of training shall not be impaired, either by its part-time nature or by the practice of private, remunerated professional activity.

The total duration of specialized training may not be curtailed in those cases where it is organized on a part-time basis.

3. The Council shall decide, not later than 25 January 1989, whether the provisions of paragraphs 1 and 2 are to be maintained or amended, in the light of a re-examination of the situation and on a proposal by the Commission, with due regard to the fact that the possibility of part-time training should continue to exist in certain circumstances to be examined specialty by specialty. (***)

*Article 4*

Member States shall ensure that the minimum length of the specialized training courses mentioned below may not be less than the following:

First group:

| | |
|---|---|
| — general surgery<br>— neuro-surgery<br>— internal medicine<br>— urology<br>— orthopaedics | five years. |

Second group:

| | |
|---|---|
| — gynaecology and obstetrics<br>— paediatrics<br>— pneumo-phthisiology | four years. |

(*) Point replaced by Directive 82/76/EEC.
(**) The rights of those concerned for the period preceding 1 January 1983 are governed by this Article of the Directive in its 16 June 1975 wording.
(***) Article replaced by Directive 82/76/EEC.

Third group:

| | |
|---|---|
| — anesthesiology and reanimation<br>— ophthalmology<br>— otorhinolaryngology | three years. |

*Article 5*

Member States which have laid down provisions by law, regulation and administrative action in this field shall ensure that the minimum length of the specialized training courses mentioned below may not be less than the following:

First group:

| | |
|---|---|
| — plastic surgery<br>— thoracic surgery<br>— vascular surgery<br>— neuro-psychiatry<br>— paediatric surgery<br>— gastroenterological surgery | five years. |

Second group:

| | |
|---|---|
| — cardiology<br>— gastroenterology<br>— neurology<br>— rheumatology<br>— psychiatry<br>— clinical biology<br>— radiology<br>— diagnostic radiology<br>— radiotherapy<br>— tropical medicine<br>— pharmacology<br>— child psychiatry<br>— microbiology-bacteriology<br>— pathological anatomy<br>— occupational medicine<br>— biological chemistry<br>— immunology<br>— dermatology<br>— venereology<br>— geriatrics<br>— renal diseases<br>— contagious diseases<br>— community medicine<br>— biological haematology | four years. |

Third group:

| | |
|---|---|
| — general haematology<br>— endocrinology<br>— physiotherapy<br>— stomatology<br>— dermato-venereology<br>— allergology | three years. |

*Article 6*

This Directive shall also apply to nationals of Member States who, in accordance with Council Regulation (EEC) No 1612/68 (¹) of 15 October 1968 on freedom of movement for workers within the Community, are pursuing or will pursue, as employed persons, one of the activities referred to in Article 1 of Directive No 75/362/EEC.

*Article 7*

As a transitional mesasure and notwithstanding Articles 2 (1) (c) and 3, Member States whose provisions, laid down by law, regulation, or administrative action, provided for part-time specialist training at the time of notification of Directives 75/362/EEC and 75/363/EEC may continue to apply these provisions to candidates who have begun training as specialists not later than 31 December 1983.

Each host Member State shall be authorized to require the beneficiaries of the above paragraph to produce, in addition to their diplomas, certificates and other evidence of formal qualifications, an attestation certifying that for at least three consecutive years out of the five years preceding the issue of the attestation they have in fact been lawfully practising as specialists in the field concerned. (*) (**)

*Article 8*

As a transitional measure and notwithstanding Article 2 (2):

(a) as regards Luxembourg, and in respect only of the Luxembourg diplomas covered by the law of 1939 of Luxembourg on the conferring of academic and university degrees, the issue of a certificate as a specialist shall be conditional simply upon the possession of the diploma of doctor of medicine, surgery and obstetrics awarded by the Luxembourg State Examining Board;

(b) as regards Denmark, and in respect only of the Danish diplomas of doctors of medicine required by law awarded by a Danish university faculty of medicine in accordance with the decree of the Ministry of the Interior of 14 May 1970, the issue of a certificate as specialist shall be conditional simply upon the possession of the above-mentioned diplomas.

(¹) OJ No L 257, 19. 10. 1968, p. 2.

(*) Article replaced by Directive 82/76/EEC.
(**) The rights of those concerned for the period preceding 1 January 1983 are governed by this Article of the Directive in its 16 June 1975 wording.

The diplomas referred to under (a) and (b) may be awarded to candidates who began their training before the end of the period referred to in Article 9

*Article 9*

1. Member States shall bring into force the measures necessary to comply with this Directive within 18 months of its notification and shall forthwith inform the Commission thereof.

2. Member States shall communicate to the Commission the texts of the main provisions of national law which they adopt in the field covered by this Directive.

*Article 10*

Where a Member State encounters major difficulties in certain fields, when applying this Directive, the Commission shall examine these difficulties in conjunction with that State and shall request the opinion of the Committee of Senior Officials on Public Health set up by Decision No 75/365/ EEC (1).

When necessary, the Commission shall submit appropriate proposals to the Council.

*Article 11*

This Directive is addressed to the Member States.

Done at Luxembourg, 16 June 1975.

*For the Council*

*The President*

R. RYAN

(1) OJ No L 167, 30.6.1975, p.19.

*ANNEX (*)*

**Characteristics of full-time and part-time training of specialists**

1. *Full-time training of specialists*

Such training shall be carried out in specific posts recognized by the competent authority.

It shall involve participation in all the medical activities of the department where the training is carried out, including on-call duties, so that the trainee specialist devotes to this practical and theoretical training all his professional activity throughout the duration of the standard working week and throughout the year according to provisions agreed by the competent authorities. Accordingly these posts shall be subject to appropriate remuneration.

Training may be interrupted for reasons such as military service, secondment, pregnancy or sickness. The total duration of the training shall not be reduced by reason of any interruption.

2. *Part-time training of specialists*

This training shall meet the same requirements as full-time training, from which it shall differ only in the possibility of limiting participation in medical activities to a period at least half of that provided for in the second subparagraph of point 1.

The competent authorities shall ensure that the total duration and quality of part-time training of specialists are not less than those of full-time trainees.

Appropriate remuneration shall consequently be attached to such part-time training.

(*) Annex added by Directive 82/76/EEC.

Official Journal of the European Communities No L 43/ 15. 2. 82

# COUNCIL DIRECTIVE

## of 26 January 1982

**amending Directive 75/362/EEC concerning the mutual recognition of diplomas, certificates and other evidence of formal qualifications in medicine, including measures to facilitate effective exercise of the right of establishment and freedom to provide services and Directive 75/363/EEC concerning the coordination of provisions laid down by law, regulation or administrative action in respect of activities of doctors**

(82/76/EEC)

•••••• (*)

*Article 14*

Part-time specialist training begun before 1 January 1983 under Article 3 of Directive 75/363/EEC may be completed in accordance with that Article.

*Article 15*

Member States which, before notification of this Directive, have repealed the provisions laid down by law, regulation or administrative action on the award of diplomas, certificates and other evidence of formal qualification in neuropsychiatry or radiology and have, before the said notification, adopted measures relating to acquired rights on behalf of their own nationals, shall accord the right to benefit from such measures to nationals of the Member States, provided their diplomas, certificates and other evidence of formal qualifications in neuropsychiatry or radiology fulfil the conditions laid down in this respect either in Article 9 (2) of Directive 75/362/EEC or in Articles 2, 3 and 5 of Directive 75/363/EEC.

*Article 16*

Member States shall take the necessary measures to comply with this Directive by 31 December 1982 at the latest. They shall forthwith inform the Commission thereof.

*Article 17*

This Directive is addressed to the Member States.

Done at Brussels, 26 January 1982.

*For the Council*

*The President*

L. TINDEMANS

(*) The remaining provisions of the Directive are incorporated in the amended Directives.

Official Journal of the European Communities No L 267/19. 9. 86

II

*(Acts whose publication is not obligatory)*

# COUNCIL

## COUNCIL DIRECTIVE
## of 15 September 1986
## on specific training in general medical practice

(86/457/EEC)

THE COUNCIL OF THE EUROPEAN COMMUNITIES,

Having regard to the Treaty establishing the European Economic Community, and in particular Articles 49, 57 and 66 thereof,

Having regard to the proposal from the Commission [1],

Having regard to the opinion of the European Parliament [2],

Having regard to the opinion of the Economic and Social Committee [3],

Whereas Council Directive 75/362/EEC [4], as last amended by the 1985 Act of Accession, and Council Directive 75/363/EEC [5], as last amended by Directive 82/76/EEC [6], on freedom of movement for medical practitioners, contain no provisions regarding the mutual recognition of diplomas attesting to specific training in general medical practice or the criteria to which such training should conform ;

Whereas, although the Council did not consider that the time was right to take appropriate measures on the matter at Community level, it nevertheless noted that in a number of Member States there was a growing tendency to emphasize the general medical practitioner's role and the importance of his training ; whereas it accordingly requested the Commission to study the problems connected with this development ;

Whereas the point has now been reached where it is almost universally recognized that there is a need for specific training for the general medical practitioner to enable him better to fulfil his function ; whereas this function, which depends to a great extent on the doctor's personal knowledge of his patients' environment, consists of giving advice on the prevention of illness and on the protection of the patient's general health, besides giving appropriate treatment ;

Whereas this need for specific training in general medical practice has emerged mainly as a result of the development of medical science, which has increasingly widened the gap between medical research and teaching on the one hand and general medical practice on the other, so that important aspects of general medical practice can no longer be taught in a satisfactory manner within the framework of the Member States' current basic medical training ;

Whereas, apart from the benefit to patients, it is also recognized that improved training for the specific function of general medical practitioner would contribute to an improvement in health care, particularly by developing a more selective approach to the consultation of specialists, use of laboratories and other highly specialized establishments and equipment ;

(1) OJ No C 13, 15. 1. 1985, p. 3 and OJ No C 125, 24. 5. 1986, p. 8.
(2) OJ No C 36, 17. 2. 1986, p. 149.
(3) OJ No C 218, 29. 8. 1985, p. 9.
(4) OJ No L 167, 30. 6. 1975, p. 1.
(5) OJ No L 167, 30. 6. 1975, p. 14.
(6) OJ No L 43, 15. 2. 1982, p. 21.

Whereas improved training for general medical practice will upgrade the status of the general medical practitioner ;

Whereas, although this situation seems irreversible, it has developed at different rates in the various Member States ; whereas it is desirable to ensure that the various trends converge in successive stages, without however forcing the pace, with a view to appropriate training for every general medical practitioner in order to satisfy the specific requirements of general medical practice ;

Whereas, to ensure the gradual introduction of this reform, it is necessary in an initial stage to institute in each Member State specific training in general medical practice which satisfies minimum quality and quantity requirements, and supplements the minimum basic training which medical practitioners must receive in accordance with Directive 75/363/EEC ; whereas it is immaterial whether this training in general medical practice is received as part of, or separately from, basic medical training as laid down nationally ; whereas, in a second stage, provision should be made to subject the exercise of general medical practice under a social security scheme to completion of specific training in general medical practice ; whereas further proposals to complete the reform should subsequently be put forward ;

Whereas this Directive does not affect the power of the Member States to organize their national social security schemes and to determine what activities are to be carried out under those schemes ;

Whereas the coordination, pursuant to this Directive, of the minimum conditions governing the issue of diplomas, certificates or other evidence of formal qualifications certifying completion of specific training in general medical practice will render possible the mutual recognition of these diplomas, certificates or other evidence of formal qualifications by the Member States ;

Whereas, under Directive 75/362/EEC, a host Member State is not entitled to require medical practitioners, in possession of diplomas obtained in another Member State and recognized under that Directive, to complete any additional training in order to practise within its social security scheme, even where such training is required of holders of diplomas of medicine obtained in its own territory ; whereas this consequence of Directive 75/362/EEC will remain in effect as regards the exercise of general medical practice under social security schemes until 1 January 1995, from which date the present Directive requires all Member States to make the exercise of general medical practice in the context of their social security schemes subject to the possession of specific training in general medical practice ; whereas medical practitioners established in practice before that date under Directive 75/362/EEC must have an acquired right to practise as general medical practitioners under the national social security scheme of the host country even if they have not completed specific training in general medical practice,

HAS ADOPTED THIS DIRECTIVE :

*Article 1*

Each Member State which dispenses the complete training referred to in Article 1 of Directive 75/363/EEC within its territory shall institute specific training in general medical practice meeting requirements at least as stringent as those laid down in Articles 2 and 3 of this Directive, in such a manner that the first diplomas, certificates or other evidence of formal qualifications awarded on completion of the course are issued not later than 1 January 1990.

*Article 2*

1. The specific training in general medical practice referred to in Article 1 must meet the following minimum requirements :

(a) entry shall be conditional upon the successful completion of at least six years' study within the framework of the training course referred to in Article 1 of Directive 75/363/EEC ;

(b) it shall be a full-time course lasting at least two years, and shall be supervised by the competent authorities or bodies ;

(c) it shall be practically rather than theoretically based ; the practical instruction shall be given, on the one hand, for at least six months in an approved hospital or clinic with suitable equipment and services and, on the other hand, for at least six months in an approved general medical practice or in an approved centre where doctors provide primary care ; it shall be carried out in contact with other health establishments or structures concerned with general medical practice ;

however, without prejudice to the aforesaid minimum periods, the practical instruction may be given for a maximum period of six months in other approved health establishments or structures concerned with general medical practice ;

(d) it shall entail the personal participation of the trainee in the professional activities and responsibilities of the persons with whom he works.

2. Member States shall be entitled to defer application of the provisions of paragraph 1 (c) relating to minimum periods of instruction until 1 January 1995 at the latest.

3. Member States shall make the issue of diplomas, certificates, or other evidence of formal qualifications awarded after specific training in general medical practice, conditional upon the candidate's holding one of the diplomas, certificates or other evidence of formal qualifications referred to in Article 3 of Directive 75/362/EEC.

4. Member States shall designate the authorities or bodies competent to issue the diplomas, certificates or other evidence of formal qualifications awarded after specific training in general medical practice.

*Article 3*

If, at the date of notification of this Directive, a Member State provides training in general medical practice by means of experience in general medical practice acquired by the medical practitioner in his own surgery under the supervision of an authorized training supervisor, that Member State may retain this type of training on an experimental basis on condition that :

— it complies with Article 2 (1) (a) and (b), and Article 2 (3),

— its duration is equal to twice the difference between the period laid down in Article 2 (1) (b) and the sum of the periods laid down in the third indent hereof,

— it involves a period in an approved hospital or clinic with suitable equipment and services and a period in an approved general medical practice or in an approved centre where doctors provide primary care ; as from 1 January 1995, each of these periods shall be of at least six months' duration.

*Article 4*

On the basis of experience acquired, and in the light of developments in training in general medical practice, the Commission shall submit to the Council, by 1 January 1996 at the latest, a report on the implementation of Articles 2 and 3 and suitable proposals in order to achieve further harmonization of the training of general medical practitioners.

The Council shall act on these proposals in accordance with procedures laid down by the Treaty before 1 January 1997.

*Article 5*

1. Without prejudice to the principle of full-time training laid down in Article 2 (1) (b), Member States may authorize specific part-time training in general medical practice in addition to full-time training where the following particular conditions are met :

— the total duration of training may not be shortened because it is being followed on a part-time basis,

— the weekly duration of part-time training may not be less than 60 % of weekly full-time training,

— part-time training must include a certain number of full-time training periods, both for the training conducted at a hospital or clinic and for the training given in an approved medical practice or in an approved centre where doctors provide primary care. These full-time training periods shall be of sufficient number and duration as to provide adequate preparation for the effective exercise of general medical practice.

2. Part-time training must be of a level of quality equivalent to that of full-time training. It shall lead to a diploma, certificate or other evidence of formal qualification, as referred to in Article 1.

*Article 6*

1. Irrespective of any acquired rights they recognize, Member States may issue the diploma, certificate or other evidence of formal qualification referred to in Article 1 to a medical practitioner who has not completed the training referred to in Articles 2 and 3 but who holds a diploma, certificate or other evidence of formal qualification issued by the competent authorities of a Member State, attesting to completion of another additonal training course ; however, the Member States may issue such diploma, certificate or other evidence of formal qualification only if it attests to a level of skill equivalent to that reached on completion of the training referred to in Articles 2 and 3.

2. In adopting their rules in accordance with paragraph 1, Member States shall specify the extent to which the additional training already completed by the candidate

and his professional experience may be taken into account in place of the training referred to in Articles 2 and 3.

Member States may issue the diploma, certificate or other evidence of formal qualification referred to in Article 1 only if the candidate has acquired at least six months' experience in general medical practice in a general medical practice or a centre where doctors provide primary care, as referred to in Article 2 (1) (c).

*Article 7*

1. From 1 January 1995, and subject to the acquired rights it has recognized, each Member State shall make the exercise of general medical practice under its national social security scheme conditional on possession of a diploma, certificate or other evidence of formal qualification as referred to in Article 1.

However, Member States may exempt from this condition persons who are undergoing specific training in general medical practice.

2. Each Member State shall specify the acquired rights that it recognizes. However, it shall recognize the right to exercise the activities of gneral medical practitioner under its national social security scheme without the diploma, certificate or other evidence of formal qualification referred to in Article 1 as having been acquired by all those doctors who on 31 December 1994 possess such a right under Directive 75/362/EEC and who are established on its territory on that date by virtue of Article 2 or Article 9 (1) of that Directive.

3. Each Member State may apply paragraph 1 before 1 January 1995, subject to the condition that any doctor who has completed the training referred to in Article 1 of Directive 75/363/EEC in another Member State shall be able to establish himself in practice on its territory until 31 December 1994 and to practise under its national social security scheme by virtue of Article 2 or Article 9 (1) of Directive 75/362/EEC.

4. The competent authorities of each Member State shall issue on request a certificate granting doctors possessing acquired rights by virtue of paragraph 2 the right to practise as general medical practitioners under its national social security scheme without the diploma, certificate or other evidence of formal qualifications referred to in Article 1.

5. Paragraph 1 shall in no way prejudice the possibility, which is open to Member States, of granting, in accordance with their own rules and in respect of their own territory, the right to practise as general practitioners under a social security scheme to persons who do not possess diplomas, certificates or other formal evidence of medical training and of specific training in general medical practice obtained in both cases in a Member State, but who possess diplomas, certificates or other evidence of either or both of these types of training obtained in a non-member country.

*Article 8*

1. Each Member State shall recognize under its national social security scheme, for the purposes of the exercise of the activities of general medical practitioner, the diplomas, certificates, or other evidence of formal qualifications referred to in Article 1, issued to nationals of Member States by other Member States in accordance with Articles 2, 3, 5 and 6.

The certificates from the competent authorities of the Federal Republic of Germany, stating that the diplomas, certificates or other evidence of formal qualifications awarded by the competent authorities of the German Democratic Republic are recognized as equivalent to those listed in the first subparagraph, shall also be recognized.

2. Each Member State shall recognize the certificates referred to in Article 7 (4) issued to nationals of Member States by other Member States, and shall consider them as equivalent within its territory to the diplomas, certificates or other evidence of formal qualifications which it issues itself, and which permit the exercise of the activities of general medical practitioner under its national social security scheme.

*Article 9*

Nationals of Member States to whom a Member State has issued the diplomas, certificates or other evidence of formal qualifications referred to in Article 1 or Article 7 (4) shall have the right to use in the host Member State the professional title existing in that State and the abbreviation thereof.

*Article 10*

1. Without prejudice to Article 9, host Member States shall ensure that the nationals of Member States covered by Article 8 have the right to use the lawful academic title, or, where appropriate, the abbreviation thereof, of their Member State of origin or of the Member State from which they come, in the language of that Member State. Host Member States may require this title to be followed by the name and location of the establishment or examining board which awarded it.

2. If the academic title of the Member State of origin, or of the Member State from which a national comes, can be confused in the host Member State with a title requiring, in that State, additional training which the person concerned has not undergone, the host Member State concerned may require such person to use the title of the Member State of origin or of the Member State from which he comes in a suitable form to be indicated by the host Member State.

*Article 11*

On the basis of experience acquired, and in the light of developments in training in general medical practice, the Commission shall submit to the Council by 1 January 1997 at the latest a report on the implementation of this Directive and, if necessary, suitable proposals with a view to appropriate training for every general medical practitioner in order to satisfy the specific requirements of general medical practice. The Council shall act on those proposals in accordance with the procedures laid down in the Treaty.

*Article 12*

1. Member States shall take the measures necessary to comply with this Directive. They shall forthwith inform the Commission thereof.

They shall also notify the Commission of the date of entry into force of these measures.

2. As soon as a Member State has notified the Commission of the date of entry into force of the measures it has taken in conformity with Article 1, the Commission shall publish an appropriate notice in the *Official Journal of the European Communities*, indicating the designations adopted by that Member State for the diploma, certificate or other evidence of formal qualifications and, where appropriate, the professional title in question.

*Article 13*

This Directive is addressed to the Member States.

Done at Brussels, 15 September 1986.

*For the Council*

*The President*

G. HOWE

Official Journal of the European Communities No L 167/30. 6. 75

# COUNCIL RECOMMENDATION

## of 16 June 1975

## concerning nationals of the Grand Duchy of Luxembourg who hold a diploma in medicine conferred in a third country

(75/366/EEC)

THE COUNCIL,

Approving Directive No 75/362/EEC [1] concerning the mutual recognition of diplomas, certificates and other evidence of formal qualifications in medicine, including measures to facilitate the effective exercise of the right of establishment and freedom to provide services;

Noting that this Directive refers only to diplomas, certificates and other evidence of formal qualifications conferred in a Member State;

Anxious, however, to take account of the special position of nationals of the Grand Duchy of Luxembourg who, since there is no complete university training in the Grand Duchy itself, have studied in a third country;

Hereby recommends that the Governments of the Member States should allow nationals of the Grand Duchy of Luxembourg who hold a diploma conferring a degree in medicine awarded in a third country and which has obtained the official recognition of the Minister for Education, in accordance with the law of 18 June 1969 on higher education and the recognition of foreign degrees and diplomas in higher education, to take up and pursue activities as doctors within the Community, by recognizing these diplomas in their territories provided that such diplomas are accompanied by the training certificates endorsed by the Minister for Public Health of the Grand Duchy of Luxembourg.

Done at Luxembourg, 16 June 1975.

*For the Council*

*The President*

R. RYAN

[1] OJ No L 167, 30.6.1975, p.1.

Official Journal of the European Communities No L 167/30. 6. 75

# COUNCIL RECOMMENDATION

of 16 June 1975

on the clinical training of doctors

(75/367/EEC)

The Council notes that in most of the Member States, after university medical training proper, the requirement of clinical training is imposed as being a condition for acquiring the unrestricted right to practise medicine.

As it is considered desirable that the possibility should exist of acquiring such clinical training in Member States other than that in which the candidate underwent his university training, the Council hereby recommends to the Member States that admission to such clinical training posts be afforded to nationals of the other Member States.

Done at Luxembourg, 16 June 1975.

*For the Council*

*The President*

R. RYAN

Official Journal of the European Communities No C 146/ 1. 7. 75

I

*(Information)*

# COUNCIL

## COUNCIL STATEMENTS

**made on adopting the texts concerning freedom of establishment and freedom to provide services for doctors within the Community**

A. *Statements regarding the Directive concerning the mutual recognition of diplomas, certificates and other evidence of formal qualifications in medicine, including measures to facilitate the effective exercise of the right of establishment and freedom to provide services (question of good character and good repute)*

1. *Council statement re Article 12*

'The Council notes that in order to apply Article 12 Member States agree to observe the principle that, except for cases relating to acts committed in its own territory, the host Member State may not suspend or withdraw the right of establishment unless the particulars communicated by the Member State of origin or Member State from which the foreign national comes include penalties which deprive the person concerned, temporarily or permanently, of his right to pursue his activity in that country.'

2. *Council statement re Article 22*

'If a Member State which has been requested to recognize the diplomas, certificates or other evidence of formal qualifications issued by an institution of another Member State has serious doubts whether those diplomas, certificates or other evidence of formal qualifications are based on training which complies with the minimum standards laid down by Directive 75/362/EEC of 16 June 1975, it shall be incumbent on the said Member State to inform the Commission thereof. The Commission shall examine the matter as soon as possible and shall confirm, if such is the case, to the Member States concerned that the training standards have been complied with.'

B. *Statement on hospital doctors:*

'THE COUNCIL,

Having regard to the fact that according to Article 48 (4) of the EEC Treaty the provisions relating to the freedom of movement of workers do not apply to employment in the public service;

Whereas in certain Member States doctors employed in public hospitals have the status of public servants; and whereas they appear for this reason to be affected by the provisions of Article 48 (4) of the EEC Treaty;

Desirous, nevertheless, of facilitating the mobility of doctors within the Community, whatever the status governing their activity;

Having regard to the resolution of the European Parliament on the definition of the concepts 'public service' and 'official authority' in the Member States and the effects of this definition on the application of Articles 48 (4) and 55 of the Treaty establishing the EEC, and in particular point 11 thereof;

Having regard to the judgement of the Court of Justice of 21 June 1974 in case No 2/74,

NOTES:

That where in a Member State the practice of the medical profession in a public hospital carries with it the status of public servant, that Member State shall, with a view to facilitating the mobility of professional persons in this sector, and this within three years at the latest after the adoption by the Council of Directives 75/362/EEC of 16 June 1975 and 75/363/EEC of 16 June 1975, undertake to enable nationals of the other Member States to take up this activity, if necessary under special conditions of employment;

Notwithstanding the nature of these special conditions, nationals of the other Member States shall have access to this activity and may practise it under the same conditions and with rights having equivalent effect to those of nationals in that professional field in the host country;

With regard to requirements as to competence, however, the Member States concerned shall take account of the special qualifications acquired by the person concerned as well as of the practice he has had in the Member States, both being vouched for by a certificate issued for this purpose;

This undertaking shall not extend to the activity of a hospital doctor which involves high-level administrative duties or which includes activities which are connected, even occasionally, with the exercise of official authority,

CALLS UPON:

The Commission to submit to it, four years after the adoption of these Directives, a report on the implementation by the Member States of this undertaking and, where appropriate, to submit suitable suggestions.'

# 4. Nurses

Official Journal of the European Communities No L 176/ 15. 7. 77

II

*(Acts whose publication is not obligatory)*

# COUNCIL

## COUNCIL DIRECTIVE

of 27 June 1977

**concerning the mutual recognition of diplomas, certificates and other evidence of the formal qualifications of nurses responsible for general care, including measures to facilitate the effective exercise of the right of establishment and freedom to provide services (*)**

(77/452/EEC)

THE COUNCIL OF THE EUROPEAN COMMUNITIES,

Having regard to the Treaty establishing the European Economic Community, and in particular Articles 49, 57, 66 and 235 thereof,

Having regard to the proposal from the Commission,

Having regard to the opinion of the European Parliament (1),

Having regard to the opinion of the Economic and Social Committee (2),

Whereas, pursuant to the Treaty, all discriminatory treatment based on nationality with regard to establishment and provision of services is prohibited as from the end of the transitional period; whereas the principle of such treatment based on nationality applies in particular to the grant of any authorization required to practise as a nurse responsible for general care and also to the registration with or membership of professional organizations or bodies;

Whereas it nevertheless seems desirable that certain provisions be introduced to facilitate the effective exercise of the right of establishment and freedom to provide services in respect of the activities of nurses responsible for general care;

Whereas, pursuant to the Treaty, the Member States are required not to grant any form of aid likely to distort the conditions of establishment;

Whereas Article 57 (1) of the Treaty provides that Directives be issued for mutual recognition of diplomas, certificates and other evidence of formal qualifications;

Whereas it would appear advisable that, contemporaneously with the mutual recognition of diplomas, provision should be made for coordinating the conditions governing the training of nurses responsibles for general care; whereas such coordination is the subject of Directive 77/453/EEC (3);

Whereas in several Member States the law makes the right to take up and pursue the activities of a

(1) OJ No C 65, 5. 6. 1970, p. 12.
(2) OJ No C 108, 26. 8. 1970, p. 23.

(3) OJ No L 176, 15.7.1977, p.8.

(*) Text as amended by:
- the Act of Accession for Greece.
- the Act of Accession for Spain and Portugal.

nurse responsible for general care dependent upon the possession of a nursing diploma; whereas in certain other Member States where this requirement does not exist, the right to use the title of nurse responsible for general care is nevertheless governed by law;

Whereas, with regard to the possession of a formal certificate of training, since a Directive on the mutual recognition of diplomas does not necessarily imply equivalence in the training covered by such diplomas, the use of such qualifications should be authorized only in the language of the Member State of origin or of the Member State from which the foreign national comes;

Whereas, to facilitate the application of this Directive by the national authorities, Member States may prescribe that, in addition to formal certificates of training, the person who satisfies the conditions of training required by this Directive must provide a certificate from the competent authorities of his country of origin or of the country from which he comes stating that these certificates of training are those covered by the Directive;

Whereas, with regard to the requirements relating to good character and good repute, a distinction should be drawn between the requirements to be satisfied on first taking up the profession and those to be satisfied to practise it;

Whereas, in the case of the provision of services, the requirement of registration with or membership of professional organizations or bodies, since it is related to the fixed and permanent nature of the activity pursued in the host country, would undoubtedly constitute an obstacle to the person wishing to provide the service, by reason of the temporary nature of his activity; whereas this requirement should therefore be abolished; whereas, however, in this event, control over professional discipline, which is the responsibility of these professional organizations or bodies, should be guaranteed; whereas, to this end, it should be provided, subject to the application of Article 62 of the Treaty, that the person concerned may be required to submit to the competent authority of the host Member State particulars relating to the provision of services;

Whereas, as far as the activities of employed nurses responsible for general care are concerned, Council Regulation (EEC) No 1612/68 of 15 October 1968 on freedom of movement for workers within the Community [1] lays down no specific provisions relating to good character or good repute, professional discipline or use of title for the professions covered; whereas, depending on the individual Member State, such rules are or may be applicable both to employed and self-employed persons; whereas the activities of a nurse responsible for general care are subject in several Member States to possession of a diploma, certificate or other evidence of formal qualification in nursing; whereas such activities are pursued by both employed and self-employed persons, or by the same persons in both capacities in the course of their professional career; whereas, in order to encourage as far as possible the free movement of those professional persons within the Community, it therefore appears necessary to extend this Directive to employed nurses,

HAS ADOPTED THIS DIRECTIVE:

## CHAPTER I

## SCOPE

### *Article 1*

1. This Directive shall apply to the activities of nurses responsible for general care.

2. For the purposes of this Directive 'activities of nurses responsible for general care' shall mean activities pursued by persons holding the following titles:

*in Germany:*

'Krankenschwester', 'Krankenpfleger';

*in Belgium:*

'hospitalier(ère)/verpleegassistent(e)', 'infirmier(ère) hospitalier(ère)/ziekenhuisverpleger (-verpleegster)';

*in Denmark:*

'sygeplejerske';

(1) OJ No L 257, 19. 10. 1968, p. 2.

*in France:*

'infirmier(ère)';

*in Ireland:*

Registered General Nurse;

*in Italy:*

'infermiere professionale';

*in Luxembourg:*

'infirmier';

*in the Netherlands:*

'verpleegkundige';

*in the United Kingdom:*

*England, Wales and Northern Ireland:*
State Registered Nurse;

*Scotland:*
Registered General Nurse;

in Greece:

διπλωματοῦχος ἀδελφή νοσοκόμος; (*)

*in Spain:*
"Enfermero/a diplomado/a; (**)

*in Portugal:*
"Enfermeiro". (**)

CHAPTER II

DIPLOMAS, CERTIFICATES AND OTHER EVIDENCE OF FORMAL QUALIFICATIONS OF NURSES RESPONSIBLE FOR GENERAL CARE

*Article 2*

Each Member State shall recognize the diplomas, certificates and other evidence of formal qualifications awarded to nationals of Member States by other Member States in accordance with Article 1 of Directive 77/453/EEC and which are listed in Article 3, by giving such qualifications, as far as the right to take up and pursue the activities of a nurse responsible for general care in a self-employed capacity is concerned, the same effect in its territory as those which the Member State itself awards.

*Article 3*

The diplomas, certificates and other evidence of formal qualifications referred to in Article 2 are the following:

(a) *in Germany:*

— the certificates awarded by the competent authorities as a result of the 'staatliche Prüfung in der Krankenpflege' (State nursing examination),

— the certificates from the competent authorities of the Federal Republic of Germany stating that the diplomas awarded after 8 May 1945 by the competent authorities of the German Democratic Republic are recognized as equivalent to those listed in the first indent;

(b) *in Belgium:*

— the certificate of 'hospitalier(ère)/verpleegassistent(e)' awarded by the State or by schools established or recognized by the State,

— the certificate of 'infirmier(ère) hospitalier(ère)/ziekenhuisverpleger (-verpleegster)' awarded by the State or by schools established or recognized by the State,

— the diploma of 'infirmier(ère) gradué(e) hospitalier(ère)/gegradueerd ziekenhuisverpleger (-verpleegster)' awarded by the State or by higher paramedical colleges established or recognized by the State;

(c) *in Denmark:*

— the diploma of 'sygeplejerske' awarded by nursing schools recognized by the 'Sundhedsstyrelsen' (State board of health);

(d) *in France:*

— the State diploma of 'infirmier(ère)' awarded by the Ministry of Health;

(e) *in Ireland:*

— the certificate of 'Registered General Nurse' awarded by 'An Bord Altranais' (the Nursing Board);

(*) Text as amended by the Act of Accession for Greece.
(**) Text as amended by the Act of Accession for Spain and Portugal.

(f) *in Italy:*

— the 'diploma di abilitazione professionale per infermiere professionale' awarded by State-recognized schools;

(g) *in Luxembourg:*

— the State diploma of 'infirmier'

— the State diploma of 'infirmier hospitalier gradué'

awarded by the Ministry of Public Health on the strength of an examining board decision;

(h) *in the Netherlands:*

— the diplomas of 'verpleger A', 'verpleegster A' or 'verpleegkundige A',

— the diploma of 'verpleegkundige MBOV (Middelbare Beroepsopleiding Verpleegkundige)' (intermediate nursing training),

— the diploma of 'verpleegkundige HBOV (Hogere Beroepsopleiding Verpleegkundige)' (higher nursing training),

awarded by one of the examining boards appointed by the public authorities;

(i) *in the United Kingdom:*

— the certificate of admission to the general part of the Register, awarded in England and Wales by the General Nursing Council for England and Wales, in Scotland by the General Nursing Council for Scotland and in Northern Ireland by the Northern Ireland Council for Nurses and Midwives;

(j) in Greece:

1. either the diploma of Ἀνωτέρας Σχολῆς Ἀδελφῶν Νοσοκόμων (college of nurses responsible for general care), recognized by the Ministry for Social Services or the diploma of τῶν παραϊατρικῶν σχολῶν τῶν Κέντρων Ἀνωτέρας Τεχνικῆς καί Ἐπαγγελματικῆς Ἐκπαιδεύσεως (paramedical schools of the Higher Technical and Vocational Education Centres) awarded by the Ministry for National Education and Religious Affairs;

2. the πιστοποιητικό πρακτικῆς ἀσκήσεως τοῦ ἐπαγγέλματος τῆς ἀδελφῆς νοσοκόμου (certificate of practical training for the nursing profession) awarded by the Ministry for Social Services; (*)

(k) *in Spain:*

"Título de Diplomado universitario en Enfermería" (university diploma in nursing) awarded by the Ministry for Education and Science; (**)

(l) *in Portugal:*

"Diploma do curso de enfermagem geral" (diploma in general nursing) awarded by State recognized educational establishments and registered by the competent authority. (**)

## CHAPTER III

## EXISTING CIRCUMSTANCES

### *Article 4* (***)

In the case of nationals of Member States whose diplomas, certificates and other evidence of formal qualifications do not satisfy all the minimum training requirements laid down in Article 1 of Directive 77/453/EEC, each Member State shall recognize, as being sufficient proof, the diplomas, certificates and other evidence of the formal qualifications of nurses responsible for general care awarded by those Member States before the implementation of Directive 77/453/EEC, accompanied by a certificate stating that those nationals have effectively and lawfully been engaged in the activities of nurses responsible for general care for at least three years during the five years prior to the date of issue of the certificate.

These activities must have included taking full responsibility for the planning, organization and carrying out of the nursing care of the patient.

## CHAPTER IV

## USE OF ACADEMIC TITLE

### *Article 5*

1. Without prejudice to Article 13, host Member States shall ensure that nationals of Member States who fulfil the conditions laid down in Articles 2 and 4 have the right to use the lawful academic title, inasmuch as it is not identical to the professional title, or,

(*) Text as amended by the Act of Accession for Greece.
(**) Text as amended by the Act of Accession for Spain and Portugal.
(***) Article 4 was supplemented by Directive 81/1057/EEC (see point 7).

where appropriate, the abbreviation thereof of their Member State of origin or of the Member State from which they come, in the language or languages of that State. Host Member States may require this title to be followed by the name and location of the establishment or examining board which awarded it.

2. If the academic title used in the Member State of origin, or in the Member State from which a foreign national comes, can be confused in the host Member State with a title requiring, in that State, additional training which the person concerned has not undergone, the host Member State may require such a person to use the title employed in the Member State of origin or the Memer State from which he comes, in suitable wording to be indicated by the host Member State.

## CHAPTER V

## PROVISIONS TO FACILITATE THE EFFECTIVE EXERCISE OF THE RIGHT OF ESTABLISHMENT AND FREEDOM TO PROVIDE SERVICES IN RESPECT OF THE ACTIVITIES OF NURSES RESPONSIBLE FOR GENERAL CARE

### A. Provisions specifically relating to the right of establishment

*Article 6*

1. A host Member State which requires of its nationals proof of good character or good repute when they take up for the first time any activity referred to in Article 1 shall accept as sufficient evidence, in respect of nationals of other Member States, a certificate issued by a competent authority in the Member State of origin or in the Member State from which the foreign national comes attesting that the requirements of the Member State as to good character or good repute for taking up the activity in question have been met.

2. Where the Member State of origin or the Member State from which the foreign national comes does not require proof of good character or good repute of persons wishing to take up the activity in question for the first time, the host Member State may require of nationals of the Member State of origin or of the Member State from which the foreign national comes an extract from the 'judicial record' or, failing this, an equivalent document issued by a competent authority in the Member State of origin or the Member State from which the foreign national comes.

3. If the host Member State has detailed knowledge of a serious matter which has occurred outside its territory and which is likely to affect the taking up within its territory of the activity concerned, it may inform the Member State of origin or the Member State from which the foreign national comes.

The Member State of origin or the Member State from which the foreign national comes shall verify the accuracy of the facts if they are likely to affect in that Member State the taking up of the activity in question. The authorities in that State shall decide on the nature and extent of the investigation to be made and shall inform the host Member State of any consequential action which they take with regard to the certificates or documents they have issued.

Member States shall ensure the confidentiality of the information which is forwarded.

*Article 7*

1. Where, in a host Member State, provisions laid down by law, regulation or administrative action are in force laying down requirements as to good character or good repute, including provisions for disciplinary action in respect of serious professional misconduct or conviction for criminal offences and relating to the pursuit of any of the activities referred to in Article 1, the Member State of origin or the Member State from which the foreign national comes shall forward to the host Member State all necessary information regarding measures or disciplinary action of a professional or administrative nature taken in respect of the person concerned, or criminal penalties imposed on him when pursuing his profession in the Member State of origin or in the Member State from which he came.

2. If the host Member State has detailed knowledge of a serious matter which has occurred outside its territory and which is likely to affect the pursuit within its territory of the activity concerned, it may inform the Member State of origin or the Member State from which the foreign national comes.

The Member State of origin or the Member State from which the foreign national comes shall verify the accuracy of the facts if they are likely to affect in that Member State the pursuit of the activity in question. The authorities in that State shall decide on the nature and extent of the investigation to be made and shall inform the host Member State of any consequential action which they take with regard to the information they have forwarded in accordance with paragraph 1.

3. Member States shall ensure the confidentiality of the information which is forwarded.

*Article 8*

Where a host Member State requires of its own nationals wishing to take up or pursue any of the activities referred to in Article 1 a certificate of physical or mental health, that State shall accept as sufficient evidence thereof the presentation of the document required in the Member State of origin or in the Member State from which the foreign national comes.

Where the Member State of origin or the Member State from which the foreign national comes does not impose any requirements of this nature on those wishing to take up or pursue the activity in question, the host Member State shall accept from such national a certificate issued by a competent authority in that State corresponding to the certificates issued in the host Member State.

*Article 9*

Documents issued in accordance with Articles 6, 7 and 8 may not be presented more than three months after their date of issue.

*Article 10*

1. The procedure for authorizing the person concerned to take up any activity referred to in Article 1, pursuant to Articles 6, 7 and 8, must be completed as soon as possible and not later than three months after presentation of all the documents relating to such person, without prejudice to delays resulting from any appeal that may be made upon the termination of this procedure.

2. In the cases referred to in Articles 6 (3) and 7 (2), a request for re-examination shall suspend the period stipulated in paragraph 1.

The Member State consulted shall give its reply within three months.

On receipt of the reply or at the end of the period the host Member State shall continue with the procedure referred to in paragraph 1.

B. Special provisions relating to the provision of services

*Article 11*

1. Where a Member State requires of its own nationals wishing to take up or pursue any of the activities referred to in Article 1 an authorization, or membership of or registration with a professional organization or body, that Member State shall in the case of the provision of services exempt the nationals of Member States from that requirement.

The person concerned shall provide services with the same rights and obligations as the nationals of the host Member State; in particular he shall be subject to the rules of conduct of a professional or administrative nature which apply in that Member State.

Where a host Member State adopts a measure pursuant to the second subparagraph or becomes aware of facts which run counter to these provisions, it shall forthwith inform the Member State where the person concerned is established.

2. The host Member State may require the person concerned to make a prior declaration to the competent authorities concerning the provision of his services where they involve a temporary stay in its territory.

In urgent cases this declaration may be made as soon as possible after the services have been provided.

3. Pursuant to paragraphs 1 and 2, the host Member State may require the person concerned to supply one or more documents containing the following particulars:

— the declaration referred to in paragraph 2,

— a certificate stating that the person concerned is lawfully pursuing the activities in question in the Member State where he is established,

— a certificate that the person concerned holds one or other of the diplomas, certificates or other evidence of formal qualification appropriate for the provision of the services in question and referred to in this Directive.

4. The document or documents specified in paragraph 3 may not be produced more than 12 months after their date of issue.

5. Where a Member State temporarily or permanently deprives, in whole or in part, one of its nationals or a national of another Member State established in its territory of the right to pursue one of the activities referred to in Article 1, it shall, as appropriate, ensure the temporary or permanent withdrawal of the certificate referred to in the second indent of paragraph 3.

*Article 12*

Where registration with a public social security body is required in a host Member State for the settlement with insurance bodies of accounts relating to services rendered to persons insured under social security schemes, that Member State shall exempt nationals of Member States established in another Member State from this requirement in cases of provision of services entailing travel on the part of the person concerned.

However, the persons concerned shall supply information to this body in advance or, in urgent cases, subsequently, concerning the services provided.

C. Provisions common to the right of establishment and freedom to provide services

*Article 13*

Where in a host Member State the use of the professional title relating to one of the activities referred to in Article 1 is subject to rules, nationals of other Member States who fulfil the conditions laid down in Articles 2 and 4 shall use the professional title of the host Member State which, in that State, corresponds to those conditions of qualification, and shall use the abbreviated title.

*Article 14*

Where a host Member State requires its own nationals wishing to take up or pursue one of the activities referred to in Article 1 to take an oath or make a solemn declaration and where the form of such oath or declaration cannot be used by nationals of other Member States, that Member State shall ensure that an appropriate and equivalent form of oath or declaration is offered to the person concerned.

*Article 15*

1. Member States shall take the necessary measures to enable the persons concerned to obtain information on the health and social security laws and, where applicable, on the professional ethics of the host Member State.

For this purpose, Member States may set up information centres from which such persons may obtain the necessary information. In the case of establishment, the host Member States may require the persons concerned to contact these centres.

2. Member States may set up the centres referred to in paragraph 1 within the competent authorities and bodies which they must designate within the period laid down in Article 19 (1).

3. Member States shall see to it that, where appropriate, the persons concerned acquire, in their own interest and in that of their patients, the linguistic knowledge necessary for the exercise of their profession in the host Member State.

CHAPTER VI

FINAL PROVISIONS

*Article 16*

In the event of justified doubts, the host Member State may require of the competent authorities of another Member State confirmation of the authenticity of the diplomas, certificates and other evidence of formal qualifications issued in that other Member State and referred to in Chapters II and III, and also confirmation of the fact that the person concerned has fulfilled all the training requirements laid down in Directive 77/453/EEC.

*Article 17*

Within the time limit laid down in Article 19 (1), Member States shall designate the authorities and bodies competent to issue or receive the diplomas, certificates and other evidence of formal qualifications as well as the documents and information referred to in this Directive, and shall forthwith inform the other Member States and the Commission thereof.

*Article 18*

This Directive shall also apply to nationals of Member States who, in accordance with Regulation (EEC) No 1612/68, are pursuing or will pursue as employed persons one of the activities referred to in Article 1.

*Article 19*

1. Member States shall bring into force the measures necessary to comply with this Directive within two years of its notification and shall forthwith inform the Commission thereof.

2. Member States shall communicate to the Commission the texts of the main provisions of national law which they adopt in the field covered by this Directive.

*Article 20*

Where a Member State encounters major difficulties in certain fields when applying this Directive, the Commission shall examine these difficulties in conjunction with that State and shall request the opinion of the Committee of Senior Officials on Public Health set up under Decision 75/365/EEC (1), as amended by Decision 77/455/EEC (2).

Where necessary, the Commission shall submit appropriate proposals to the Council.

*Article 21*

This Directive is addressed to the Member States.

Done at Luxembourg, 27 June 1977.

*For the Council*

*The President*

J. SILKIN

(1) OJ No L 167, 30. 6. 1975, p. 19.
(2) OJ No L 176, 15.7.1977, p.13.

Official Journal of the European Communities No L 176/ 15. 7. 77

# COUNCIL DIRECTIVE

of 27 June 1977

**concerning the coordination of provisions laid down by law, regulation or administrative action in respect of the activities of nurses responsible for general care**

(77/453/EEC)

THE COUNCIL OF THE EUROPEAN COMMUNITIES,

Having regard to the Treaty establishing the European Economic Community, and in particular Articles 49, 57, 66 and 235 thereof,

Having regard to the proposal from the Commission,

Having regard to the opinion of the European Parliament (1),

Having regard to the opinion of the Economic and Social Committee (2),

Whereas, with a view to achieving the mutual recognition of diplomas, certificates and other evidence of formal qualifications of nurses responsible for general care laid down in Council Directive 77/452/EEC (3), the comparable nature of training courses in the Member States enables coordination in this field to be confined to the requirement that minimum standards be observed, which then leaves the Member States freedom of organization as regards teaching;

Whereas the coordination envisaged by this Directive does not exclude any subsequent coordination;

Whereas the coordination envisaged by this Directive covers the professional training of nurses responsible for general care; whereas, as far as training is concerned, most Member States do not at present distinguish between nurses who pursue their activities as employed persons and those who are self-employed; whereas for this reason and in order to encourage as far as possible the free movement of professional persons within the Community, it appears necessary to extend the application of this Directive to employed nurses,

HAS ADOPTED THIS DIRECTIVE:

*Article 1*

1. Member States shall make the award of diplomas, certificates and other evidence of the formal qualifications of nurses responsible for general care as specified in Article 3 of Directive 77/452/EEC subject to passing an examination which guarantees that during his training period the person concerned has acquired:

(a) adequate knowledge of the sciences on which general nursing is based, including sufficient understanding of the structure, physiological functions and behaviour of healthy and sick persons, and of the relationship between the state of health and the physical and social environment of the human being;

(b) sufficient knowledge of the nature and ethics of the profession and of the general principles of health and nursing;

(c) adequate clinical experience; such experience, which should be selected for its training value, should be gained under the supervision of qualified nursing staff and in places where the number of qualified staff and equipment are appropriate for the nursing care of the patients;

(d) the ability to participate in the practical training of health personnel and experience of working with such personnel;

(e) experience of working with members of other professions in the health sector.

2. The training referred to in paragraph 1 shall include at least:

(a) a general school education of 10 years' duration attested by a diploma, certificate or other formal qualification awarded by the competent authorities or bodies in a Member State, or a certificate

(1) OJ No C 65, 5. 6. 1970, p. 12.
(2) OJ No C 108, 26. 8. 1970, p. 23.
(3) OJ No L 176, 15.7.1977, p.1.

resulting from a qualifying examination of an equivalent standard for entrance to a nurses' training school;

(b) full-time training, of a specifically vocational nature, which must cover the subjects of the training programme set out in the Annex to this Directive and comprise a three-year course or 4 600 hours of theoretical and practical instruction.

3. Member States shall ensure that the institution training nurses is responsible for the coordination of theory and practice throughout the programme.

The theoretical and technical training mentioned in part A of the Annex shall be balanced and coordinated with the clinical training of nurses mentioned in part B of the same Annex in such a way that the knowledge and experience listed in paragraph 1 may be acquired in an adequate manner.

Clinical instruction in nursing shall take the form of supervised in-service training in hospital departments or other health services, including home nursing services, approved by the competent authorities or bodies. During this training student nurses shall participate in the activities of the departments concerned in so far as those activities contribute to their training. They shall be informed of the responsibilities of nursing care.

4. Five years at the latest after notification of this Directive and in the light of a review of the situation, the Council, acting on a proposal from the Commission, shall decide whether the provisions of paragraph 3 on the balance between theoretical and technical training on the one hand and clinical training of nurses on the other should be retained or amended.

5. Member States may grant partial exemption to persons who have undergone part of the training referred to in paragraph 2 (b) in the form of other training which is of at least equivalent standard.

*Article 2*

Notwithstanding the provisions of Article 1, Member States may permit part-time training under conditions approved by the competent national authorities.

The total period of part-time training may not be shorter than that of full-time training. The standard of the training may not be impaired by its part-time nature.

*Article 3*

This Directive shall also apply to nationals of Member States who, in accordance with Council Regulation (EEC) No 1612/68 of 15 October 1968 on freedom of movement for workers within the Community ([1]), are pursuing or will pursue, as employed persons, one of the activities referred to in Article 1 of Directive 77/452/EEC.

*Article 4*

1. Member States shall bring into force the measures necessary to comply with this Directive within two years of its notification and shall forthwith inform the Commission thereof.

2. Member States shall communicate to the Commission the texts of the main provisions of national law which they adopt in the field covered by this Directive.

*Article 5*

Where a Member State encounters major difficulties in certain fields when applying this Directive, the Commission shall examine these difficulties in conjunction with that State and shall request the opinion of the Committee of Senior Officials on Public Health set up by Decision 75/365/EEC ([2]), as amended by Decision 77/455/EEC ([3]).

Where necessary, the Commission shall submit appropriate proposals to the Council.

*Article 6*

This Directive is addressed to the Member States.

Done at Luxembourg, 27 June 1977.

*For the Council*

*The President*

J. SILKIN

([1]) OJ No L 257, 19. 10. 1968, p. 2.

([2]) OJ No L 167, 30. 6. 1975, p. 19.

([3]) OJ No L 176, 15.7.1977, p.13.

*ANNEX*

## TRAINING PROGRAMME FOR NURSES RESPONSIBLE FOR GENERAL CARE

The training leading to the award of a diploma, certificate or other formal qualification of nurses responsible for general care shall consist of the following two parts:

### A. Theoretical and technical instruction:

(a) *nursing:*

nature and ethics of the profession,

general principles of health and nursing,

nursing principles in relation to:
- general and specialist medicine,
- general and specialist surgery,
- child care and peadiatrics,
- maternity care,
- mental health and psychiatry,
- care of the old and geriatrics;

(b) *basic sciences:*

anatomy and physiology,

pathology,

bacteriology, virology and parasitology,

biophysics, biochemistry and radiology,

dietetics,

hygiene:
- preventive medicine,
- health education,

pharmacology;

(c) *social sciences:*

sociology,

psychology,

principles of administration,

principles of teaching,

social and health legislation,

legal aspects of nursing,

### B. Clinical instruction:

Nursing in relation to:
- general and specialist medicine,
- general and specialist surgery,
- child care and peadiatrics,
- maternity care,
- mental health and psychiatry,
- care of the old and geriatrics,
- home nursing.

# 5. Dental practitioners

Official Journal of the European Communities No L 233/ 24. 8. 78

II

*(Acts whose publication is not obligatory)*

# COUNCIL

## COUNCIL DIRECTIVE

**of 25 July 1978**

**concerning the mutual recognition of diplomas, certificates and other evidence of the formal qualifications of pratitioners of dentistry, including measures to facilitate the effective exercise of the right of establishment and freedom to provide services** (*)

(78/686/EEC)

THE COUNCIL OF THE EUROPEAN COMMUNITIES,

Having regard to the Treaty establishing the European Economic Community, and in particular Articles 49, 57, 66 and 235 thereof,

Having regard to the proposal from the Commission,

Having regard to the opinion of the European Parliament (1),

Having regard to the opinion of the Economic and Social Committee (2),

Whereas, pursuant to the Treaty, all discriminatory treatment based on nationality with regard to establishment and provision of services is prohibited as from the end of the transitional period; whereas the principle of such treatment based on nationality applies in particular to the grant of any authorization required to practise as a dental practitioner and also to registration with or membership of professional organizations or bodies;

Whereas it nevertheless seems desirable that certain provisions be introduced to facilitate the effective exercise of the right of establishment and freedom to provide services in respect of the activities of dental practitioners;

Whereas, pursuant to the Treaty, the Member States are required not to grant any form of aid likely to distort the conditions of establishment;

Whereas Article 57 (1) of the Treaty provides that Directives shall be issued for the mutual recognition of diplomas, certificates and other evidence of formal qualifications; whereas the aim of this Directive is the recognition of diplomas, certificates and other evidence of formal qualifications of a dental practitioner enabling activities in the field of dentistry to be taken up and pursued and the recognition of diplomas, certificates and other evidence of formal qualifications in respect of practitioners of specialized dentistry;

Whereas, with regard to the training of practitioners of specialized dentistry, the mutual recognition of training qualifications is advisable where these qualifications, while not being a condition for taking up the activities of practitioner of specialized dentistry, are nonetheless a condition for the use of a specialist title;

Whereas, in view of the current differences between the Member States regarding the number of specializations in dentistry and the type or the length of training courses for such specializations, certain coordinating provisions intended to enable Member States to proceed with the mutual recognition of diplomas, certificates and other evidence of formal qualifications should be laid down; whereas such coordination has been effected by Council Directive 78/687/EEC of 25 August 1978 concerning the coordination of provisions laid down by law, regulation or administrative action in respect of the activities of dental practitioners (3);

(*) Text as amended by:
- the Act of Accession for Greece.
- the Act of Accession for Spain and Portugal.

(1) OJ No C 101, 4. 8. 1970, p. 19.

(2) OJ No C 36, 28. 3. 1970, p. 17.

(3) OJ No L 233, 24.8.1978, p.10.

Whereas, although the coordination referred to above was not intended to harmonize all the provisions of the Member States on the training of practitioners of specialized dentistry, it is nevertheless appropriate to proceed with the mutual recognition of diplomas, certificates and other evidence of formal qualifications as a pratitioner of specialized dentistry which are not common to all the Member States, without however excluding the possibility of subsequent harmonization in this field; whereas it was considered in this connection that recognition of diplomas, certificates and other evidence of formal qualifications as a practitioner of specialized dentistry must be restricted to those Member States where such specialization is known;

Whereas, with regard to the use of academic titles, since a Directive on the mutual recognition of diplomas does not necessarily imply equivalence in the training covered by such diplomas, the use of such titles should be authorized only in the language of the Member State of origin or of the Member State from which the foreign national comes;

Whereas, to facilitate the application of this Directive by national authorities, Member States may prescribe that, in addition to formal certificates of training, a person who satisfies the conditions of training required by these authorities must provide a certificate from the competent authorities of his Member State of origin or of the Member State from which he comes stating that these certificates of training are those covered by this Directive;

Whereas, in the case of the provision of services, the requirement of registration with or membership of professional organizations or bodies since it is related to the fixed and permanent nature of activities pursued in the host country would thus undoubtedly constitute an obstacle to the persons wishing to provide the service, by reason of the temporary nature of his activity; whereas this requirement should therefore be abolished; whereas, however, in this event, control over professional discipline which is the responsibility of these professional organizations or bodies, should be guaranteed; whereas, to this end, it should be provided, subject to the application of Article 62 of the Treaty, that the person concerned may be required to submit to the competent authority of the host Member State particulars relating to the provision of services;

Whereas, with regard to the requirements relating to good character and good repute, a distinction should be drawn between the requirements to be satisfied on first taking up the profession and those to be satisfied for its practice;

Whereas, as far as the activities of employed dental practitioners are concerned, Council Regulation (EEC) No 1612/68 of 15 October 1968 on freedom of movement for workers within the Community [1] lays down no specific provisions relating to good character or good repute, professional discipline or use of title for the professions covered; whereas, depending on the individual Member State, such rules are or may be applicable both to employed and self-employed persons; whereas the activities of dental practitioners are or will be subject in all Member States to possession of a diploma, certificate or other evidence of formal qualification in dentistry; whereas such activities are pursued by both employed and self-employed persons, or by the same persons in both capacities in the course of their professional career; whereas, in order to encourage as far as possible their free movement within the Community, it therefore appears necessary to extend this Directive to cover employed dental practitioners;

Whereas the dental profession is not yet organized in Italy; whereas it is therefore necessary to grant Italy an additional period for recognizing the diplomas of dental practitioners awarded by the other Member States;

Whereas, moreover, this means that holders of a doctor's diploma awarded in Italy may not acquire a certificate meeting the requirements of Article 19 of this Directive;

Whereas, in these circumstances, it is necessary to defer on the one hand the obligation of Italy to recognize diplomas awarded by the other Member States and on the other hand that of the Member States to recognize diplomas awarded in Italy as referred to in Article 19,

HAS ADOPTED THIS DIRECTIVE:

## CHAPTER I

## SCOPE

### *Article 1*

This Directive shall apply to the activities of dental practitioners as defined in Article 5 of Directive 78/687/EEC pursued under the following titles:

— in Germany:

Zahnarzt,

---

[1] OJ No L 257, 19. 10. 1968, p. 2.

— in Belgium:

licencié en science dentaire/licentiaat in de tandheelkunde,

— in Denmark:

tandlæge,

— in France:

chirurgien-dentiste,

— in Ireland:

dentist, dental practitioner or dental surgeon,

— in Italy:

the diploma the title of which will be notified by Italy to the Member States and the Commission within the time limit laid down in Article 24 (1),

— in Luxembourg:

médecin-dentiste,

— in the Netherlands:

tandarts,

— in the United Kingdom:

dentist, dental practitioner or dental surgeon,

— in Greece:

ὀδοντίατρος ἤ χειρούργος ὀδοντίατρος, (*)

— *in Spain:*

Licenciado en Odontología, (**)

— *in Portugal:*

médico dentista. (**)

CHAPTER II

## DIPLOMAS, CERTIFICATES AND OTHER EVIDENCE OF FORMAL QUALIFICATIONS IN DENTISTRY

*Article 2*

Each Member State shall recognize the diplomas, certificates and other evidence of formal qualifications in dentistry awarded to nationals of Member States by the other Member States in accordance with Article 1 of Directive 78/687/EEC and which are listed in Article 3 of this Directive, by giving such qualifications, as far as the right to take up and pursue the activities of a dental practitioner is concerned, the same effect in its territory as those which the Member States itself awards.

*Article 3*

The diplomas, certificates and other evidence of formal qualification referred to in Article 2 are as follows:

(a) *in Germany*

1. 'Zeugnis über die zahnärztliche Staatsprüfung' (the State examination certificate in dentistry), awarded by the competent authorities;
2. the certificates from the competent authorities of the Federal Republic of Germany stating that the diplomas awarded after 8 May 1945 by the competent authorities of the German Democratic Republic are recognized as equivalent to those listed in point 1;

(b) *in Belgium*

'diplôme légal de licencié en science dentaire/wettelijk diploma van licentiaat in de tandheelkunde' (the official diploma of graduate in dental science), awarded by the university faculties of medicine, or by the Central Board or by the State boards of university examiners;

(c) *in Denmark*

'bevis for tandlægeeksamen (kandidateksamen)' (official diploma certifying that the holder has passed the examination in dentistry), issued by schools of dentistry together with the document issued by the 'Sundhedsstyrelsen' (State Board of Health) certifying that he has worked as an assistant for the required length of time;

(d) *in France*

1. 'diplôme d'État de chirurgien-dentiste' (State diploma of dental surgeon), awarded until 1973 by the university faculties of medicine or the university joint faculties of medicine and pharmacy;
2. 'diplôme d'État de docteur en chirurgie dentaire' (State diploma of doctor of dental surgery), awarded by the universities;

(e) *in Ireland*

the diploma of:

— Bachelor in Dental Science (B.Dent.Sc.),

— Bachelor of Dental Surgery (BDS), or

— Licentiate in Dental Surgery (LDS),

awarded by the universities or the Royal College of Surgeons in Ireland;

(*) Text as amended by the Act of Accession for Greece.
(**) Text as amended by the Act of Accession for Spain and Portugal.

(f) *in Italy*

the diploma the title of which will be notified by Italy to the Member States and to the Commission within the time limit laid down in Article 24 (1);

(g) *in Luxembourg*

'diplôme d'État de docteur en médecine dentaire' (State diploma of doctor of dental medicine), issued by the State Board of Examiners;

(h) *in the Netherlands*

'universitair getuigschrift van een met goed gevolg afgelegd tandartsexamen' (university certificate certifying success in the dental surgeon's examination);

(i) *in the United Kingdom*

the diploma of:

— Bachelor of Dental Surgery (BDS or B.Ch.D), or

— Licentiate in Dental Surgery (LDS),

issued by the universities and the royal colleges;

(j) in Greece:

πτυχίο ὀδοντιατρικῆς τοῦ Πανεπιστημίου; (*)

(k) *in Spain:*

the diploma, the name of which will be notified by Spain to the Member States and to the Commission on accession; (**)

(l) *in Portugal:*

"carta de curso de licenciatura em medicina dentária" (diploma conferring official recognition of completion of studies in dentistry) awarded by an establishment of higher education. (**)

CHAPTER III

## DIPLOMAS, CERTIFICATES AND OTHER EVIDENCE OF FORMAL QUALIFICATIONS IN SPECIALIZED DENTISTRY PECULIAR TO TWO OR MORE MEMBER STATES

*Article 4*

Each Member State with provisions in this field laid down by laws, regulations or administrative provisions shall recognize the diplomas, certificates and other evidence of formal qualifications of dental practitioners specializing in orthodontics and oral surgery awarded to nationals of Member States by other Member States in accordance with Articles 2 and 3 of Directive 78/687/EEC and which are listed in Article 5, by granting such qualifications the same effect in its territory as the diplomas, certificates and other formal qualifications which it itself awards.

*Article 5*

The diplomas, certificates and other evidence of formal qualifications referred to in Article 4 are as follows:

1. **Orthodontics**

— *in Germany*

'fachzahnärztliche Anerkennung für Kieferorthopädie' (certificate of orthodontist), issued by the 'Landeszahnärztekammern' (Chamber of Dental Practitioners of the 'Länder'),

— *in Denmark*

'bevis for tilladelse til at betegne sig som specialtandlæge i ortodonti' (certificate awarding the right to use the title of dental practitioner specializing in orthodontics), issued by the 'Sundhedsstyrelsen' (State Board of Health),

— *in France*

'le titre de spécialiste en orthodontie' (the title of orthodontic specialist), issued by the authority recognized competent for this purpose,

— *in Ireland*

certificate of specialist dentist in orthodontics, issued by the competent authority recognized for this purpose by the competent minister,

— *in the Netherlands*

'getuigschrift van erkenning en inschrijving als orthodontist in het Specialistenregister' (certificate showing that the person concerned is officially recognized and that his name is entered as a orthodontist in the specialists' register), issued by the 'Specialisten-Registratiecommissie (SRC)' (Specialists Registration Board),

— *in the United Kingdom*

certificate of completion of specialist training in orthodontics, issued by the competent authority recognized for this purpose.

(*) Text as amended by the Act of Accession for Greece.
(**) Text as amended by the Act of Accession for Spain and Portugal.

2. **Oral surgery**

— *in Germany*

'fachzahnärztliche Anerkennung für Oralchirurgie/Mundchirurgie' (certificate of oral surgery), issued by the 'Landeszahnärztekammern' (Chamber of Dental Practitioners of the 'Länder'),

— *in Denmark*

'bevis for tilladelse til at betegne sig som specialtandlæge i hospitalsodontologi' (certificate conferring the right to use the title of dental practitioner specialized in hospital odontology), issued by the 'Sundhedsstyrelsen' (State Board of Health),

— *in Ireland*

certificate of specialist dentist in oral surgery, issued by the competent authority recognized for this purpose by the competent Minister,

— *in the Netherlands*

'getuigschrift van erkenning en inschrijving als kaakchirurg in het Specialistenregister' (certificate showing that the person concerned is officially recognized and that his name is entered as an oral surgeon in the specialists' register), issued by the 'Specialisten-Registratiecommissie (SRC)' (Specialists Registration Board),

— *in the United Kingdom*

certificate of completion of specialist training in oral surgery, issued by the competent authority recognized for this purpose.

*Article 6*

1. Nationals of Member States wishing to acquire one of the diplomas, certificates or other evidence of formal qualification of practitioner of specialized dentistry which are not awarded in the Member State of origin or the Member State from which the foreign national comes, may be required by a host Member State to fulfil the conditions of training laid down in respect of the speciality by its own laws, regulations or administrative provisions.

2. The host Member State shall, however, take into account, in whole or in part, the training periods completed by the nationals referred to in paragraph 1 and attested by possession of a diploma, certificate or other evidence of formal training awarded by the competent authorities of the Member State of origin or the Member State from which the foreign national comes, provided such training periods correspond to those required in the host Member State for the specialized training in question.

3. The competent authorities or bodies of the host Member State, having verified the content and duration of the specialist training of the person concerned on the basis of the diplomas, certificates and other evidence of formal qualifications submitted, shall inform him of the period of additional training required and of the fields to be covered by it.

CHAPTER IV

EXISTING CIRCUMSTANCES

*Article 7* (*)

1. In the case of nationals of Member States whose diplomas, certificates and other evidence of formal qualifications do not satisfy all the minimum training requirements laid down in Article 1 of Directive 78/687/EEC, each Member State shall recognize as being sufficient proof the diplomas, certificates and other evidence of formal qualifications in dentistry awarded by those Member States before the implementation of Directive 78/687/EEC, accompanied by a certificate stating that those nationals have effectively and lawfully been engaged in the activities in question for at least three consecutive years during the five years prior to the date of issue of the certificate.

2. In the case of nationals of Member States whose diplomas, certificates and other evidence of formal qualifications in specialized dentistry do not satisfy the minimum training requirements under Articles 2 and 3 of Directive 78/687/EEC, each Member State shall recognize as sufficient proof the diplomas, certificates and other evidence of formal qualifications in specialized dentistry awarded by those Member States before the implementation of Directive 78/687/EEC. The Member State may, however, require that such diplomas, certificates and other evidence of formal qualifications be accompanied by a certificate issued by the competent authorities or bodies of the Member State of origin or of the Member State from which the foreign national comes, stating that he has been engaged in activities of specialized dentistry for a period equal to twice the difference between the length of specialized training in the Member State of origin or in the Member State from which the foreign national comes and the minimum training period referred to in Directive

(*) Article 7 was supplemented by Directive 81/1057/EEC (see point 7).

78/687/EEC where these diplomas, certificates and other evidence of formal qualifications do not satisfy the minimum training period laid down in Article 2 of Directive 78/687/EEC.

However, if before this Directive is implemented, the host Member State requires a minimum training period of shorter duration than that referred to in Article 2 of Directive 78/687/EEC, the difference mentioned in the first subparagraph can be determined only by reference to the minimum training period laid down by that State.

## CHAPTER V

## USE OF ACADEMIC TITLE

### *Article 8*

1. Without prejudice to Article 17, host Member States shall ensure that the nationals of Member States who fulfil the conditions laid down in Articles 2, 4, 7 and 19 have the right to use the lawful academic title in so far as this is not identical with the professional title or, where appropriate, the abbreviation thereof, of their Member State of origin or of the Member State from which they come, in the language of that State. Host Member States may require this title to be followed by the name and location of the establishment or examining board which awarded it.

2. If the academic title used in the Member State of origin or in the Member State from which a foreign national comes can be confused in the host Member State with a title requiring in that State additional training which the person concerned has not undergone, the host Member State may require such a person to use the title employed in the Member State of origin or the Member State from which he comes in suitable wording to be drawn up by the host Member State.

## CHAPTER VI

## PROVISIONS TO FACILITATE THE EFFECTIVE EXERCISE OF THE RIGHT OF ESTABLISHMENT AND FREEDOM TO PROVIDE SERVICES IN RESPECT OF THE ACTIVITIES OF DENTAL PRACTITIONERS

### A. Provisions relating specifically to the right of establishment

### *Article 9*

1. A host Member State which requires of its nationals proof of good character or good repute when they take up for the first time any of the activities referred to in Article 1 shall accept as sufficient evidence, in respect of nationals of other Member States, a certificate issued by a competent authority in the Member State of origin or the Member State from which the foreign national comes attesting that the requirements of the Member State as to good character or good repute for taking up the activity in question have been met.

2. Where the Member State of origin or the Member State from which the foreign national comes does not require proof of good character or good repute of persons wishing to take up the activity in question for the first time, the host Member State may require of nationals of the Member State of origin or the Member State from which the foreign national comes an extract from the 'judicial record' or, failing this, an equivalent document issued by a competent authority in the Member State of origin or the Member State from which the foreign national comes.

3. If the host Member State has detailed knowledge of a serious matter which has occurred prior to the establishment of the person concerned in that State outside its territory and which is likely to affect the taking up within its territory of the activity concerned, it may inform the Member State of origin or the Member State from which the foreign national comes.

The Member State of origin or the Member State from which the foreign national comes shall verify the accuracy of the facts if they are likely to affect in that Member State the taking up of the activity in question. The authorities in that State shall decide on the nature and extent of the investigation to be made and shall inform the host Member State of any consequential action which they take with regard to the certificates or documents they have issued.

4. Member States shall ensure the confidentiality of the information forwarded.

### *Article 10*

1. Where, in a host Member State, provisions laid down by law, regulation or administrative action are in force laying down requirements as to good character or good repute, including provision for disciplinary action in the event of serious professional misconduct or conviction for criminal offences and relating to the pursuit of any of the activities referred to in Article 1, the Member State of origin or the Member State from which the foreign national comes shall forward to the host Member State all necessary information regarding

measures or disciplinary action of a professional or administrative nature taken in respect of the person concerned or regarding criminal penalties imposed on him when pursuing his profession in the Member State of origin or in the Member State from which he comes.

2. If the host Member State has detailed knowledge of a serious matter which has occurred prior to the establishment of the person concerned in the State outside its territory and which is likely to affect the pursuit within its territory of the activity concerned, it may inform the Member State of origin or the Member State from which the foreign national comes.

The Member State of origin or the Member State from which the foreign national comes shall verify the accuracy of the facts if they are likely to affect in that Member State the pursuit of the activity in question. The authorities in that State shall decide on the nature and extent of the investigation to be made and shall inform the host Member State of any consequential action which they take with regard to the information they have forwarded in accordance with paragraph 1.

3. Member States shall ensure the confidentiality of the information forwarded.

*Article 11*

Where a host Member State requires of its own nationals wishing to take up or pursue any of the activities referred to in Article 1 a certificate of physical or mental health, that State shall accept as sufficient evidence thereof the presentation of the document required in the Member State of origin or the Member State from which the foreign national comes.

Where the Member State of origin or the Member State from which the foreign national comes does not impose any requirements of this nature on those wishing to take up or pursue the activity in question, the host Member State shall accept from such national a certificate issued by a competent authority in that State corresponding to the certificates issued in the host Member State.

*Article 12*

Documents issued in accordance with Articles 9, 10 and 11 may not be presented more than three months after their date of issue.

*Article 13*

1. The procedure for authorizing the person concerned to take up any activity referred to in Article 1, pursuant to Articles 9, 10 and 11, must be completed as soon as possible and not later than three months after presentation of all the documents relating to such person, without prejudice to delays resulting from any appeal that may be made upon the termination of this procedure.

2. In the cases referred to in Articles 9 (3) and 10 (2), a request for re-examination shall suspend the period laid down in paragraph 1.

The Member State consulted shall give its reply within a period of three months.

On receipt of the reply or at the end of the period the host Member State shall continue with the procedure referred to in paragraph 1.

*Article 14*

Where a host Member State requires its own nationals wishing to take up or pursue any of the activities referred to in Article 1 to take an oath or make a solemn declaration and where the form of such oath or declaration cannot be used by nationals of other Member States, that Member State shall ensure that an appropriate and equivalent form of oath or declaration is offered to the person concerned.

**B. Provisions relating specifically to the provision of services**

*Article 15*

1. Where a Member State requires of its own nationals wishing to take up or pursue any of the activities referred to in Article 1 an authorization or membership of or registration with a professional organization or body, that Member State shall in the case of the provision of services exempt the nationals of the other Member States from that requirement.

The person concerned shall provide services with the same rights and obligations as the nationals of the host Member State; in particular he shall be subject to the rules of conduct of a professional or administrative nature which apply in that Member State.

To this end and in addition to the declaration relating to the provision of services referred to in paragraph 2 Member States may, so as to permit the implementation of the provisions relating to professional conduct in force in their territory, provide for automatic temporary registration with or *pro forma* membership of a professional organization or body or entry in a register, provided that such registration does not delay or in any way complicate the provision of services or impose any additional costs on the person providing the services.

Where a host Member State adopts a measure pursuant to the second subparagraph or becomes aware of facts which run counter to these provisions, it shall forthwith inform the Member State where the person concerned is established.

2. The host Member State may require the person concerned to make a prior declaration to the competent authorities concerning the provision of his services where they involve a temporary stay in its territory.

In urgent cases this declaration may be made as soon as possible after the services have been provided.

3. Pursuant to paragraphs 1 and 2, the host Member State may require the person concerned to supply one or more documents containing the following particulars:

— the declaration referred to in paragraph 2,

— a certificate stating that the person concerned is lawfully pursuing the activities in question in the Member State where he is established,

— a certificate that the person concerned holds one or other of the diplomas, certificates or other evidence of formal qualifications appropriate for the provision of the services in question and referred to in this Directive.

4. The document or documents specified in paragraph 3 may not be presented more than 12 months after their date of issue.

5. Where a Member State temporarily or permanently deprives, in whole or in part, one of its nationals or a national of another Member State established in its territory of the right to pursue any of the activities referred to in Article 1, it shall, as appropriate, ensure the temporary or permanent withdrawal of the certificate referred to in the second indent of paragraph 3.

*Article 16*

Where registration with a public social security body is required in a host Member State for the settlement with insurance bodies of accounts relating to services rendered to persons insured under social security schemes, that Member State shall exempt nationals of Member States established in another Member State from this requirement in cases of provision of services entailing travel on the part of the person concerned.

In all cases of provision of services entailing travel on the part of the person concerned, the host Member State may require him to supply information to this body in advance, or, in urgent cases, at the earliest opportunity, concerning the services provided.

**C. Provisions common to the right of establishment and freedom to provide services**

*Article 17*

1. Where in a host Member State the use of the professional title relating to any of the activities referred to in Article 1 is subject to rules, nationals of other Member States who fulfil the conditions laid down in Articles 2, 7 (1) and 19 shall use the professional title of the host Member State which, in that State, corresponds to those conditions of qualification and shall use the abbreviated title.

2. Paragraph 1 shall also apply to the use of professional titles of practitioner of specialized dentistry by those who fulfil the conditions laid down in Articles 4 and 7 (2) respectively.

*Article 18*

1. Member States shall take the necessary measures to enable the persons concerned to obtain information on the health and social security laws and, where applicable, on the professional ethics of the host Member State.

For this purpose Member States may set up information centres from which such persons may obtain the necessary information. In the case of establishment, the host Member States may require the person concerned to contact these centres.

2. Member States may set up the centres referred to in paragraph 1 within the competent authorities and bodies which they must designate within the period laid down in Article 24 (1).

3. Member States shall see to it that, where appropriate, the persons concerned acquire, in their interest and

in that of their patients, the linguistic knowledge necessary for the exercise of their profession in the host Member State.

CHAPTER VII

## TRANSITIONAL PROVISIONS COVERING THE SPECIAL CASE OF ITALY

*Article 19*

From the date on which Italy takes the measures necessary to comply with this Directive, Member States shall recognize, for the purposes of carrying out the activities referred to in Article 1 of this Directive, the diplomas, certificates and other evidence of formal qualifications in medicine awarded in Italy to persons who had begun their university medical training not later than 18 months after notification of this Directive, accompanied by a certificate issued by the competent Italian authorities, certifying that these persons have effectively, lawfully and principally been engaged in Italy in the activities specified in Article 5 of Directive 78/687/EEC for at least three consecutive years during the five years prior to the issue of the certificate and that these persons are authorized to carry out the said activites under the same conditions as holders of the diploma, certificate or other evidence of formal qualifications referred to in Article 3 (f) of this Directive.

The requirement of three years' experience referred to in the first subparagraph shall be waived in the case of persons who have successfully completed at least three years of study which are certified by the competent authorities as being equivalent to the training referred to in Article 1 of Directive 78/687/EEC.

*Article 19a* (*)

From the date on which the Kingdom of Spain takes the measures necessary to comply with this Directive, Member States shall recognize, for the purposes of carrying out the activities referred to in Article 1 of this Directive, the diplomas, certificates and other evidence of formal qualifications in medicine awarded in Spain to persons who had begun their university medical training before accession, accompanied by a certificate issued by the competent Spanish authorities, certifying that these persons have effectively, lawfully and principally been engaged in Spain in the activities specified in Article 5 of Directive 78/687/EEC for at least three consecutive years during the five years prior to the issue of the certificate and that these persons are authorized to carry out the said activities under the same conditions as holders of the diploma, certificate or other evidence of formal qualifications referred to in Article 3 (k) of this Directive.

The requirement of three years' experience referred to in the first subparagraph shall be waived in the case of persons who have successfully completed at least three years of study which are certified by the competent authorities as being equivalent to the training referred to in Article 1 of Directive 78/687/EEC.

CHAPTER VIII

## FINAL PROVISIONS

*Article 20*

Member States which require their own nationals to complete a preparatory training period in order to become eligible for appointment as a dental practitioner of a social security scheme may impose the same requirement on nationals of the other Member States for a period of eight years following notification of this Directive. The training period may not, however, exceed six months.

*Article 21*

In the event of justified doubts, the host Member State may require of the competent authorities of another Member State confirmation of the authenticity of the diplomas, certificates and other evidence of formal qualifications issued in that other Member State and referred to in Chapters II, III and IV, and also confirmation that the person concerned has fulfilled all the training requirements laid down in Directive 78/687/EEC.

*Article 22*

Within the time limit laid down in Article 24 (1), Member States shall designate the authorities and bodies competent to issue or receive the diplomas, certificates and other evidence of formal qualifications as well as the documents and information referred to in this Directive and shall forthwith inform the other Member States and the Commission thereof.

(*) Article added by the Act of Accession for Spain and Portugal.

*Article 23*

The Directive shall also apply to the nationals of Member States who, in accordance with Regulation (EEC) No 1612/68, are or will be pursuing as employed persons any of the activities referred to in Article 1.

*Article 24*

1. Member States shall take the measures necessary to comply with this Directive within 18 months of its notification and shall forthwith inform the Commission thereof. However, Italy shall take these measures within a maximum period of six years and in any event when it takes those necessary to comply with Directive 78/687/EEC.

2. Member States shall forward to the Commission the texts of the main provisions of national law which they adopt in the field covered by this Directive.(*)

*Article 25*

Where a Member State encounters major difficulties in certain fields when applying this Directive, the Commission shall examine these difficulties in conjunction with that State and shall request the opinion of the Committee of Senior Officials on Public Health set up by Decision 75/365/EEC ([1]), as last amended by Decision 78/689/EEC ([2]).

Where necessary, the Commission shall submit appropriate proposals to the Council.

*Article 26*

This Directive is addressed to the Member States.

Done at Brussels, 25 July 1978.

*For the Council*

*The President*

K. von DOHNANYI

([1]) OJ No L 167, 30. 6. 1975, p. 19.

([2]) OJ No L 233, 24.8.1978, p.17.

(*) For Spain = 1 January 1991 (Annex XXXVI to the Act of Accession for Spain and Portugal). With regard to Spain, see also point 5.4.

Official Journal of the European Communities No L 233/ 24. 8. 78

# COUNCIL DIRECTIVE

## of 25 July 1978

## concerning the coordination of provisions laid down by law, regulation or administrative action in respect of the activities of dental practitioners

(78/687/EEC)

THE COUNCIL OF THE EUROPEAN COMMUNITIES,

Having regard to the Treaty establishing the European Economic Community, and in particular Articles 49, 57, 66 and 235 thereof,

Having regard to the proposal from the Commission,

Having regard to the opinion of the European Parliament [1],

Having regard to the opinion of the Economic and Social Committee [2],

Whereas, with a view to achieving the mutual recognition of diplomas, certificates and other evidence of the formal qualifications in dentistry, laid down by Council Directive 78/686/EEC of 25 July 1978 concerning the mutual recognition of diplomas, certificates and other evidence of the formal qualifications of practitioners of dentistry, including measures to facilitate the effective exercise of the right of establishment and freedom to provide services [3], the comparable nature of training courses in the Member States enables coordination in this field to be confined to the requirement that minimum standards be observed, which then leaves the Member States freedom of organization as regards teaching;

Whereas, with a view to mutual recognition of diplomas, certificates and other evidence of formal qualifications of a practitioner of specialized dentistry and in order to put all members of the profession who are nationals of the Member States on an equal footing within the Community, some coordination of the requirements for training as a practitioner of specialized dentistry is necessary; whereas certain minimum criteria should be laid down for this purpose concerning the right to take up specialized training, the minimum training period, the method by which such training is given and the place where it is to be carried out, as well as the supervision to which it should be subject; whereas these criteria only concern the specializations common to several Member States;

Whereas it is necessary for reasons of public health to move within the Community towards a common definition of the field of activity of the professional persons concerned; whereas this Directive does not at this stage enable complete coordination to be achieved as regards the field of activity of dental practitioners in the various Member States;

Whereas Member States will ensure that, as from the implementation of this Directive, the training of dental practitioners will provide them with the skills necessary for carrying out all activities involving the prevention, diagnosis and treatment of anomalies and diseases of the teeth, mouth, jaws and associated tissues;

Whereas coordination of the conditions for the pursuit of these activities, as provided for under this Directive, does not exclude any subsequent coordination;

Whereas the coordination envisaged by this Directive covers the professional training of dental practitioners; whereas, as far as training is concerned, most Member States do not at present distinguish between dental practitioners who pursue their activities as employed persons and those who are self-employed; whereas for this reason and in order to encourage as far as possible the free movement of professional persons within the Community, it appears necessary to extend the application of this Directive to dental practitioners pursuing their activities as employed persons;

Whereas, at the time of notification of this Directive, dentistry is practised in Italy solely by doctors, whether or not specializing in odontostomatology; whereas, under this Directive, Italy is obliged to create a new category of professional persons entitled to practise dentistry under a title other than that of doctor; whereas in creating a new profession Italy must not only introduce a specific system of training complying with the criteria laid down in this Directive, but also set up structures proper to this new profession, such as a council, for example; whereas, therefore, in view of the extent of the measures to be taken, Italy should be granted an additional period to allow it to comply with this Directive,

(1) OJ No C 101, 4. 8. 1970, p. 19.
(2) OJ No C 36, 28. 3. 1970, p. 19.
(3) OJ No L 233, 24.8.1978, p.1.

HAS ADOPTED THIS DIRECTIVE:

CHAPTER I

TRAINING REQUIREMENTS

*Article 1*

1. The Member States shall require persons wishing to take up and pursue a dental profession under the titles referred to in Article 1 of Directive 78/686/EEC to hold a diploma, certificate or other evidence of formal qualifications referred to in Article 3 of the same Directive which guarantees that during his complete training period the person concerned has acquired:

(a) adequate knowledge of the sciences on which dentistry is based and a good understanding of scientific methods, including the principles of measuring biological functions, the evaluation of scientifically established facts and the analysis of data;

(b) adequate knowledge of the constitution, physiology and behaviour of healthy and sick persons as well as the influence of the natural and social environment on the state of health of the human being, in so far as these factors affect dentistry;

(c) adequate knowledge of the structure and function of the teeth, mouth, jaws and associated tissues, both healthy and diseased, and their relationship to the general state of health and to the physical and social well-being of the patient;

(d) adequate knowledge of clinical disciplines and methods, providing the dentist with a coherent picture of anomalies, lesions and diseases of the teeth, mouth, jaws and associated tissues and of preventive, diagnostic and therapeutic dentistry;

(e) suitable clinical experience under appropriate supervision.

This training shall provide him with the skills necessary for carrying out all activities involving the prevention, diagnosis and treatment of anomalies and diseases of the teeth, mouth, jaws and associated tissues.

2. A complete period of dental training of this kind shall comprise at least a five-year full time course of theoretical and practical instruction given in a university, in a higher-education institution recognized as having equivalent status or under the supervision of a university and shall include the subjects listed in the Annex.

3. In order to be accepted for such training, the candidate must have a diploma or a certificate which entitles him to be admitted for the course of study concerned to the universities of a Member State or to the higher education institutions recognized as having equivalent status.

4. Nothing in this Directive shall prejudice any facility which may be granted in accordance with their own rules by Member States in respect of their own territory to authorize holders of diplomas, certificates or other evidence of formal qualifications which have not been obtained in a Member State to take up and pursue the activities of a dental practitioner.

*Article 2*

1. Member States shall ensure that the training leading to a diploma, certificate or other evidence of formal qualifications as a practitioner of specialized dentistry meets the following requirements at least:

(a) it shall entail the completion and validation of a five-year full-time course of theoretical and practical instruction within the framework of the training referred to in Article 1, or possession of the documents referred to in Article 7 (1) of Directive 78/686/EEC.

(b) it shall comprise theoretical and practical instruction;

(c) it shall be a full-time course of a minimum of three years' duration supervised by the competent authorities or bodies;

(d) it shall be in a university centre, in a treatment, teaching and research centre or, where appropriate, in a health establishment approved for this purpose by the competent authorities or bodies;

(e) it shall involve the personal participation of the dental practitioner training to be a specialist in the activity and in the responsibilities of the establishments concerned.

2. Member States shall make the award of a diploma, certificate or other evidence of formal qualifications as a practitioner of specialized dentistry subject to the possession of one of the diplomas, certificates or other evidence of formal qualifications in dentistry referred to in Article 1, or to the possession of the documents referred to in Article 7 (1) of Directive 78/686/EEC.

3. Within the time limit laid down in Article 8 Member States shall designate the authorities or bodies competent to issue the diplomas, certificates or other evidence of formal qualifications referred to in paragraph 1.

4. Member States may derogate from paragraph 1 (a). Persons in respect of whom such derogation is made shall not be entitled to avail themselves of Article 4 of Directive 78/686/EEC.

*Article 3*

1. Without prejudice to the principle of full-time training as set out in Article 2 (1) (c), and until such time as the Council takes a decision in accordance with paragraph 3, Member States may permit part-time specialist training, under conditions approved by the competent national authorities, when training on a full-time basis would not be practicable for well-founded reasons.

2. The total period of specialized training may not be shortened by virtue of paragraph 1. The standard of the training may not be impaired, either by its part-time nature or by the practice of private, remunerated professional activity.

3. Four years at the latest after notification of this Directive and in the light of a review of the situation, acting on a proposal from the Commission, and bearing in mind that the possibility of part-time training should continue to exist in certain circumstances to be examined separately for each specialization, the Council shall decide whether the provisions of paragraphs 1 and 2 should be retained or amended.

*Article 4*

As a transitional measure and notwithstanding Articles 2 (1) (c) and 3, Member States whose provisions laid down by law, regulation or administrative action permit a method of part-time specialist training at the time of notification of this Directive may continue to apply these provisions to candidates who have begun their training as specialists no later than four years after the notification of this Directive. This period may be extended if the Council has not taken a decision in accordance with Article 3 (3).

CHAPTER II

## FIELD OF ACTIVITY

*Article 5*

Member States shall ensure that dental surgeons shall generally be entitled to take up and pursue activities involving the prevention, diagnosis and treatment of anomalies and diseases of the teeth, mouth, jaws and associated tissues in accordance with the regulatory provisions and the rules of professional conduct governing the profession at the time of notification of this Directive.

Those Member States which do not have such provisions or rules may define or limit the pursuit of certain activities referred to in the first subparagraph to an extent which is comparable to that existing in the other Member States.

CHAPTER III

## FINAL PROVISIONS

*Article 6*

Persons covered by Article 19 of Directive 78/686/EEC shall be regarded as fulfilling the requirements laid down in Article 2 (1) (a).

For the purposes of applying Article 2 (2), persons covered by Article 19 of Directive 78/686/EEC shall be treated in the same way as those holding one of the diplomas, certificates or other evidence of formal qualifications in dentistry referred to in Article 1.

*Article 7*

This Directive shall also apply to nationals of Member States who, in accordance with Council Regulation (EEC) No 1612/68 of 15 October 1968 on freedom of movement for workers within the Community (1), are or will be pursuing, as employed persons, any of the activities referred to in Article 1 of Directive 78/686/EEC.

(1) OJ No L 257, 19. 10. 1968, p. 2.

*Article 8*

1. Member States shall take the measures necessary to comply with this Directive within 18 months of its notification and shall forthwith inform the Commission thereof. However, Italy shall take these measures within a maximum of six years.

2. Member States shall communicate to the Commission the texts of the main provisions of national law which they adopt in the field covered by this Directive.

*Article 9*

Where a Member State encounters major difficulties in certain fields when applying this Directive, the Commission shall examine these difficulties in conjunction with that State and shall request the opinion of the Committee of Senior Officials on Public Health set up by Decision 75/365/EEC (1), as last amended by Decision 78/689/EEC (2).

Where necessary, the Commission shall submit appropriate proposals to the Council.

*Article 10*

This Directive is addressed to the Member States.

Done at Brussels, 25 July 1978.

*For the Council*

*The President*

K. von DOHNANYI

(1) OJ No L 167, 30. 6. 1975, p. 19.

(2) OJ No L 233, 24.8.1978, p.17.

*ANNEX*

**Study programme for dental practitioners**

The programme of studies leading to a diploma, certificate or other evidence of formal qualifications in dentistry shall include at least the following subjects. One or more of these subjects may be taught in the context of the other disciplines or in conjunction therewith.

(a) *Basic subjects*

chemistry,
physics,
biology.

(b) *Medico-biological subjects and general medical subjects*

anatomy,
embryology,
histology, including cytology,
physiology,
biochemistry (or physiological chemistry),
pathological anatomy,
general pathology,
pharmacology,
microbiology,
hygiene,
preventive medicine and epidemiology,
radiology,
physiotherapy,
general surgery,
general medicine, including paediatrics,
oto-rhino-laryngology,
dermato-venereology,
general psychology — psychopathology — neuropathology,
anaesthetics.

(c) *Subjects directly related to dentistry*

prosthodontics,
dental materials and equipment,
conservative dentistry,
preventive dentistry,
anaesthetics and sedation in dentistry,
special surgery,
special pathology,
clinical practice,
paedodontics,
orthodontics,
periodontics,
dental radiology,
dental occlusion and function of the jaw,
professional organization, ethics and legislation,
social aspects of dental practice.

Official Journal of the European Communities No C 202/ 24. 8. 78

I

*(Information)*

# COUNCIL

**Statement on the Directive concerning the coordination of provisions laid down by law, regulation or administrative action in respect of the activities of dental surgeons**

*Council statement on Article 1 (2):*

The Council has adopted the idea of full-time instruction since, unlike the Directive on coordination for doctors, this provision makes no reference to a number of hours.

The Council states that a year of full-time instruction means theoretical and practical instruction covering a normal, complete annual course of study at university level comprising the programme of studies given in the Annex to this Directive.

*ANNEX XXXII*

**List provided for in Article 378 of the Act of Accession**

3. Council Directive 78/686/EEC of 25 July 1978 (OJ No L 233, 24. 8. 1978, p. 1).

Until such time as the training of dental practitioners in Spain under the conditions laid down pursuant to Directive 78/687/EEC is completed and until 31 December 1990 at the latest, freedom of establishment and freedom to provide services shall be deferred for qualified dental practitioners from the other Member States in Spain and for qualified Spanish doctors practising dentistry in the other Member States.

During the temporary derogation provided for above, general or special facilities concerning the right of estabilishment and the freedom to provide services which would exist pursuant to Spanish provisions or Conventions governing relations between the Kingdom of Spain and any other Member State will be maintained and applied on a non-discriminatory basis with regard to all other Member States. (*)

(*) Official Journal of the European Communities, No L 302, 15.11.1985, p.381.

# 6. Veterinary surgeons

Official Journal of the European Communities No L 362/ 23. 12. 78

II

*(Acts whose publication is not obligatory)*

# COUNCIL

## COUNCIL DIRECTIVE

**of 18 December 1978**

**concerning the mutual recognition of diplomas, certificates and other evidence of formal qualifications in veterinary medicine, including measures to facilitate the effective exercise of the right of establishment and freedom to provide services (*)**

(78/1026/EEC)

THE COUNCIL OF THE EUROPEAN COMMUNITIES,

Having regard to the Treaty establishing the European Economic Community, and in particular Articles 49, 57, 66 and 235 thereof,

Having regard to the proposal from the Commission [1],

Having regard to the opinion of the European Parliament [2],

Having regard to the opinion of the Economic and Social Committee [3],

Whereas, pursuant to the Treaty, all discriminatory treatment based on nationality with regard to establishment and provision of services is prohibited as from the end of the transitional period; whereas the principle of such treatment based on nationality applies in particular to the grant of any authorization required to practise as a veterinary surgeon and also to the registration with or membership of professional organizations or bodies;

Whereas it nevertheless seems desirable that certain provisions be introduced to facilitate the effective exercise of the right of establishment and freedom to provide services in respect of the activities of veterinary surgeons;

Whereas, pursuant to the Treaty, the Member States are required not to grant any form of aid likely to distort the conditions of establishment;

Whereas Article 57 (1) of the Treaty provides that Directives be issued for mutual recognition of diplomas, certificates and other evidence of formal qualifications; whereas the aim of this Directive is the recognition of diplomas, certificates and other evidence of formal qualifications whereby activities in the field of veterinary medicine may be taken up and pursued;

Whereas, in view of the differences between the Member States regarding the nature and duration of the training of veterinary surgeons, certain coordinating provisions designed to enable Member States to proceed with the mutual recognition of diplomas, certificates and other evidence of formal qualifications should be laid down; whereas such coordination has been effected by Council Directive 78/1027/EEC of 18 December 1978 concerning the coordination of provisions laid down by law, regulation or administrative action in respect of the activities of veterinary surgeons [4];

Whereas, with regard to the possession of a formal certificate of training, since a Directive on the mutual recognition of diplomas does not necessarily imply equivalence in the training covered by such diplomas, the use of such qualifications should be authorized only in the language of the Member State of origin or of the Member State from which the foreign national comes;

Whereas, to facilitate the application of this Directive by the national authorities, Member States may prescribe that, in addition to formal certificates of training, the person who satisfies the conditions of training required by this Directive must provide a certificate from the competent authorities of his country of origin or of

(1) OJ No C 92, 20. 7. 1970, p. 18.
(2) OJ No C 19, 28. 2. 1972, p. 10.
(3) OJ No C 60, 14. 6. 1971, p. 3.

(4) OJ No L 362, 23.12.1978, p.7.

(*) Text as amended by:
– the Act of Accession for Greece.
– the Act of Accession for Spain and Portugal.

the country from which he comes stating that these certificates of training are those covered by the Directive;

Whereas, in the case of the provision of services, the requirement of registration with or membership of professional organizations or bodies, since it is related to the fixed and permanent nature of the activity pursued in the host country, would undoubtedly constitute an obstacle to the person wishing to provide the service, by reason of the temporary nature of his activity; whereas this requirement should therefore be abolished; whereas, however, in this event, control over professional discipline, which is the responsibility of these professional organizations or bodies, should be guaranteed; whereas, to this end, it should be provided, subject to the application of Article 62 of the Treaty, that the person concerned may be required to submit to the competent authority of the host Member State particulars relating to the provision of services;

Whereas, with regard to the requirements relating to good character and good repute, a distinction should be drawn between the requirements to be satisfied on first taking up the profession and those to be satisfied in order to practise it;

Whereas, as far as the activities of employed veterinary surgeons are concerned, Council Regulation (EEC) No 1612/68 of 15 October 1968 on freedom of movement for workers within the Community ([1]) lays down no specific provisions relating to good character or good repute, professional discipline or use of title for the professions covered; whereas, depending on the individual Member State, such rules are or may be applicable both to employed and self-employed persons; whereas the activities of veterinary surgeons are subject in all Member States to possession of a diploma, certificate or other evidence of formal qualification as a veterinary surgeon; whereas such activities are pursued by both employed and self-employed persons or by the same persons in both capacities in the course of their professional career; whereas, in order to encourage as far as possible the free movement of those professional persons within the Community, it therefore appears necessary to extend this Directive to employed veterinary surgeons,

HAS ADOPTED THIS DIRECTIVE:

## CHAPTER I

## SCOPE

### *Article 1*

This Directive shall apply to the activities of veterinary surgeons.

## CHAPTER II

## DIPLOMAS, CERTIFICATES AND OTHER EVIDENCE OF FORMAL QUALIFICATIONS IN VETERINARY MEDICINE

### *Article 2*

Each Member State shall recognize the diplomas, certificates and other evidence of formal qualifications awarded to nationals of Member States by the other Member States in accordance with Article 1 of Directive 78/1027/EEC and which are listed in Article 3, by giving such qualifications, as far as the right to take up and pursue the activities of a veterinary surgeon is concerned, the same effect in its territory as those which the Member State itself awards.

Where a diploma, certificate or other evidence of formal qualifications as listed in Article 3 was issued before the implementation of this Directive, it shall be accompanied by a certificate from the competent authorities of the issuing country stating that it complies with Article 1 of Directive 78/1027/EEC.

### *Article 3*

The diplomas, certificates and other evidence of formal qualifications referred to in Article 2 are as follows:

(a) *in Germany*

1. Zeugnis über die tierärztliche Staatsprüfung (the State examination certificate in veterinary medicine) awarded by the competent authorities;
2. the certificates from the competent authorities of the Federal Republic of Germany stating that the diplomas awarded after 8 May 1945 by the competent authorities of the German Democratic Republic are recognized as equivalent to that listed in point 1 above;

(b) *in Belgium*

le diplôme légal de docteur en médecine vétérinaire — het wettelijke diploma van doctor in de veeartsenijkunde of doctor in de diergeneeskunde (diploma of doctor of veterinary medicine, required by law) awarded by the State Universities, the Central Examining Board, or the State University Education Examining Boards;

(c) *in Denmark*

bevis for bestået kandidateksamen i veterinaervidenskab (cand. med. vet.) (the certificate proving the passing of the examination for candidates in veterinary medicine) awarded by the 'Kongelige Veterinaer- og Landbohøjskole';

([1]) OJ No L 257, 19. 10. 1968, p. 2.

(d) *in France*

le diplôme de docteur vétérinaire d'État (State degree in veterinary medicine);

(e) *in Ireland*

1. the degree of Bachelor in/of Veterinary Medicine (MVB);

2. the diploma of membership of the Royal College of Veterinary Surgeons (MRCVS) gained by examination after a full course of study at a veterinary school in Ireland;

(f) *in Italy*

il diploma di laurea di dottore in medicina veterinaria accompagnato dal diploma d'abilitazione all'esercizio della medicina veterinaria awarded by the Minister of Education on the basis of the findings of the competent State Examining Board;

(g) *in Luxembourg*

1. le diplôme d'État de docteur en médecine vétérinaire (the State diploma in veterinary medicine) awarded by the State Examining Board and endorsed by the Minister of Education;
2. diplomas conferring a higher education degree in veterinary medicine awarded in one of the countries of the Community and giving the right to take up training but not to practise the profession, and officially recognized by the Minister of Education in accordance with the law of 18 June 1969 on higher education and recognition of foreign degrees and diplomas, together with the certificate of practical training endorsed by the Minister of Public Health;

(h) *in the Netherlands*

1. het getuigschrift van met goed gevolg afgelegd diergeneeskundig examen (certificate proving the passing of the examination in veterinary medicine);
2. het getuigschrift van met goed gevolg afgelegd veeartsenijkundig examen (certificate proving the passing of the examination in veterinary medicine);

(i) *in the United Kingdom*

the degrees:

— Bachelor of Veterinary Science (BVSc.),

— Bachelor of Veterinary Medicine (Vet.MB or BVet.Med.),

— Bachelor of Veterinary Medicine and Surgery (BVM and S or BVMS),

— the diploma of membership of the Royal College of Veterinary Surgeons (MRCVS) gained by examination after a full course of study at a veterinary school in the United Kingdom;

(j) in Greece:

Δίπλωμα Κτηνιατρικῆς Σχολῆς τοῦ Πανεπιστημίου Θεσσαλονίκης; (*)

(k) *in Spain:*

título de Licenciado en Veterinaria (University degree in veterinary medicine) awarded by the Ministry for Education and Science; (**)

(l) *in Portugal:*

carta de curso de licenciatura em medicina veterinária (diploma conferring official recognition of completion of studies in veterinary medicine) awarded by a University. (**)

## CHAPTER III

## EXISTING CIRCUMSTANCES

### *Article 4* (***)

In the case of nationals of Member States whose diplomas, certificates and other evidence of formal qualifications do not satisfy all the minimum training requirements laid down in Article 1 of Directive 78/1027/EEC, each Member State shall recognize, as being sufficient proof, the diplomas, certificates and other evidence of formal qualifications in veterinary medicine awarded by those Member States before the implementation of Directive 78/1027/EEC, accompanied by a certificate stating that those nationals have effectively and lawfully been engaged in the activities in question for at least three consecutive years during the five years prior to the date of issue of the certificate.

## CHAPTER IV

## USE OF ACADEMIC TITLE

### *Article 5*

1. Without prejudice to Article 13, host Member States shall ensure that the nationals of Member States who fulfil the conditions laid down in Articles 2 and 4 have the right to use the lawful academic title or, where appropriate, the abbreviation thereof, of their Member State of origin or of the Member State from which they

(*) Text as amended by the Act of Accession for Greece.
(**) Text as amended by the Act of Accession for Spain and Portugal.
(***) Article 4 was supplemented by Directive 81/1057/EEC (see point 7).

come, in the language of that State. Host Member States may require this title to be followed by the name and location of the establishment or examining board which awarded it.

2. If the academic title used in the Member State of origin, or in the Member State from which a foreign national comes, can be confused in the host Member State with a title requiring in that State additional training which the person concerned has not undergone, the host Member State may require such person to use the title employed in the Member State of origin or the Member State from which he comes in suitable wording to be indicated by the host Member State.

## CHAPTER V

## PROVISIONS TO FACILITATE THE EFFECTIVE EXERCISE OF THE RIGHT OF ESTABLISHMENT AND FREEDOM TO PROVIDE SERVICES IN RESPECT OF THE ACTIVITIES OF VETERINARY SURGEONS

### A. Provisions specifically relating to the right of establishment

*Article 6*

1. A host Member State which requires of its nationals proof of good character or good repute when they take up for the first time the activities referred to in Article 1 shall accept as sufficient evidence, in respect of nationals of other Member States, a certificate issued by a competent authority in the Member State of origin or in the Member State from which the foreign national comes attesting that the requirements of the Member State as to good character or good repute for taking up the activities in question have been met.

2. Where the Member State of origin or the Member State from which the foreign national comes does not require proof of good character or good repute of persons wishing to take up the activities in question for the first time, the host Member State may require of nationals of the Member State of origin or of the Member State from which the foreign national comes an extract from the 'judicial record' or, failing this, an equivalent document issued by a competent authority in the Member State of origin or the Member State from which the foreign national comes.

3. If the host Member State has detailed knowledge of a serious matter which has occurred outside its territory and which is likely to affect the taking up within its territory of the activities concerned, it may inform the Member State of origin or the Member State from which the foreign national comes.

The Member State of origin or the Member State from which the foreign national comes shall verify the accuracy of the facts. The authorities in that State shall themselves decide on the nature and extent of the investigation to be made and shall inform the host Member State of any consequential action which they take with regard to the certificates or documents they have issued.

4. Member States shall ensure the confidentiality of the information which is forwarded.

*Article 7*

1. Where, in a host Member State, provisions laid down by law, regulation or administrative action are in force laying down requirements as to good character or good repute, including provisions for disciplinary action in respect of serious professional misconduct or conviction for criminal offences and relating to the pursuit of the activities referred to in Article 1, the Member State of origin or the Member State from which the foreign national comes shall forward to the host Member State all necessary information regarding measures or disciplinary action of a professional or administrative nature taken in respect of the person concerned, or criminal penalties imposed on him when pursuing his profession in the Member State of origin or in the Member State from which he came.

2. If the host Member State has detailed knowledge of a serious matter which has occurred outside its territory and which is likely to affect the pursuit within its territory of the activities concerned, it may inform the Member State of origin or the Member State from which the foreign national comes.

The Member State of origin or the Member State from which the foreign national comes shall verify the accuracy of the facts. The authorities in that State shall themselves decide on the nature and extent of the investigation to be made and shall inform the host Member State of any consequential action which they take with regard to the information they have forwarded in accordance with paragraph 1.

3. Member States shall ensure the confidentiality of the information which is forwarded.

*Article 8*

Where a host Member State requires of its own nationals wishing to take up or pursue the activities referred to in Article 1, a certificate of physical or mental health, that State shall accept as sufficient evidence thereof the presentation of the document required in the Member State of origin or the Member State from which the foreign national comes.

Where the Member State of origin or the Member State from which the foreign national comes does not impose any requirements of this nature on those wishing to take up or pursue the activities in question, the host Member State shall accept from such national a certificate issued by a competent authority in that State corresponding to the certificates issued in the host Member State.

*Article 9*

The documents referred to in Articles 6, 7 and 8 may not be presented more than three months after their date of issue.

*Article 10*

1. The procedure for authorizing the person concerned to take up the activities referred to in Article 1, in accordance with Articles 6, 7 and 8, must be completed as soon as possible and not later than three months after presentation of all the documents relating to such person, without prejudice to delays resulting from any appeal that may be made upon termination of this procedure.

2. In the cases referred to in Articles 6 (3) and 7 (2), a request for re-examination shall suspend the period laid down in paragraph 1.

The Member State consulted shall give its reply within a period of three months. If it does not, the host Member State may take action in consequence of its detailed knowledge of the serious matter involved.

On receipt of the reply or at the end of the period the host Member State shall continue with the procedure referred to in paragraph 1.

*Article 11*

Where a host Member State requires its own nationals wishing to take up or pursue the activities referred to in Article 1 to take an oath or make a solemn declaration and where the form of such oath or declaration cannot be used by nationals of other Member States, that Member State shall ensure that an appropriate and equivalent form of oath or declaration is offered to the person concerned.

B. Special provisions relating to the provision of services

*Article 12*

1. Where a Member State requires of its own nationals wishing to take up or pursue the activities referred to in Article 1, an authorization or membership of, or registration with, a professional organization or body, that Member State shall in the case of the provision of services exempt the nationals of Member States from that requirement.

The person concerned shall provide services with the same rights and obligations as the nationals of the host Member State; in particular he shall be subject to the rules of conduct of a professional or administrative nature which apply in that Member State.

For this purpose and in addition to the declaration provided for in paragraph 2 relating to the services to be provided, Member States may, so as to permit the implementation of the provisions relating to professional conduct in force in their territory, require either automatic temporary registration or *pro forma* membership of a professional organization or body or, in the alternative, registration in a register, provided that such registration or membership does not delay or in any way complicate the provision of services or impose any additional costs on the person providing the services.

Where a host Member State adopts a measure pursuant to the second subparagraph or becomes aware of facts which run counter to these provisions, it shall forthwith inform the Member State where the person concerned is established.

2. The host Member State may require the person concerned to make a prior declaration to the competent authorities concerning the provision of his services where they involve a temporary stay in its territory. The host Member State may in all cases require a veterinary surgeon established in another Member State to supply a prior declaration of provision of services in the form of a prescription or of veterinary certificates not involving the examination of animals, provided such

practice is permissible under the legal and administrative provisions and professional rules applied in the host State.

The host Member State requiring such prior declaration shall take the steps necessary to provide the possibility that the declaration is made, where appropriate, for a series of services provided within one and the same region and in respect of one or more recipients within a given period of not more than one year.

In urgent cases this declaration may be made as soon as possible after the services have been provided.

3. Pursuant to paragraphs 1 and 2, the host Member State may require the person concerned to supply one or more documents containing the following particulars:

— the declaration referred to in paragraph 2,

— a certificate stating that the person concerned is lawfully pursuing the activities in question in the Member State where he is established,

— a certificate that the person concerned holds one or other of the diplomas, certificates or other evidence of formal qualification appropriate for the provision of the services in question and referred to in this Directive.

4. The document or documents specified in paragraph 3 may not be produced more than 12 months after their date of issue.

5. Where a Member State temporarily or permanently deprives, in whole or in part, one of its nationals or a national of another Member State established in its territory of the right to pursue one of the activities referred to in Article 1, it shall, as appropriate, ensure the temporary or permanent withdrawal of the certificate referred to in the second indent of paragraph 3.

### C. Provisions common to the right of establishment and freedom to provide services

*Article 13*

Where in a host Member State the use of the professional title relating to the activities referred to in Article 1 is subject to rules, nationals of other Member States who fulfil the conditions laid down in Articles 2 and 4 shall use the professional title of the host Member State which, in that State, corresponds to those conditions of qualification and shall use the abbreviated title.

*Article 14*

1. Member States shall take the necessary measures to enable the persons concerned to obtain information on veterinary legislation and, where applicable, on professional ethics by the host Member State.

For this purpose, Member States may set up information centres from which such persons may obtain the necessary information. In the case of establishment, the host Member States may require the persons concerned to contact these centres.

2. Member States may set up the centres referred to in paragraph 1 within the competent authorities and bodies which they must designate within the period laid down in Article 18 (1).

3. Member States shall see to it that, where appropriate, the persons concerned acquire, in their interest and in that of their clients, the linguistic knowledge necessary for the pursuit of their profession in the host Member State.

## CHAPTER VI

## FINAL PROVISIONS

*Article 15*

When it has ground for doubt, the host Member State may require of the competent authorities of another Member State confirmation of the authenticity of the diplomas, certificates and other evidence of formal qualifications awarded in that other Member State and referred to in Chapter II and also confirmation of the fact that the person concerned has fulfilled all the training requirements laid down in Directive 78/1027/EEC.

*Article 16*

Within the time limit laid down in Article 18 (1), Member States shall designate the authorities and bodies competent to award or receive the diplomas, certificates and other evidence of formal qualifications as well as the documents and information referred to in this Directive and shall forthwith inform the other Member States and the Commission thereof.

*Article 17*

This Directive shall also apply to nationals of Member States who, in accordance with Regulation (EEC) No 1612/68, are pursuing or will pursue as employed persons the activities referred to in Article 1.

*Article 18*

1. Member States shall bring into force the measures necessary to comply with this Directive within two years of its notification and shall forthwith inform the Commission thereof.

2. Member States shall communicate to the Commission the texts of the main provisions of national law which they adopt in the field covered by this Directive.

*Article 19*

This Directive is addressed to the Member States.

Done at Brussels, 18 December 1978.

*For the Council*

*The President*

H.-D. GENSCHER

Official Journal of the European Communities No L 362/23. 12. 78

# COUNCIL DIRECTIVE

## of 18 December 1978

## concerning the coordination of provisions laid down by law, regulation or administrative action in respect of the activities of veterinary surgeons

(78/1027/EEC)

THE COUNCIL OF THE EUROPEAN COMMUNITIES,

Having regard to the Treaty establishing the European Economic Community, and in particular Articles 49, 57, 66 and 235 thereof,

Having regard to the proposal from the Commission [1],

Having regard to the opinion of the European Parliament [2],

Having regard to the opinion of the Economic and Social Committee [3],

Whereas, with a view to achieving the mutual recognition of diplomas, certificates and other evidence of formal qualifications in veterinary medicine laid down in Council Directive 78/1026/EEC of 18 December 1978 concerning the mutual recognition of diplomas, certificates and other evidence of formal qualifications in veterinary medicine, including measures to facilitate the effective exercise of the right of establishment and freedom to provide services [4], the comparable nature of training courses in the Member States enables coordination in this field to be confined to the requirement that minimum standards be observed, which then leaves the Member States freedom of organization as regards instruction;

Whereas the coordination of the conditions for the pursuit of these activities, as envisaged by this Directive, does not exclude any subsequent coordination;

Whereas the coordination envisaged by this Directive covers the professional training of veterinary surgeons; whereas, as far as training is concerned, most Member States do not at present distinguish between veterinary surgeons who pursue their activities as employed persons and those who are self-employed; whereas, for this reason and in order to encourage as far as possible the free movement of professional persons within the Community, it appears necessary to extend the application of this Directive to employed veterinary surgeons,

HAS ADOPTED THIS DIRECTIVE:

*Article 1*

1. The Member States shall require persons wishing to take up and pursue the profession of veterinary surgeon to hold a diploma, certificate or other evidence of formal qualifications in veterinary medicine referred to in Article 3 of Directive 78/1026/EEC which guarantees that during his complete training period the person concerned has acquired:

(a) adequate knowledge of the sciences on which the activities of the veterinary surgeon are based;

(b) adequate knowledge of the structure and functions of healthy animals, of their husbandry, reproduction and hygiene in general, as well as their feeding, including the technology involved in the manufacture and preservation of foods corresponding to their needs;

(c) adequate knowledge of the behaviour and protection of animals;

(d) adequate knowledge of the causes, nature, course, effects, diagnosis and treatment of the diseases of animals, whether considered individually or in groups, including a special knowledge of the diseases which may be transmitted to humans;

(e) adequate knowledge of preventive medicine;

(f) adequate knowledge of the hygiene and technology involved in the production, manufacture and putting into circulation of animal foodstuffs or foodstuffs of animal origin intended for human consumption;

(g) adequate knowledge of the laws, regulations and administrative provisions relating to the subjects listed above;

(h) adequate clinical and other practical experience under appropriate supervision.

2. Veterinary training of this kind shall comprise in all

(1) OJ No C 92, 20. 7. 1970, p. 18.
(2) OJ No C 19, 28. 2. 1972, p. 10.
(3) OJ No C 60, 14. 6. 1971, p. 3.
(4) OJ No L 362, 23.12.1978, p.1.

at least five years' theoretical and practical full-time instruction given in a university, a higher education institution recognized as having equivalent status, or under the supervision of a university, and shall include at least the subjects listed in the Annex.

3. In order to be accepted for this training, the candidate must have a diploma or a certificate which entitles him to be admitted to the universities or higher education institutions recognized as having equivalent status of a Member State for the course of study concerned.

4. Nothing in this Directive shall prejudice any facility which may be granted in accordance with their own rules by Member States in respect of their own territory to authorize holders of diplomas, certificates or other evidence of formal qualifications which have not been obtained in a Member State to take up and pursue the activities of a veterinary surgeon.

*Article 2*

This Directive shall also apply to nationals of Member States who, in accordance with Council Regulation (EEC) No 1612/68 of 15 October 1968 on freedom of movement for workers within the Community [1], are pursuing or will pursue as employed persons the activities referred to in Article 1 of Directive 78/1026/EEC.

*Article 3*

1. Member States shall bring into force the measures necessary to comply with this Directive within two years of its notification and shall forthwith inform the Commission thereof.

2. Member States shall communicate to the Commission the texts of the main provisions of national law which they adopt in the field covered by this Directive.

*Article 4*

This Directive is addressed to the Member States.

Done at Brussels, 18 December 1978.

*For the Council*

*The President*

H.-D. GENSCHER

(1) OJ No L 257, 19. 10. 1968, p. 2.

*ANNEX*

## STUDY PROGRAMME FOR VETERINARY SURGEONS

The programme of studies leading to the diploma, certificate or other evidence of formal qualifications in veterinary medicine shall include at least the subjects listed below. Instruction in one or more of these subjects may be given as part of, or in association with, other courses.

A. **Basic subjects**

— Physics,
— Chemistry,
— Animal biology,
— Plant biology,
— Biomathematics.

B. **Specific subjects**

**Group 1:** Basic sciences

— Anatomy (including histology and embryology),
— Physiology,
— Bio-chemistry,
— Genetics,
— Pharmacology,
— Pharmacy,
— Toxicology,
— Microbiology,
— Immunology,
— Epidemiology,
— Professional ethics.

**Group 2:** Clinical sciences

— Obstetrics,
— Pathology (including pathological anatomy),
— Parasitology,
— Clinical medicine and surgery (including anaesthetics),
— Clinical lectures on the various domestic animals, poultry and other animal species,
— Preventive medicine,
— Radiology,
— Reproduction and reproductive disorders,
— Veterinary state medicine and public health,
— Veterinary legislation and forensic medicine,
— Therapeutics,
— Propaedeutics.

**Group 3:** Animal production

— Animal production,
— Animal nutrition,
— Agronomy,
— Rural economics,
— Animal husbandry,
— Veterinary hygiene,
— Animal ethology and protection.

**Group 4:** Food hygiene

— Inspection and control of animal foodstuffs or foodstuffs of animal origin,
— Food hygiene and technology,
— Practical work (including practical work in places where slaughtering and processing of foodstuffs takes place).

Practical training may be in the form of a training period, provided that such training is full-time and under the direct control of the competent authority, and does not exceed six months within the aggregate training period of five years study.

The distribution of the theoretical and practical training among the various groups of subjects shall be balanced and coordinated in such a way that the knowledge and experience listed in Article 1 (1) of this Directive may be acquired in a manner which will adequately enable veterinary surgeons to perform all their various duties.

Official Journal of the European Communities No L 362/23. 12. 78

# COUNCIL RECOMMENDATION

## of 18 December 1978

## concerning nationals of the Grand Duchy of Luxembourg who hold a diploma in veterinary medicine conferred in a third country

(78/1029/EEC)

THE COUNCIL OF THE EUROPEAN COMMUNITIES,

Approving Directive 78/1026/EEC concerning the mutual recognition of diplomas, certificates and other evidence of formal qualifications in veterinary medicine, including measures to facilitate the effective exercise of the right of establishment and freedom to provide services (1),

Noting that this Directive refers only to diplomas, certificates and evidence of formal qualifications conferred in a Member State,

Anxious, however, to take account of the special position of nationals of the Grand Duchy of Luxembourg who, since there is no complete university training in the Grand Duchy itself, have studied in a third country,

Hereby recommends that the Governments of the other Member States should allow nationals of the Grand Duchy of Luxembourg who hold a final diploma of studies in veterinary medicine conferred in a third country and recognized under the Luxembourg law of 18 June 1969, to take up and pursue activities as self-employed veterinary surgeons within the Community, by recognizing these diplomas in their territories.

Done at Brussels, 18 December 1978.

*For the Council*

*The President*

H.-D. GENSCHER

(1) OJ No L 362, 23.12.1978, p.1.

Official Journal of the European Communities No C 308/23. 12. 78

I

*(Information)*

# COUNCIL

**Statements on the Directive concerning the mutual recognition of diplomas, certificates and other evidence of formal qualifications in veterinary medicine, including measures to facilitate the effective exercise of the right of establishment and freedom to provide services (¹)**

*Council statement on prophylaxis and the inspection of animal foodstuffs and foodstuffs of animal origin*

'The Member States undertake to treat nationals of the other Member States as their own nationals with regard to activities in the field of prophylaxis and, therefore, to refrain from invoking the first paragraph of Article 55, provided that such activities are covered by these provisions, in so far as these tasks are assigned to nationals pursuing activities as self-employed or employed veterinary surgeons.

In addition, noting that in the Member States veterinary surgeons who are nationals of a Member State may be authorized by their national authorities to pursue activities in the field of inspection of animal foodstuffs and foodstuffs of animal origin in addition to their other activities, the Member States also undertake in this connection to treat veterinary surgeons who are nationals of the other Member States as their own veterinary surgeons, and consequently to refrain from invoking the first paragraph of Article 55 of the Treaty for the purpose of applying different types of treatment.

By the same token, the Member States also undertake not to invoke Article 48 (4) where self-employed veterinary surgeons thus authorized are regarded as being employed in the public service within the meaning of that Article.

The Member States may, however, make the right to take up these activities conditional upon attendance at an interview in which the veterinary surgeon must prove to the competent authority that he has acquainted himself with the legal provisions applying in the host country in the matter.'

(¹) OJ No L 362, 23. 12. 1978, p. 1.

# 7. Acquired rights

**(doctors, nurses, dentists, veterinary surgeons)**

Official Journal of the European Communities No L 385/31. 12. 81

# COUNCIL DIRECTIVE

**of 14 December 1981**

**supplementing Directives 75/362/EEC, 77/452/EEC, 78/686/EEC and 78/1026/EEC concerning the mutual recognition of diplomas, certificates and other evidence of the formal qualifications of doctors, nurses responsible for general care, dental practitioners and veterinary surgeons respectively, with regard to acquired rights**

(81/1057/EEC)

THE COUNCIL OF THE EUROPEAN COMMUNITIES,

Having regard to the Treaty establishing the European Economic Community, and in particular Articles 49, 57 and 66 thereof,

Having regard to the proposal from the Commission [1],

Having regard to the opinion of the European Parliament [2],

Having regard to the opinion of the Economic and Social Committee [3],

Whereas in Directives 75/362/EEC [4], 77/452/EEC [5], 78/686/EEC [6] and 78/1026/EEC [7] concerning the mutual recognition of diplomas, certificates and other evidence of the formal qualifications of doctors, nurses responsible for general care, dental practitioners and veterinary surgeons respectively, and including measures to facilitate the effective exercise of the right of establishment and freedom to provide services, the provisions relating to acquired rights refer to diplomas, certificates and other evidence of formal qualifications of doctors, nurses responsible for general care, dental practitioners and veterinary surgeons issued by the Member States before the implementation of the said Directives;

Whereas these provisions therefore do not expressly cover the diplomas, certificates and other evidence of formal qualifications which are evidence of training not meeting the minimum training requirements provided for in Directives 75/363/EEC [8], 77/453/EEC [9], 78/687/EEC [10] and 78/1027/EEC [11] which was completed after the implementation of the said Directives, but which had commenced before their implementation;

Whereas it is advisable to make good this omission,

HAS ADOPTED THIS DIRECTIVE:

*Article 1*

Article 9 (1) and (2) of Directive 75/362/EEC, Article 4 of Directive 77/452/EEC, Article 7 (1) and (2) of Directive 78/686/EEC and Article 4 of Directive 78/1026/EEC shall also apply to the diplomas, certificates and other evidence of formal qualifications which are evidence of training which does not meet the minimum training requirements provided for respectively in Articles 1, 2, 3, 4 and 5 of Directive 75/363/EEC, Article 1 of Directive 77/453/FEC, Articles 1, 2 and 3 of Directive 78/687/EEC and Article 1 of Directive 78/1027/EEC and which was completed after the implementation of these Directives but has commenced before the said implementation.

(1) OJ No C 121, 23. 5. 1981, p. 3.
(2) OJ No C 172, 13. 7. 1981, p. 114.
(3) OJ No C 185, 27. 7. 1981, p. 7.
(4) OJ No L 167, 30. 6. 1975, p. 1.
(5) OJ No L 176, 15. 7. 1977, p. 1.
(6) OJ No L 233, 24. 8. 1978, p. 1.
(7) OJ No L 362, 23. 12. 1978, p. 1.
(8) OJ No L 167, 30. 6. 1975, p. 14.
(9) OJ No L 176, 15. 7. 1977, p. 8.
(10) OJ No L 233, 24. 8. 1978, p. 10.
(11) OJ No L 362, 23. 12. 1978, p. 7.

*Article 2*

Member States shall take the measures necessary to comply with this Directive by 30 June 1982 at the latest. They shall forthwith inform the Commission thereof.

*Article 3*

This Directive is addressed to the Member States.

Done at Brussels, 14 December 1981.

*For the Council*

*The President*

G. HOWE

# 8. Midwives

Official Journal of the European Communities No L 33/ 11. 2. 80

II

*(Acts whose publication is not obligatory)*

# COUNCIL

## COUNCIL DIRECTIVE

**of 21 January 1980**

**concerning the mutual recognition of diplomas, certificates and other evidence of formal qualifications in midwifery and including measures to facilitate the effective exercise of the right of establishment and freedom to provide services** (*)

(80/154/EEC)

THE COUNCIL OF THE EUROPEAN COMMUNITIES,

Having regard to the Treaty establishing the European Economic Community, and in particular Articles 49, 57 and 66 thereof,

Having regard to the proposal from the Commission [1],

Having regard to the opinion of the European Parliament [2],

Having regard to the opinion of the Economic and Social Committee [3],

Whereas, pursuant to the Treaty, all discriminatory treatment based on nationality with regard to establishment and provision of services is prohibited as from the end of the transitional period; whereas the principle of such treatment based on nationality applies in particular to the grant of any authorization required to practise as a midwife and also to the registration with or membership of professional organizations or bodies;

Whereas it nevertheless seems desirable that certain provisions be introduced to facilitate the effective exercise of the right of establishment and freedom to provide services in respect of the activities of midwives;

Whereas, pursuant to the Treaty, the Member States are required not to grant any form of aid likely to distort the conditions of establishment;

Whereas Article 57 (1) of the Treaty provides that Directives be issued for mutual recognition of diplomas, certificates and other evidence of formal qualifications;

Whereas it would appear advisable that, contemporaneously with the mutual recognition of diplomas, provision should be made for coordinating the conditions governing the training of midwives; whereas such coordination is the subject of Directive 80/155/EEC [4];

Whereas in the Member States the law makes the right to take up and pursue the activities of midwife dependent upon the possession of a midwifery diploma;

Whereas, with regard to the possession of a formal certificate of training, since a Directive on the mutual recognition of diplomas does not necessarily imply equivalence in the training covered by such diplomas, the use of such qualifications should be authorized only in the language of the Member State of origin or of the Member State from which the foreign national comes;

Whereas, to facilitate the application of this Directive by the national authorities, Member States may prescribe that, in addition to formal certificates of training, the person who satisfies the conditions of

[1] OJ No C 18, 12. 2. 1970, p. 1.
[2] OJ No C 101, 4. 8. 1970, p. 26.
[3] OJ No C 146, 11. 12. 1970, p. 17.

[4] OJ No L 33, 11.2.1980, p.8.

(*) Text as amended by:
- Directive 80/1273/EEC of 22 December 1980 (Official Journal of the European Communities No L 375, 31.12.1980, p.74).
- the Act of Accession for Spain and Portugal.

training required by this Directive must provide a certificate from the competent authorities of his country of origin or of the country from which he comes stating that these certificates of training are those covered by the Directive;

Whereas, in the case of the provision of services, the requirement of registration with or membership of professional organizations or bodies, since it is related to the fixed and permanent nature of the activity pursued in the host country, would undoubtedly constitute an obstacle to the person wishing to provide the service, by reason of the temporary nature of his activity; whereas this requirement should therefore be abolished; whereas however, in this event, control over professional discipline, which is the responsibility of these professional organizations or bodies, should be guaranteed; whereas, to this end, it should be provided, subject to the application of Article 62 of the Treaty, that the person concerned may be required to submit to the competent authority of the host Member State particulars relating to the provision of services;

Whereas, with regard to the requirements relating to good character and good repute, a distinction should be drawn between the requirements to be satisfied on first taking up the profession and those to be satisfied to practise it;

Whereas, as far as the activities of employed midwives are concerned, Council Regulation (EEC) No 1612/68 of 15 October 1968 on freedom of movement for workers within the Community (1) lays down no specific provisions relating to good character or good repute, professional discipline or use of title for the professions covered; whereas, depending on the individual Member State, such rules are or may be applicable both to employed and self-employed persons; whereas the activities of midwives are subject in all Member States to possession of a diploma, certificate or other evidence of formal qualification in midwifery; whereas such activities are pursued by both employed and self-employed persons, or by the same persons in both capacities in the course of their professional career; whereas, in order to encourage as far as possible the free movement of those professional persons within the Community, it therefore appears necessary to extend this Directive to employed midwives,

HAS ADOPTED THIS DIRECTIVE:

## CHAPTER I

## SCOPE

### *Article 1*

1. This Directive shall apply to the activities of midwives as defined by each Member State, without prejudice to Article 4 of Directive 80/155/EEC, and pursued under the following professional titles:

*in the Federal Republic of Germany:*

— 'Hebamme';

*in Belgium:*

— 'accoucheuse/vroedvrouw';

*in Denmark:*

— 'jordemoder';

*in France:*

— 'sage-femme';

*in Ireland:*

— midwife;

*in Italy:*

— 'ostetrica';

*in Luxembourg:*

— 'sage-femme';

*in the Netherlands*

— 'verloskundige';

*in the United Kingdom:*

— midwife;

in Greece:

‚Μαία'; (*)

*in Spain:*

"matrona" or "asistente obstétrico"; (**)

---

(1) OJ No L 257, 19. 10. 1968, p. 2.

(*) Text as amended by Directive 80/1273/EEC.
(**) Text as amended by the Act of Accession for Spain and Portugal.

*in Portugal:*

"enfermeiro especialista em enfermagem de saúde materna e obstétrica".(*)

CHAPTER II

DIPLOMAS, CERTIFICATES AND OTHER EVIDENCE OF FORMAL QUALIFICATIONS IN MIDWIFERY

*Article 2*

1. Each Member State shall recognize the diplomas, certificates and other evidence of formal qualifications in midwifery awarded to nationals of Member States by the other Member States and listed in Article 3 which satisfy the minimum programme mentioned in Article 1 (1), (3) and (4) of Directive 80/155/EEC and comply with one of the following conditions:

- full-time training in midwifery lasting at least three years:
  - either subject to possession of a diploma, certificate or other evidence of formal qualifications giving right of admittance to university or higher-education establishments or, failing this, attesting an equivalent level of knowledge,
  - or followed by professional practice for which the certificate referred to in Article 4 of this Directive is issued,
- full-time training in midwifery lasting at least two years or 3 600 hours subject to possession of a diploma, certificate or other evidence of formal qualifications as a nurse responsible for general care, referred to in Article 3 of Directive 77/452/EEC [1],
- full-time training in midwifery lasting at least 18 months or 3 000 hours subject to possession of a diploma, certificate or other evidence of formal qualifications as a nurse responsible for general care referred to in Article 3 of Directive 77/452/EEC and followed by professional practice for which the certificate referred to in Article 4 of this Directive is issued.

2. Each Member State shall, as far as the right to take up and pursue the activities of midwives in a self-employed capacity is concerned, give diplomas, certificates and other evidence of formal qualifications recognized by it the same effect in its territory as those which the Member State itself awards.

*Article 3*

The diplomas, certificates and other evidence of formal qualifications referred to in Article 2 are the following:

(a) *in the Federal Republic of Germany:*

- the 'Hebammenprüfungszeugnis' awarded by the State-appointed examining board,
- the certificates issued by the competent authorities of the Federal Republic of Germany, stating that the diplomas awarded after 8 May 1945 by the competent authorities of the German Democratic Republic are recognized as equivalent to those listed in the first indent;

(b) *in Belgium:*

the 'diplôme d'accoucheuse/vroedvrouwdiploma' awarded by schools set up or approved by the State or by the 'Jury central';

(c) *in Denmark:*

the 'bevis for bestået jordemodereksamen' awarded by 'Danmarks Jordemoderskole';

(d) *in France:*

the 'diplôme de sage-femme' awarded by the State;

(e) *in Ireland:*

the certificate in midwifery awarded by 'An Bord Altranais';

(f) in Italy:

the 'diploma d'ostetrica' awarded by schools approved by the State;

(g) *in Luxembourg:*

the 'diplôme de sage-femme' awarded by the Minister for Health following a decision by the examining board;

(h) *in the Netherlands:*

the 'vroedvrouwdiploma' awarded by the examining body designated by the State;

(i) *in the United Kingdom:*

the certificate of admission to the Roll of Midwives, awarded in England and Wales by the Central Midwives Board for England and Wales, in Scotland by the Central Midwives Board for Scotland, and in Northern Ireland by the Northern Ireland Council for Nurses and Midwives;

---

[1] OJ No L 176, 15. 7. 1977, p. 1.

(*) Text as amended by the Act of Accession for Spain and Portugal.

j. in Greece:

— the πτυχίο μαίας authenticated by the Ministry of Social Services,

— the πτυχίο 'Ανωτέρας Σχολῆς Στελεχῶν 'Υγείας καί Κοινωνικῆς Προνοίας, Τμήματος Μαιῶν' issued by the KATEE; (*)

(k) *in Spain:*

the diploma of "asistencia obstétrica" awarded by the Ministero de Educación y Ciencia; (**)

(l) *in Portugal:*

the diploma of "enfermeiro especialista em enfermagem de saúde materna e obstétrica".(**)

*Article 4*

The certificate provided for in Article 2 shall be issued by the competent authorities of the Member State of origin or of the Member State from which the foreign national comes. It shall certify that the holder has satisfactorily, after qualifying as a midwife, carried out all the activities of a midwife in a hospital or other health establishment approved for this purpose, for a period fixed as follows:

— two years in the case provided for in the second sub-indent of the first indent of Article 2 (1),

— one year in the case provided for in the third indent of Article 2 (1).

CHAPTER III

EXISTING CIRCUMSTANCES

*Article 5*

1. In the case of nationals of Member States whose diplomas, certificates and other evidence of formal qualifications do not satisfy all the minimum training requirements laid down in Article 1 of Directive 80/155/EEC, each Member State shall recognize as sufficient evidence the diplomas, certificates and other evidence of the formal qualifications of midwives awarded by those Member States prior to and during a period of not more than six years after the notification of this Directive, accompanied by a certificate stating that those nationals have effectively and lawfully been engaged in the activities in question for at least three years during the five years prior to the date of issue of the certificate.

2. In the case of nationals of Member States whose diplomas, certificates and other evidence of formal qualifications satisfy all the minimum training requirements laid down in Article 1 of Directive 80/155/EEC, but, by virtue of Article 2 of the present Directive, need be recognized only if they are accompanied by the certificate of professional practice referred to in Article 4, each Member State shall recognize as sufficient evidence the diplomas, certificates and other evidence of formal qualifications of midwives awarded by those Member States prior to the entry into force of the present Directive, accompanied by a certificate stating that those nationals have effectively and lawfully been engaged in the activities in question for at least two years during the five years prior to the date of issue of the certificate.

CHAPTER IV

USE OF ACADEMIC TITLE

*Article 6*

1. Without prejudice to Article 15, host Member States shall ensure that nationals of Member States who fulfil the conditions laid down in Articles 2 and 5 have the right to use the lawful academic title, inasmuch as it is not identical to the professional title, or, where appropriate, the abbreviation thereof of their Member State of origin or of the Member State from which they come, in the language or languages of that State. Host Member States may require this title to be followed by the name and location of the establishment or examining board which awarded it.

2. If the academic title used in the Member State of origin, or in the Member State from which a foreign national comes, can be confused in the host Member State with a title requiring, in that State, additional training which the person concerned has not undergone, the host Member State may require such a person to use the title employed in the Member State of origin or the Member State from which he comes in a suitable form to be indicated by the host Member State.

(*) Text as amended by Directive 80/1273/EEC.
(**) Text as amended by the Act of Accession for Spain and Portugal.

CHAPTER V

PROVISIONS TO FACILITATE THE EFFECTIVE EXERCISE OF THE RIGHT OF ESTABLISHMENT AND FREEDOM TO PROVIDE SERVICES IN RESPECT OF THE ACTIVITIES OF MIDWIVES

A. Provisions specifically relating to the right of establishment

*Article 7*

1. A host Member State which requires of its nationals proof of good character or good repute when they take up for the first time any activity referred to in Article 1 shall accept as sufficient evidence, in respect of nationals of other Member States, a certificate issued by a competent authority in the Member State of origin or in the Member State from which the foreign national comes, attesting that the requirements of the Member State as to good character or good repute for taking up the activity in question have been met.

2. Where the Member State of origin or the Member State from which the foreign national comes does not require proof of good character or good repute of persons wishing to take up the activity in question for the first time, the host Member State may require of nationals of the Member State of origin or of the Member State from which the foreign national comes an extract from the judicial record or, failing this, an equivalent document issued by a competent authority in the Member State of origin or the Member State from which the foreign national comes.

3. If the host Member State has detailed knowledge of a serious matter which occurred outside its territory prior to the establishment of the person concerned in that State and which is likely to affect the taking up within its territory of the activity concerned, it may inform the Member State of origin or the Member State from which the foreign national comes.

The Member State of origin or the Member State from which the foreign national comes shall verify the accuracy of the facts if they are likely to affect in that Member State the taking up of the activity in question. The authorities in that State shall decide on the nature and extent of the investigation to be made and shall inform the host Member State of any consequential action which they take with regard to the certificates or documents they have issued.

4. Member States shall ensure the confidentiality of the information which is forwarded.

*Article 8*

1. Where, in a host Member State, provisions laid down by law, regulation or administrative action are in force laying down requirements as to good character or good repute, including provisions for disciplinary action in respect of serious professional misconduct or conviction for criminal offences and relating to the pursuit of any of the activities referred to in Article 1, the Member State of origin or the Member State from which the foreign national comes shall forward to the host Member State all necessary information regarding measures or disciplinary action of a professional or administrative nature taken in respect of the person concerned, or criminal penalties imposed on him when pursuing his profession in the Member State of origin or in the Member State from which he came.

2. If the host Member State has detailed knowledge of a serious matter which has occurred prior to the establishment of the person concerned in that State outside its territory and which is likely to affect the pursuit within its territory of the activity concerned, it may inform the Member State of origin or the Member State from which the foreign national comes.

The Member State of origin or the Member State from which the foreign national comes shall verify the accuracy of the facts if they are likely to affect in that Member State the pursuit of the activity in question. The authorities in that State shall decide on the nature and extent of the investigation to be made and shall inform the host Member State of any consequential action which they take with regard to the information they have forwarded in accordance with paragraph 1.

3. Member States shall ensure the confidentiality of the information which is forwarded.

*Article 9*

Where a host Member State requires of its own nationals wishing to take up or pursue any of the activities referred to in Article 1 a certificate of physical or mental health, that State shall accept as sufficient evidence thereof the presentation of the document required in the Member State of origin or in the Member State from which the foreign national comes.

Where the Member State of origin or the Member State from which the foreign national comes does not impose any requirements of this nature on those wishing to take up or pursue the activity in question, the host Member State shall accept from such national a certificate issued by a competent authority in that State corresponding to the certificates issued in the host Member State.

*Article 10*

Documents issued in accordance with Articles 7, 8 and 9 may not be presented more than three months after their date of issue.

*Article 11*

1. The procedure for authorizing the person concerned to take up any activity referred to in Article 1, pursuant to Articles 7, 8 and 9 must be completed as soon as possible and not later than three months after presentation of all the documents relating to such person, without prejudice to delays resulting from any appeal that may be made upon the termination of this procedure.

2. In the cases referred to in Articles 7 (3) and 8 (2), a request for re-examination shall suspend the period stipulated in paragraph 1.

The Member State consulted shall give its reply within three months.

On receipt of the reply or at the end of the period the host Member State shall continue with the procedure referred to in paragraph 1.

*Article 12*

Where a host Member State requires its own nationals wishing to take up or pursue one of the activities referred to in Article 1 to take an oath or make a solemn declaration and where the form of such oath or declaration cannot be used by nationals of other Member States, that Member State shall ensure that an appropriate and equivalent form of oath or declaration is offered to the person concerned.

**B. Provisions specifically relating to the provision of services**

*Article 13*

1. Where a Member State requires of its own nationals wishing to take up or pursue any of the activities referred to in Article 1 an authorization, or membership of or registration with a professional organization or body, that Member State shall in the case of the provision of services exempt the nationals of Member States from that requirement.

The person concerned shall provide services with the same rights and obligations as the nationals of the host Member State; in particular he shall be subject to the rules of conduct of a professional or administrative nature which apply in that Member State.

Where a host Member State adopts a measure pursuant to the second subparagraph or becomes aware of facts which run counter to these provisions, it shall forthwith inform the Member State where the person concerned is established.

2. The host Member State may require the person concerned to make a prior declaration to the competent authorities concerning the provision of his services where they involve a temporary stay in its territory.

In urgent cases this declaration may be made as soon as possible after the services have been provided.

3. Pursuant to paragraphs 1 and 2, the host Member State may require the person concerned to supply one or more documents containing the following particulars:

— the declaration referred to in paragraph 2,

— a certificate stating that the person concerned is lawfully pursuing the activities in question in the Member State where he is established,

— a certificate that the person concerned holds one or other of the diplomas, certificates of other evidence of formal qualification appropriate for the provision of the services in question and referred to in this Directive.

4. The document or documents specified in paragraph 3 may not be produced more than 12 months after their date of issue.

5. Where a Member State temporarily or permanently deprives, in whole or in part, one of its nationals or a national of another Member State established in its territory of the right to pursue one of the activities referred to in Article 1, it shall, as appropriate, ensure the temporary or permanent withdrawal of the certificate referred to in the second indent of paragraph 3.

*Article 14*

Where registration with a public social security body is required in a host Member State for the settlement with insurance bodies of accounts relating to services rendered to persons insured under social security schemes, that Member State shall exempt nationals of Member States established in another Member State from this requirement in cases of provision of services entailing travel on the part of the person concerned.

However, the persons concerned shall supply information to this body in advance, or, in urgent cases, subsequently, concerning the services provided.

**C. Provisions common to the right of establishment and freedom to provide services**

*Article 15*

Where in a host Member State the use of the professional title relating to one of the activities referred to in Article 1 is subject to rules, nationals of other Member States who fulfil the conditions laid down in Articles 2 and 5 shall use the professional title of the host Member State which, in that State, corresponds to those conditions of qualification, and shall use the abbreviated title.

*Article 16*

1. Member States shall take the necessary measures to enable the persons concerned to obtain information on the health and social security laws and, where applicable, on the professional ethics of the host Member State.

For this purpose, Member States may set up information centres from which such persons may obtain the necessary information. In the case of establishment, the host Member States may require the persons concerned to contact these centres.

2. Member States may set up the centres referred to in paragraph 1 within the competent authorities and bodies which they must designate within the period laid down in Article 20 (1).

3. Member States shall see to it that, where appropriate, the persons concerned acquire, in their own interest and in that of their patients, the linguistic knowledge necessary for the exercise of their profession in the host Member State.

CHAPTER VI

**FINAL PROVISIONS**

*Article 17*

In the event of justified doubts, the host Member State may require of the competent authorities of another Member State confirmation of the authenticity of the diplomas, certificates and other evidence of formal qualifications issued in that other Member State and referred to in Chapters II and III, and also confirmation of the fact that the person concerned has fulfilled all the training requirements laid down in Directive 80/155/EEC.

*Article 18*

Within the time limit laid down in Article 20 (1) Member States shall designate the authorities and bodies competent to issue or receive the diplomas, certificates and other evidence of formal qualifications as well as the documents and information referred to in this Directive, and shall forthwith inform the other Member States and the Commission thereof.

*Article 19*

This Directive shall also apply to nationals of Member States who, in accordance with Regulation (EEC) No 1612/68, are pursuing or will pursue as employed persons one of the activities referred to in Article 1.

*Article 20*

1. Member States shall bring into force the measures necessary to comply with this Directive within three years of its notification and shall forthwith inform the Commission thereof.

2. Member States shall communicate to the Commission the texts of the main provisions of national law which they adopt in the field covered by this Directive.

*Article 21*

Where a Member State encounters major difficulties in certain fields when applying this Directive, the Commission shall examine these difficulties in conjunction with that State and shall request the opinion of the Committee of Senior Officials on Public Health set up under Decision 75/365/EEC (1), as last amended by Decision 80/157/EEC (2).

Where necessary, the Commission shall submit appropriate proposals to the Council.

*Article 22*

This Directive is addressed to the Member States.

Done at Brussels, 21 January 1980.

*For the Council*

*The President*

G. MARCORA

(1) OJ No L 167, 30. 6. 1975, p. 19.
(2) OJ No L 33, 11.2.1980, p.15.

Official Journal of the European Communities No L 33/11. 2. 80

# COUNCIL DIRECTIVE

## of 21 January 1980

## concerning the coordination of provisions laid down by law, regulation or administrative action relating to the taking up and pursuit of the activities of midwives

(80/155/EEC)

THE COUNCIL OF THE EUROPEAN COMMUNITIES,

Having regard to the Treaty establishing the European Economic Community, and in particular Articles 49, 57 and 66 thereof,

Having regard to the proposal from the Commission (1),

Having regard to the opinion of the European Parliament (2),

Having regard to the opinion of the Economic and Social Committee (3),

Whereas, under Article 57 of the Treaty, the provisions laid down by law, regulation or administrative action relating to the taking up and pursuit of the activities of midwives must be coordinated; whereas it is necessary for reasons of public health to move within the Community towards a common definition of the field of activity of the professional persons concerned and of their training; whereas it has not been thought desirable to impose to that end a unified training programme for all Member States; whereas they should on the contrary be allowed the greatest possible freedom in organizing training; whereas the best solution is therefore to lay down minimum standards;

Whereas the coordination of these activities, as envisaged by this Directive, does not exclude subsequent coordination;

Whereas, as far as training is concerned, most Member States do not at present distinguish between midwives who pursue their activities as employed persons and those who are self-employed; whereas for this reason it appears necessary to extend the application of this Directive to employed midwives,

HAS ADOPTED THIS DIRECTIVE:

*Article 1*

1. Member States shall make the taking up and pursuit of midwifery activities under the titles referred to in Article 1 of Directive 80/154/EEC (4) conditional on the possession of a diploma, certificate or other evidence of formal qualifications in midwifery as listed in Article 3 of the said Directive, guaranteeing that the person concerned has acquired during the total duration of training:

(a) adequate knowledge of the sciences on which the activities of midwives are based, particularly obstetrics and gynaecology;

(b) adequate knowledge of the ethics of the profession and the professional legislation;

(c) detailed knowledge of biological functions, anatomy and physiology in the field of obstetrics and of the newly born, and also a knowledge of the relationship between the state of health and the physical and social environment of the human being, and of his behaviour;

(d) adequate clinical experience gained in approved institutions under the supervision of staff qualified in midwifery and obstetrics;

(e) adequate understanding of the training of health personnel and experience of working with such personnel.

2. The training referred to in paragraph 1 shall comprise:

— either a full-time course in midwifery comprising at least three years of practical and theoretical studies, admission to which is subject to completion of at least the first 10 years of general school education,

— or a full-time course in midwifery lasting at least 18 months, admission to which is subject to possession of a diploma, certificate or other evidence of formal qualifications of nurses responsible for general care referred to in Article 3 of Directive 77/452/EEC (5).

3. The course in midwifery provided for in the first indent of paragraph 2 shall cover at least the subjects of the training programme set out in the Annex.

(1) OJ No C 18, 12. 2. 1970, p. 1.
(2) OJ No C 101, 4. 8. 1970, p. 26.
(3) OJ No C 146, 11. 12. 1970, p. 17.
(4) OJ No L 33, 11.2.1980, p.1.
(5) OJ No L 176, 15. 7. 1977, p. 1.

The course provided for in the second indent of paragraph 2 shall cover at least the subjects of the training programme set out in the Annex which did not form part of an equivalent course in the training of nurses.

4. Member States shall ensure that the institution training midwives is responsible for the coordination of theory and practice throughout the programme.

The theoretical and technical training mentioned in Part A of the Annex shall be balanced and coordinated with the clinical training of midwives mentioned in Part B of the same Annex in such a way that the knowledge and experience listed in paragraph 1 may be acquired in an adequate manner.

Clinical instruction shall take the form of supervised in-service training in hospital departments or other health services approved by the competent authorities or bodies. As part of this training, student midwives shall participate in the activities of the departments concerned in so far as those activities contribute to their training. They shall be taught the responsibilities involved in the activities of midwives.

*Article 2*

After a periodical examination of the results of the various training courses provided for in Article 1 (2), the Commission shall make its first report to the Council six years after notification of this Directive. The said examination shall be carried out with the assistance of the Advisory Committee on the Training of Midwives.

In the light of the results of this examination, the Commission shall present proposals for amendments aimed at aligning the minimum criteria laid down for the said training courses on the conditions prescribed in the first sub-indent of the first indent and in the second indent of Article 2 (1) of Directive 80/154/EEC. The Council shall act forthwith on these proposals.

*Article 3*

Notwithstanding Article 1, Member States may permit part-time training under conditions approved by the competent national authorities.

The total period of part-time training may not be less than that of full-time training. The standard of the training may not be impaired by its part-time nature.

*Article 4*

Member States shall ensure that midwives are at least entitled to take up and pursue the following activities:

1. to provide sound family planning information and advice;
2. to diagnose pregnancies and monitor normal pregnancies; to carry out the examinations necessary for the monitoring of the development of normal pregnancies;
3. to prescribe or advise on the examinations necessary for the earliest possible diagnosis of pregnancies at risk;
4. to provide a programme of parenthood preparation and a complete preparation for childbirth including advice on hygiene and nutrition;
5. to care for and assist the mother during labour and to monitor the condition of the foetus in utero by the appropriate clinical and technical means;
6. to conduct spontaneous deliveries including where required an episiotomy and in urgent cases a breech delivery;
7. to recognize the warning signs of abnormality in the mother or infant which necessitate referral to a doctor and to assist the latter where appropriate; to take the necessary emergency measures in the doctor's absence, in particular the manual removal of the placenta, possibly followed by manual examination of the uterus;
8. to examine and care for the new-born infant; to take all initiatives which are necessary in case of need and to carry out where necessary immediate resuscitation;
9. to care for and monitor the progress of the mother in the post-natal period and to give all necessary advice to the mother on infant care to enable her to ensure the optimum progress of the new-born infant;
10. to carry out the treatment prescribed by a doctor;
11. to maintain all necessary records.

*Article 5*

This Directive shall also apply to nationals of Member States who, in accordance with Council Regulation (EEC) No 1612/68 of 15 October 1968 on freedom of movement for workers within the Community ([1]), are pursuing or will pursue, as employed persons, one of the activities referred to in Article 1 of Directive 80/154/EEC.

*Article 6*

1. Member States shall take the measures necessary to comply with this Directive within three years of its notification and shall forthwith inform the Commission thereof.

2. Member States shall communicate to the Commission the texts of the main provisions of national law which they adopt in the field covered by this Directive.

*Article 7*

Where a Member State encounters major difficulties in certain fields when applying this Directive, the Commission shall examine these difficulties in conjunction with that State and shall request the opinion of the Committee of Senior Officials on Public Health set up under Decision 75/365/EEC([2]), as last amended by Decision 80/157/EEC([3]).

Where necessary, the Commission shall submit appropriate proposals to the Council.

*Article 8*

Not later than six years after notification of this Directive, the Council, acting on a proposal from the Commission, and after having sought the opinion of the Advisory Committee, shall decide whether the derogation provided for in the third item in Part B of the Annex should be withdrawn or its scope reduced.

*Article 9*

This Directive is addressed to the Member States.

Done at Brussels, 21 January 1980.

*For the Council*

*The President*

G. MARCORA

([1]) OJ No L 257, 19. 10. 1968, p. 2.

([2]) OJ No L 167, 30. 6. 1975, p. 19.

([3]) OJ No L 33, 11.2.1980, p.15.

## ANNEX

### TRAINING PROGRAMME FOR MIDWIVES

The training programme for obtaining a diploma, certificate or other evidence of formal qualifications in midwifery consists of the following two parts:

A. THEORETICAL AND TECHNICAL INSTRUCTION

(a) **General subjects**

1. Basic anatomy and physiology
2. Basic pathology
3. Basic bacteriology, virology and parasitology
4. Basic biophysics, biochemistry and radiology
5. Paediatrics, with particular reference to new-born infants
6. Hygiene, health education, preventive medicine, early diagnosis of diseases
7. Nutrition and dietetics, with particular reference to women, new-born and young babies
8. Basic sociology and socio-medical questions
9. Basic pharmacology
10. Psychology
11. Principles and methods of teaching
12. Health and social legislation and health organization
13. Professional ethics and professional legislation
14. Sex education and family planning
15. Legal protection of mother and infant

(b) **Subjects specific to the activities of midwives**

1. Anatomy and physiology
2. Embryology and development of the foetus
3. Pregnancy, childbirth and puerperium
4. Gynaecological and obstetrical pathology
5. Preparation for childbirth and parenthood, including psychological aspects
6. Preparation for delivery (including knowledge and use of technical equipment in obstetrics)
7. Analgesia, anaesthesia and resuscitation
8. Physiology and pathology of the new-born infant
9. Care and supervision of the new-born infant
10. Psychological and social factors

B. PRACTICAL AND CLINICAL TRAINING

This training is to be dispensed under appropriate supervision:

1. Advising of pregnant women, involving at least 100 pre-natal examinations
2. Supervision and care of at least 40 pregnant women

3. Conduct by the student of at least 40 deliveries; where this number cannot be reached owing to the lack of available women in labour, it may be reduced to a minimum of 30, provided that the student assists with 20 further deliveries
4. Assistance with one or two breech deliveries
5. Experience of episiotomy and initiation into suturing
6. Supervision and care of 40 pregnant women at risk
7. At least 100 post-natal examinations and examinations of normal new-born infants
8. Supervision and care of mothers and new-born infants, including pre-term, post-term, underweight and ill new-born infants
9. Care of pathological cases in the fields of gynaecology and obstetrics, and diseases of new-born and young babies
10. Initiation into the care of general pathological cases in medicine and surgery.

# 9. Architects

Official Journal of the European Communities No L 223/21. 8. 85

II

*(Acts whose publication is not obligatory)*

# COUNCIL

## COUNCIL DIRECTIVE

**of 10 June 1985**

**on the mutual recognition of diplomas, certificates and other evidence of formal qualifications in architecture, including measures to facilitate the effective exercise of the right of establishment and freedom to provide services** (*)

(85/384/EEC)

THE COUNCIL OF THE EUROPEAN COMMUNITIES,

Having regard to the Treaty establishing the European Economic Community, and in particular Articles 49, 57 and 66 thereof,

Having regard to the proposal from the Commission ([1]),

Having regard to the opinion of the European Parliament ([2]),

Having regard to the opinion of the Economic and Social Committee ([3]),

Whereas, pursuant to the Treaty, all discriminatory treatment based on nationality with regard to establishment and provision of services is prohibited as from the end of the transitional period; whereas the resulting principle of non-discriminatory treatment as regards nationality applies *inter alia* to the grant of any authorization required to take up activities in the field of architecture and also to the registration with or membership of professional organizations or bodies;

Whereas it nevertheless seems desirable that certain provisions be introduced to facilitate the effective exercise of the right of establishment and freedom to provide services in respect of activities in the field of architecture;

Whereas, pursuant to the Treaty, Member States are required not to grant any form of aid likely to distort the conditions of establishment;

Whereas Article 57 (1) of the Treaty provides that directives be issued for the mutual recognition of diplomas, certificates and other evidence of formal qualifications;

Whereas architecture, the quality of buildings, the way they blend in with their surroundings, respect for the natural and urban environment and the collective and individual cultural heritage are matters of public concern; whereas, therefore, the mutual recognition of diplomas, certificates and other evidence of formal qualifications must be founded on qualitative and quantitative criteria ensuring that the holders of recognized diplomas, certificates and other evidence of formal qualifications are able to understand and give practical expression to the needs of individuals, social groups and communities as regards spatial planning, the design, organization and construction of buildings, the conservation and enhancement of the architectural heritage and preservation of the natural balance;

Whereas methods of education and training for those practising professionally in the field of architecture are at present very varied; whereas, however, provision should be made for progressive alignment of education and training leading to the pursuit of activities under the professional title of architect;

(*) Text as amended by:
- Directive 85/614/EEC of 20 December 1980 (Official Journal of the European Communities No L 376, 31.12.1980, p.1).
- Directive 86/17/EEC of 27 January 1986 (Official Journal of the European Communities No L 27, 1.2.1986, p.71).

([1]) OJ No C 239, 4. 10. 1967, p. 15.
([2]) OJ No C 72, 19. 7. 1968, p. 3.
([3]) OJ No C 24, 22. 3. 1968, p. 3.

Whereas, in some Member States, the taking up and pursuit of the activities of architect are by law conditional upon the possession of a diploma in architecture ; where, in certain other Member States where this condition does not exist, the right to hold the professional title of architect is none the less governed by law ; whereas, finally, in some Member States where neither the former nor the latter is the case, laws and regulations are being prepared on the taking up and pursuit of these activities under the professional title of architect ; whereas, therefore, the conditions under which such activities may be taken up and pursued in those Member States have not yet been laid down ; whereas the mutual recognition of diplomas, certificates and other evidence of formal qualifications presupposes that such diplomas, certificates and other evidence of formal qualifications authorize the taking up and pursuit of certain activities in the Member State of issue ; whereas, therefore, the recognition of certain certificates under this Directive should continue to apply only in so far as the holders of such certificates will be authorized, in accordance with legal provisions still to be adopted in the Member State of issue, to take up activities under the professional title of architect ;

Whereas acquisition of the lawful professional title of architect is subject in some Member States to completion of a period of practical experience in addition to the possession of a diploma, certificate or other evidence of formal qualifications ; whereas, since practice in this respect of present varies from one Member State to another, to obviate possible difficulties completion of an equal period of appropriate practical experience in another Member State should be recognized as meeting this condition ;

Whereas the reference in Article 1 (2) to 'activities in the field of architecture' as being 'those activities usually pursued under the professional title of architect', the justification for which lies in the conditions prevailing in certain Member States, is intended solely to indicate the scope of this Directive, without claiming to give a legal definition of activities in the field of architecture ;

Whereas, in most Member States, activities in the field of architecture are pursued, in law or in fact, by persons who hold the title of architect, whether alone or together with another title, without those persons having a monopoly in pursuing those activities save where there are laws to the contrary ; whereas the aforementioned activities, or some of them, may also be pursued by members of other professions, in particular by engineers who have received special training in construction engineering or building ;

Whereas the mutual recognition of qualifications will facilitate the taking up and pursuit of the activities in question ;

Whereas in some Member States there is legislation allowing the lawful professional title of architect, by way of exception and notwithstanding the usual educational and training requirements for access to the title, to be granted to certain distinguished persons in the field, who are very few in number and whose work shows exceptional architectural talent ; whereas the case of these architects should be covered in this Directive, particularly since they frequently enjoy an international reputation ;

Whereas the recognition of a number of the existing diplomas, certificates and other evidence of formal qualifications in architecture listed in Articles 10 to 12 is intended to enable the holders thereof to establish themselves or provide services in other Member States with immediate effect ; whereas the sudden introduction of this provision in the Grand Duchy of Luxembourg could, in view of the country's small size, lead to distortion of competition and disturb the organization of the profession ; whereas, as a result, there appears to be justification for allowing this Member State an addiitional period of adjustment ;

Whereas, since a Directive on the mutual recognition of diplomas, certificates and other evidence of formal qualifications in architecture does not necessarily imply practical equivalence in the education and training covered by such diplomas, certificates and evidence, the use of titles should be authorized only in the language of the Member State of origin or of the Member State from which a foreign national comes ;

Whereas, to facilitate the application of this Directive by the national authorities, Member States may prescribe that, in addition to evidence of qualifications, persons who satisfy the educational and training requirements of this Directive must provide a certificate from the competent authorities of their Member State of origin or of the country from which they come stating that these qualifications are those referred to by the Directive ;

Whereas the national provisions with regard to good repute and good character may be applied as standards for the taking up of activities if establishment takes place ; whereas, moreover, in the circumstances a distinction should be drawn between cases in which the persons concerned have never yet exercised any activities in the field of architecture and those in which they have already exercised such activities in another Member State ;

Whereas, in the case of the provision of services, the requirement of registration with, or membership of, professional organizations or bodies would, since it is related to the fixed and permanent nature of the activity pursued in the host Member State, undoubtedly constitute an obstacle to the provider of services by reason of the temporary nature of his activity ; whereas this requirement should therefore be abolished ; whereas, however, in this event control over professional discipline, which is the responsibility of these professional organizations or bodies, should be guaranteed ; whereas, to this end, it should be provided, subject to the application of Article 62 of the Treaty, that the person concerned may be required to notify the provision of services to the competent authority of the host Member State ;

Whereas, as far as the activities of employed persons in the field of architecture are concerned, Council Regulation (EEC) No 1612/68 of 15 October 1968 on freedom of movement for workers within the Community [1] lays down no specific provisions relating to good character or good repute, professional discipline or use of title for the professions covered ; whereas, depending on the individual Member State, such rules are or may be applicable both to employed and to self-employed persons ; whereas activities in the field of architecture are subject in several Member States to possession of a diploma, certificate or other evidence of formal qualifications ; whereas such activities are pursued by both employed and self-employed persons, or by the same persons in both capacities in the course of their professional career ; whereas, in order to encourage fully the free movement of members of the profession within the Community, it therefore appears necessary to extend this Directive to employed persons in the field of architecture ;

Whereas this Directive introduces mutual recognition of diplomas, certificates and other evidence of formal qualifications giving access to professional activities, without concomitant coordination of national provisions relating to education and training ; whereas, moreover, the number of members of the profession who are concerned varies considerably from one Member State to another ; whereas the first few years of application of this Directive must therefore be followed particularly attentively by the Commission,

HAS ADOPTED THIS DIRECTIVE :

## CHAPTER I

## SCOPE

### *Article 1*

1. This Directive shall apply to activities in the field of architecture.

2. For the purposes of this Directive, activities in the field of architecture shall be those activities usually pursued under the professional title of architect.

## CHAPTER II

## DIPLOMAS, CERTIFICATES AND OTHER EVIDENCE OF FORMAL QUALIFICATIONS ENABLING THE HOLDER TO TAKE UP ACTIVITIES IN THE FIELD OF ARCHITECTURE UNDER THE PROFESSIONAL TITLE OF ARCHITECT

### *Article 2*

Each Member State shall recognize the diplomas, certificates and other evidence of formal qualifications acquired as a result of education and training fulfilling the requirements of Articles 3 and 4 and awarded to nationals of Member States by other Member States, by giving such diplomas, certificates and other evidence of formal qualifications, as regards the right to take up activities referred to in Article 1 and pursue them under the professional title of architect pursuant to Article 23 (1), the same effect in its territory as those awarded by the Member State itself.

(1) OJ No L 257, 19. 10. 1968, p. 2.

*Article 3*

Education and training leading to diplomas, certificates and other evidence of formal qualifications referred to in Article 2 shall be provided through courses of studies at university level concerned principally with architecture. Such studies shall be balanced between the theoretical and practical aspects of architectural training and shall ensure the acquisition of :

1. an ability to create architectural designs that satisfy both aesthetic and technical requirements,
2. an adequate knowledge of the history and theories of architecture and the related arts, technologies and human sciences,
3. a knowledge of the fine arts as an influence on the quality of architectural design,
4. an adequate knowledge of urban design, planning and the skills involved in the planning process,
5. an understanding of the relationship between people and buildings, and between buildings and their environment, and of the need to relate buildings and the spaces between them to human needs and scale,
6. an understanding of the profession of architecture and the role of the architect in society, in particular in preparing briefs that take account of social factors,
7. an understanding of the methods of investigation and preparation of the brief for a design project,
8. an understanding of the structural design, constructional and engineering problems associated with building design,
9. an adequate knowledge of physical problems and technologies and of the function of buildings so as to provide them with internal conditions of comfort and protection against the climate,
10. the necessary design skills to meet building users' requirements within the constraints imposed by cost factors and building regulations,
11. an adequate knowledge of the industries, organizations, regulations and procedures involved in translating design concepts into buildings and integrating plans into overall planning.

*Article 4*

1. The education and training referred to in Article 2 must satisfy the requirements defined in Article 3 and also the following conditions :

(a) the total length of education and training shall consist of a minimum of either four years of full-time studies at a university or comparable educational establishment, or at least six years of study at a university or comparable educational establishment of which at least three must be full time ;

(b) such education and training shall be concluded by successful completion of an examination of degree standard.

Notwithstanding the first subparagraph, recognition under Article 2 shall also be accorded to the training given over three years in the 'Fachhochschulen' in the Federal Republic of Germany in the form in which it exists at the time of notification of this Directive and in so far as it satisfies the requirements laid down in Article 3, giving access to the activities referred to in Article 1 in that Member State with the professional title of architect, provided that such training is supplemented by a four-year period of professional experience in the Federal Republic of Germany sanctioned by a certificate issued by the professional body on whose list the architect wishing to benefit from the provisions of this Directive is registered. The body shall previously have established that the work carried out by the architect concerned in the field of architecture constitutes conclusive proof of the practical application of all the knowledge referred to in Article 3. The certificate shall be issued according to the same procedure as that which applies to registration on the list of architects.

On the basis of the experience gained and bearing in mind developments in architectural training, the Commission shall, eight years after the end of the period specified in the first subparagraph of Article 31 (1), submit a report to the Council on the application of this derogation and the appropriate proposals on which the Council shall decide in accordance with the procedures laid down by the Treaty within a period of six months.

2. Recognition under Article 2 shall also be accorded to education and training which, as part of a social betterment scheme or a part-time university course, conforms to the requirements of Article 3 and leads to an examination in architecture successfully completed by persons who have been employed in architecture for not less than seven years under the supervision of an architect or firm of architects. This examination must be of degree standard and be equivalent to the final examination referred to in paragraph 1 (b).

*Article 5*

1. Nationals of a Member State authorized to hold the professional title of architect pursuant to a law giving the competent authority of a Member State the possibility of conferring this title on nationals of Member States who have particularly distinguished themselves by their achievements in the field of architecture shall be considered as meeting the requirements laid down for the pursuit of architectural activities under the professional title of architect.

2. In the case of those persons referred to in paragraph 1, a certificate issued by the Member State of which the holder is a national, or from which he comes, shall constitute proof of the status of architect.

*Article 6*

Certificates issued by the competent authorities of the Federal Republic of Germany attesting the equivalence of qualifications awarded after 8 May 1945 by the competent authorities of the German Democratic Republic with the formal qualifications referred to in Article 2 shall be recognized under the conditions laid down in that Article.

*Article 7*

1. Each Member State shall communicate as soon as possible, simultaneously to the other Member States and to the Commission, the list of diplomas, certificates and other evidence of formal qualifications which are awarded within its territory and which meet the criteria laid down in Articles 3 and 4, together with the establishments and authorities awarding them.

The first list shall be sent within 12 months of notification of this Directive.

Each Member State shall likewise communicate any amendments made as regards the diplomas, certificates and other evidence of formal qualifications which are awarded within its territory, in particular those which no longer meet the requirements of Articles 3 and 4.

2. For information purposes, the lists and the updating thereof shall be published by the Commission in the *Official Journal of the European Communities* after expiry of a three-month period following their communication. However, in the cases referred to in Article 8, the publication of a diploma, certificate or other evidence of formal qualifications shall be deferred. Consolidated lists shall be published periodically by the Commission.

*Article 8*

If a Member State or the Commission has doubts as to whether a diploma, certificate or other evidence of formal qualifications meets the criteria laid down in Articles 3 and 4, the Commission shall bring the matter before the Advisory Committee on Education and Training in the Field of Architecture within three months of communication pursuant to Article 7 (1). The Committee shall deliver its opinion within three months.

The diploma, certificate or other evidence of formal qualifications shall be published within the three months following delivery of the opinion or expiry of the deadline for delivery thereof except in the following two cases:

— where the awarding Member State amends the communication made pursuant to Article 7 (1)

or

— where a Member State or the Commission implements Articles 169 or 170 of the Treaty with a view to bringing the matter before the Court of Justice of the European Communities.

*Article 9*

1. The Advisory Committee may be consulted by a Member State or the Commission whenever a Member State or the Commission has doubts as to whether a diploma, certificate or other evidence of formal qualifications included on one of the lists published in the *Official Journal of the European Communities* still meets the requirements of Articles 3 and 4. The Committee shall deliver its opinion within three months.

2. The Commission shall withdraw a diploma from one of the lists published in the *Official Journal of the European Communities* either in agreement with the Member State concerned or following a ruling by the Court of Justice.

## CHAPTER III

## DIPLOMAS, CERTIFICATES AND OTHER EVIDENCE OF FORMAL QUALIFICATIONS ENABLING THE HOLDER TO TAKE UP ACTIVITIES IN THE FIELD OF ARCHITECTURE BY VIRTUE OF ESTABLISHED RIGHTS OR EXISTING NATIONAL PROVISIONS

*Article 10*

Each Member State shall recognize the diplomas, certificates and other evidence of formal qualifications set out in Article 11, awarded by other Member States to nationals of the Member States, where such nationals already possess these qualifications at the time of notification of this Directive or their studies leading to such diplomas, certificates and other evidence of formal qualifications commences during the third academic year at the latest following such notification, even if those qualifications do not fulfil the minimum requirements laid down in Chapter II, by giving them as regards the taking up and pursuit of the activities referred to in Article 1 and subject to compliance with Article 23, the same effect within its territory as the diplomas, certificates and other evidence of formal qualifications which it awards in architecture.

*Article 11*

The diplomas, certificates and other evidence of formal qualifications referred to in Article 10 shall be as follows:

(a) *in Germany*

— the diplomas awarded by higher institutes of fine arts (Dipl.-Ing., Architekt (HfbK));

— the diplomas awarded by the departments of architecture (Architektur/Hochbau) of 'Technische Hochschulen', of technical universities, of universities and, in so far as these institutions have been merged into 'Gesamthochschulen', of 'Gesamthochschulen' (Dipl.-Ing. and any other title which may be laid down later for holders of these diplomas);

— the diplomas awarded by the departments of architecture (Architektur/Hochbau) of 'Fachhochschulen' and, in so far as these institutions have been merged into 'Gesamthochschulen', by the departments of architecture (Architektur/Hochbau) of 'Gesamthochschulen', accompanied, where the period of study is less than four years but at least three years, by a certificate attesting to a four-year period of professional experience in the Federal Republic of Germany issued by the professional body in accordance with the second subparagraph of Article 4 (1) (Ingenieur grad. and any other title which may be laid down later for holders of these diplomas);

— the diplomas (Prüfungszeugnisse) awarded before 1 January 1973 by the departments of architecture of 'Ingenieurschulen' and of 'Werkkunstschulen', accompanied by a certificate from the competent authorities to the effect that the person concerned has passed a test of his formal qualifications in accordance with Article 13;

(b) *in Belgium*

— the diplomas awarded by the higher national schools of architecture or the higher national institutes of architecture (architecte — architect);

— the diplomas awarded by the higher provincial school of architecture of Hasselt (architect);

— the diplomas awarded by the Royal Academies of Fine Arts (architecte — architect);

— the diplomas awarded by the 'écoles Saint-Luc' (architecte — architect);

— university diplomas in civil engineering, accompanied by a traineeship certificate awarded by the association of architects entitling the holder to hold the professional title of architect (architecte — architect);

— the diplomas in architecture awarded by the central or State examining board for architecture (architecte — architect);

— the civil engineering/architecture diplomas and architecture/engineering diplomas awarded by the faculties of applied sciences of the universities and by the Polytechnical Faculty of Mons (ingénieur-architecte, ingenieur-architect);

(c) *in Denmark*

— the diplomas awarded by the National Schools of Architecture in Copenhagen and Århus (arkitekt);

— the certificate of registration issued by the Board of Architects pursuant to Law No 202 of 28 May 1975 (registreret arkitekt);

— diplomas awarded by the Higher Schools of Civil Engineering (bygningskonstruktør), accompanied by a certificate from the competent authorities to the effect that the person concerned has passed a test of his formal qualifications in accordance with Article 13;

(d) *in France*

— the Government architect's diploma awarded by the Ministry of Education until 1959, and subsequently by the Ministry of Cultural Affairs (architecte DPLG);

— the diplomas awarded by the 'Ecole spéciale d'architecture' (architecte DESA);

— the diplomas awarded since 1955 by the department of architecture of the 'Ecole nationale supérieure des Arts et Industries de Strasbourg' (formerly the 'Ecole nationale d'ingénieurs de Strasbourg') (architecte ENSAIS);

(e) *in Greece*

— the engineering/architecture diplomas awarded by the METSOVION POLYTECHNION of Athens, together with a certificate issued by Greece's Technical Chamber conferring the right to pursue activities in the field of architecture;

— the engineering/architecture diplomas awarded by the ARISTOTELION PANEPISTIMION of Thessaloniki, together with a certificate issued by Greece's Technical Chamber conferring the right to pursue activities in the field of architecture;

— the engineering/civil engineering diplomas awarded by the METSOVION POLYTECHNION of Athens, together with a certificate issued by Greece's Technical Chamber conferring the right to pursue activities in the field of architecture;

— the engineering/civil engineering diplomas awarded by the ARISTOTELION PANEPISTIMION of Thessaloniki, together with a certificate issued by Greece's Technical Chamber conferring the right to pursue activities in the field of architecture;

— the engineering/civil engineering diplomas awarded by the PANEPISTIMION THRAKIS, together with a certificate issued by Greece's Technical Chamber conferring the right to pursue activities in the field of architecture;

— the engineering/civil engineering diplomas awarded by the PANEPISTIMION PATRON, together with a certificate issued by Greece's Technical Chamber conferring the right to pursue activities in the field of architecture;

(f) *in Ireland*

— the degree of Bachelor of Architecture awarded by the National University of Ireland (B Arch. (NUI)) to architecture graduates of University College, Dublin;

— the diploma of degree standard in architecture awarded by the College of Technology, Bolton Street, Dublin (Dipl. Arch.);

— the Certificate of Associateship of the Royal Institute of Architects of Ireland (ARIAI);

— the Certificate of Membership of the Royal Institute of Architects of Ireland (MRIAI);

(g) *in Italy*

— 'laurea in architettura' diplomas awarded by universities, polytechnic institutes and the higher institutes of architecture of Venice and Reggio Calabria, accompanied by the diploma entitling the holder to pursue independently the profession of architect, awarded by the Minister for Education after the candidate has passed, before a competent board, the State examination entitling him to pursue independently the profession of architect (dott. Architetto);

— 'laurea in ingegneria' diplomas in building construction ('sezione costenzione civile') awarded by universities and polytechnic institutes, accompanied by the diploma entitling the holder to pursue independently a profession in the field of architecture, awarded by the Minister for Education after the candidate has passed, before a competent board, the State examination entitling him to pursue the profession independently (dott. Ing. Architetto or dott. Ing. in ingegneria civile);

(h) *in the Netherlands*

— the certificate stating that its holder has passed the degree examination in architecture awarded by the departments of architecture of the technical colleges of Delft or Eindhoven (bouwkundig ingenieur);

— the diplomas awarded by State-recognized architectural academies (architect);

— the diplomas awarded until 1971 by the former architectural colleges (Hoger Bouwkunstonderricht) (architect HBO);

— the diplomas awarded until 1970 by the former architectural colleges (Voortgezet Bouwkunstonderricht) (architect VBO);

— the certificate stating that the person concerned has passed an examination organized by the Architects Council of the 'Bond van Nederlandse Architecten' (Order of Dutch Architects, BNA) (architect);

— the diploma of the 'Stichting Instituut voor Architectuur' ('Institute of Architecture' Foundation) (IVA) awarded on completion of a course organized by this foundation and extending over a minimum period of four years (architect), accompanied by a certificate from the competent authorities to the effect that the person concerned has passed a test of his formal qualifications in accordance with Article 13;

— a certificate issued by the competent authorities to the effect that, before the date of entry into force of this Directive, the person concerned passed the degree examination of 'Kandidaat in de bouwkunde' organized by the technical colleges of Delft or Eindhoven and that, over a period of at least five years immediately prior to that date, he pursued architectural activities the nature and importance of which, in accordance with Netherlands requirements, guarantee that he is competent to pursue those activities (architect);

— a certificate issued by the competent authorities only to persons who have reached the age of 40 years before the date of entry into force of this Directive, certifying that, over a period of at least five years immediately prior to that date, the person concerned had pursued architectural activities the nature and importance of which, in accordance with Netherlands requirements, guarantee that he is competent to pursue those activities (architect);

the certificates referred to in the seventh and eighth indents need no longer be recognized as from the date of entry into force of laws and regulations in the Netherlands governing the taking up and pursuit of architectural activities under the professional title of architect, in so far as under such provisions those certificates do not authorize the taking up of such activities under that professional title;

(i) *in the United Kingdom*

— the qualifications awarded following the passing of examinations of:

— the Royal Institute of British Architects;

— schools of architecture at:

— universities,

— polytechnics,

— colleges,

— academies,

— schools of technology and art,

which were, or are at the time of the adoption of this Directive, recognized by the Architects Registration Council of the United Kingdom for the purpose of admission to the Register (Architect);

— a certificate stating that its holder has an established right to hold the professional title of architect by virtue of section 6 (1) a, 6 (1) b or 6 (1) d of the Architects Registration Act 1931 (Architect);

— a certificate stating that its holder has an established right to hold the professional title of architect by virue of section 2 of the Architects Registration Act 1938 (Architect);

(j) *in Spain*

— the official formal qualification of an architect (título oficial de arquitecto) awarded by the Ministry of Education and Science or by the universities; (*)

(k) *in Portugal*

— the Diploma "diploma do curso especial de arquitectura" awarded by the Schools of Fine Arts of Lisbon and of Porto, (*)

— the Architects Diploma "diploma de arquitecto" awarded by the Schools of Fine Arts of Lisbon and of Porto, (*)

— the Diploma "diploma do curso de arquitectura" awarded by the Higher Schools of Fine Arts of Lisbon and Porto, (*)

— the Diploma "diploma de licenciatura em arquitectura" awarded by the Higher School of Fine Arts of Lisbon, (*)

— the Diploma "carta de curso de licenciatura em arquitectura" awarded by the Technical University of Lisbon and the University of Porto. (*)

— the university diploma in civil engineering awarded by the Higher Technical Institute of the Technical University of Lisbon (Licenciatura em engenharia civil), (**)

— the university diploma in civil engineering awarded by the Faculty of Engineering (Engenharia) of the University of Porto (Licenciatura em engenharia civil), (**) (***)

— the university diploma in civil engineering awarded by the Faculty of Science and Technology of the University of Coimbra (Licenciatura em engenharia civil), (**)

(*) Text as amended by Directive 85/614/EEC.
(**) Text as amended by Directive 86/17/EEC.
(***) Corrigendum published in OJ No L 87, 2.4.1986, p.36.

— the university diploma in civil engineering (production) awarded by the University of Minho (Licenciatura em engenharia civil (produção)). (*)

*Article 12*

Without prejudice to Article 10, each Member State shall recognize, by giving them as regards the taking up and pursuit under the professional title of architect of the activities referred to in Article 1, the same effect within its territory as the diplomas, certificates and other evidence of formal architectural qualifications which it issues :

— certificates issued to nationals of Member States by Member States in which there are regulations at the time of notification of this Directive governing the taking up and pursuit of the activities referred to in Article 1 under the professional title of architect, stating that the holder has received authorization to bear the professional title of architect before the implementation of this Directive and has effectively exercised the activities in question under such regulations for at least three consecutive years during the five years preceding the issue of the certificate ;

— certificates issued to nationals of Member States by Member States which between the time of notification and implementation of the Directive introduce regulations governing the taking up and pursuit of the activities referred to in Article 1 under the professional title of architect, stating that the holder has received authorization to bear the professional title of architect at the time when this Directive is implemented and has effectively exercised the activities in question under such regulations for at least three consecutive years during the five years preceding the issue of the certificate.

*Article 13*

The test of formal qualifications referred to in Article 11 (a), fourth indent, Article 11 (c), third indent, and Article 11 (h), sixth indent, shall comprise an appraisal of plans drawn up and carried out by the person concerned while actually pursuing the activities referred to in Article 1 for not less than six years.

*Article 14*

Certificates issued by the competent authorities of the Federal Republic of Germany attesting the equivalence of qualifications awarded from 8 May 1945 onwards by the competent authorities of the German Democratic Republic with the formal qualifications listed in Article 11 shall be recognized under the conditions listed in that Article.

*Article 15*

The Grand Duchy of Luxembourg shall be authorized, without prejudice to Article 5, to suspend application of Articles 10, 11 and 12 as regards the recognition of non-university diplomas, certificates and other evidence of formal qualifications, in order to avoid distortions of competition, for a transitional period of four-and-a-half years from the date of notification of this Directive.

CHAPTER IV

## USE OF ACADEMIC TITLE

*Article 16*

1. Without prejudice to Article 23, host Member States shall ensure that the nationals of Member States who fulfil the conditions laid down in Chapter II or Chapter III have the right to use their lawful academic title and, where appropriate, the abbreviation thereof deriving from their Member State of origin or the Member State from which they come, in the language of that State. Host Member States may require this title to be followed by the name and location of the establishment or examining board which awarded it.

2. If the academic title used in the Member State of origin, or in the Member State from which a foreign national comes, can be confused in the host Member State with a title requiring, in that State, additional education or training which the person concerned has not undergone, the host Member State may require such a person to use the title employed in the Member State of origin or the Member State from which he comes in a suitable form to be specified by the host Member State.

CHAPTER V

## PROVISIONS TO FACILITATE THE EFFECTIVE EXERCISE OF THE RIGHT OF ESTABLISHMENT AND FREEDOM TO PROVIDE SERVICES

### A. Provisions specific to the right of establishment

*Article 17*

1. A host Member State which requires of its nationals proof of good character or good repute when

(*) Text as amended by Directive 86/17/EEC.

they take up for the first time the activities referred to in Article 1 shall accept as sufficient evidence, in respect of nationals of other Member States, a certificate issued by a competent authoritiy in the Member State of origin or in the Member State from which the foreign national comes, attesting that the requirements of that Member State as to good character or good repute for taking up the activity in question have been met.

2. Where the Member State of origin or the Member State from which the foreign national comes does not require proof of good character or good repute of persons wishing to take up the activity in question for the first time, the host Member State may require of nationals of the Member State of origin or of the Member State from which the foreign national comes an extract from the 'judicial record' or, failing this, an equivalent document issued by a competent authority in the Member State of origin or the Member State from which the foreign national comes.

3. Where the Member State of origin or the Member State from which the foreign national comes does not issue the documentary proof referred to in paragraph 2, such proof may be replaced by a declaration on oath — or, in States where there is no provision for declaration on oath, by a solemn declaration — made by the person concerned before a competent judicial or administrative authority or, where appropriate, a notary or qualified professional body of the Member State of origin or the Member State from which the person comes; such authority or notary shall issue a certificate attesting the authenticity of the declaration on oath or solemn declaration.

4. If the host Member State has detailed knowledge of a serious matter which has occurred outside its territory prior to the establishment of the person concerned in that State, or if it knows that the declaration referred to in paragraph 3 contains incorrect information and if the matter or information is likely to affect the taking up within its territory of the activity concerned, it may inform the Member State of origin or the Member State from which the foreign national comes.

The Member State of origin or the Member State from which the foreign national ccmes shall verify the accuracy of the facts in so far as they might affect the taking up of the activity in question in that Member State. The authorities in that State shall themselves decide on the nature and extent of the investigation to be made and shall inform the host Member State of any consequential action which they take with regard to the certificates or documents they have issued.

5. Member States shall ensure the confidentiality of the information forwarded.

*Article 18*

1. Where, in a host Member State, laws, regulations or administrative provisions impose requirements as to good character or good repute, including provisions in relation to the pursuit of the activities referred to in Article 1 for disciplinary action in respect of serious professional misconduct or conviction on criminal offences, the Member State of origin or the Member State from which the foreign national comes shall forward to the host Member State all necessary information regarding any measures or disciplinary action of a professional or administrative nature taken against the person concerned or any criminal penalties concerning the practise of his profession in the Member State of origin or in the Member State from which he came.

2. If the host Member State has detailed knowledge of a serious matter which has occurred outside its territory prior to the establishment of the person concerned in that State and which is likely to affect the pursuit of the activity concerned in that State, it may inform the Member State of origin or the Member State from which the foreign national comes.

The Member State of origin or the Member State from which the foreign national comes shall verify the accuracy of the facts in so far as they might affect the pursuit of the activity concerned in that State. The authorities of that State shall themselves decide on the nature and extent of the investigation to be made and shall inform the host Member State of any consequential action which they take with regard to the information forwarded under paragraph 1.

3. Member States shall ensure the confidentiality of the information forwarded.

*Article 19*

Documents issued in accordance with Articles 17 and 18 may not be presented more than three months after their date of issue.

*Article 20*

1. The procedure for authorizing the person concerned to take up the activities referred to in Article 1, pursuant to Article 17 and 18, must be completed as soon as possible and not later than three months after presentation of all the documents rela-

ting to that person, without prejudice to delays resulting from any appeal that may be made upon termination of this procedure.

2. In the cases referred to in Article 17 (4) and Article 18 (2), a request for re-examination shall suspend the period laid down in paragraph 1.

The Member State consulted shall give its reply within a period of three months.

On receipt of the reply or at the end of the period the host Member State shall continue with the procedure referred to in paragraph 1.

*Article 21*

Where a host Member State requires its own nationals wishing to take up or pursue the activities referred to in Article 1 to take an oath or make a solemn declaration and where the form of such oath or declaration cannot be used by nationals of other Member States, that Member State shall ensure that an appropriate and equivalent form of oath or declaration is offered to the person concerned.

**B. Provisions specific to the provision of services**

*Article 22*

1. Where a Member State requires of its own nationals wishing to take up or pursue the activities referred to in Article 1 either an authorization from or membership of or registration with a professional organization or body, that Member State shall, in the case of provision of services, exempt nationals of other Member States from that requirement.

The person concerned shall provide services with the same rights and obligations as nationals of the host Member State ; in particular he shall be subject to the rules of conduct of a professional or administrative nature which apply in that Member State.

For this purpose and in addition to the declaration referred to in paragraph 2 relating to the provision of services, Member States may, so as to permit the implementation of the provisions relating to professional conduct in force in their territory, require automatic temporary registration or *pro forma* registration with a professional organization or body or in a register, provided that this registration does not delay or in any way complicate the provision of services or impose any additional costs on the person providing the services.

Where a host Member State adopts a measure pursuant to the second subparagraph or becomes aware of facts which run counter to these provisions, it shall forthwith inform the Member State in which the person concerned is established.

2. The host Member State may require the person concerned to make a prior declaration to the competent authorities about the services to be provided where they involve the execution of a project in its territory.

3. Pursuant to paragraphs 1 and 2, the host Member State may require the person concerned to supply one or more documents containing the following particulars :

— the declaration referred to in paragraph 2,

— a certificate stating that the person concerned is lawfully pursuing the activities in question in the Member State where he is established,

— a certificate that the person concerned holds the diploma(s), certificate(s) or other evidence of formal qualifications required for the provision of the services in question and that those qualifications comply with the criteria in Chapter II or are as listed in Chapter III of this Directive ;

— where appropriate, the certificate referred to in Article 23 (2).

4. The document or documents specified in paragraph 3 may not be produced more than 12 months after their date of issue.

5. Where a Member State temporarily or permanently deprives, in whole or in part, one of its nationals or a national of another Member State established in its territory of the right to pursue the activities referred to in Article 1, it shall, as appropriate, ensure the temporary or permanent withdrawal of the certificate referred to in the second indent of paragraph 3.

**C. Provisions common to the right of establishment and freedom to provide services**

*Article 23*

1. Where in a host Member State the use of the professional title of architect relating to the activities referred to in Article 1 is regulated, nationals of other Member States who fulfil the conditions laid down in Chapter II or whose diplomas, certificates or other evidence of formal qualifications referred to in Article

11 have been recognized under Article 10 shall be vested with the professional title of the host Member State and the abbreviated form thereof once they have fulfilled any conditions as to practical training experience laid down by that State.

2. If in a Member State the taking up of the activities referred to in Article 1 or the pursuit of such activities under the title of architect is subject, in addition to the requirements set out in Chapter II or to the possession of a diploma, certificate or other evidence of formal qualifications as referred to in Article 11, to the completion of a given period of practical experience, the Member State concerned shall accept as sufficient evidence a certificate from the Member State of origin or previous residence stating that appropriate practical experience for a corresponding period has been acquired in that country. The certificate referred to in the second subparagraph of Article 4 (1) shall be recognized as sufficient proof within the meaning of this paragraph.

*Article 24*

1. Where the host Member State requires its nationals wishing to take up or pursue the activities referred to in Article 1 to furnish proof of no previous bankruptcy and where the information provided pursuant to Articles 17 and 18 does not contain proof thereof, that state shall accept a declaration on oath — or, in States where there is no provision for declaration on oath, a solemn declaration — made by the person concerned before a competent judicial or administrative authority, a notary or qualified professional body of the Member State of origin or of the Member State from which the person comes; such authority or notary shall issue a certificate attesting the authenticity of the declaration on oath or solemn declaration.

Where, in the host Member State, sound financial standing must be proved, that Member State shall accept attestations issued by banks of other Member States as being equivalent to attestations issued in its own territory.

2. The documents referred to in paragraph 1 may not be produced later than three months after their date of issue.

*Article 25*

1. Where a host Member State requires its nationals wishing to take up or pursue the activities referred to in Article 1 to furnish proof that they are covered by insurance against the financial consequences of their professional liability, that State shall accept certificates issued by the insurance undertakings of other Member States as being equivalent to certificates issued in its own territory. Such certificates must specify that the insurer has complied with the laws and regulations in force in the host Member State as regards the conditions and extent of cover.

2. The certificates referred to in paragraph 1 may not be produced latter than three months after their date of issue.

*Article 26*

1. Member States shall take the measures necessary to enable the persons concerned to obtain information on the laws and, where applicable, on the professional ethics of the host Member State.

For this purpose, Member States may set up information centres from which such persons may obtain the necessary information. In the event of establishment, the host Member States may require them to contact these centres.

2. Member States may set up the centres referred to in paragraph 1 under the auspices of the competent authorities and bodies which they designate before expiry of the time limit laid down in the first subparagraph of 31 (1).

3. Member States shall ensure that, where appropriate, the persons concerned acquire, in their own interest and in that of their clients, the linguistic knowledge needed to follow their profession in the host Member State.

## CHAPTER VI

## FINAL PROVISIONS

*Article 27*

Where legitimate doubt exists, the host Member State may require the competent authorities of another Member State to confirm the authenticity of the diplomas, certificates and other evidence of formal qualifications awarded in that other Member State and referred to in Chapters II and III.

*Article 28*

Within the time limit laid down in the first subparagraph of Article 31 (1), Member States shall designate the authorities and bodies empowered to issue or receive diplomas, certificates and other evidence of formal qualifications as well as the documents and information referred to in this Directive, and shall forthwith inform the other Member States and the Commission thereof.

*Article 29*

This Directive shall also apply to nationals of Member States who, in accordance with Regulation (EEC) No 1612/68, are pursuing or will pursue as employed persons the activities referred to in Article 1.

*Article 30*

Not more than three years after the end of the period provided for in the first subparagraph of Article 31 (1), the Commission shall review this Directive on the basis of experience and if necessary submit to the Council proposals for amendments after consulting the Advisory Committee. The Council shall examine any such proposals within one year.

*Article 31*

1. Member States shall take the measures necessary to comply with this Directive within 24 months of its notification and shall forthwith inform the Commission thereof.

Member States shall, however, have three years from the date of notification within which to comply with Article 22.

2. Member States shall communicate to the Commission the texts of the main provisions of national law which they adopt in the field covered by this Directive.

*Article 32*

This Directive is addressed to the Member States.

Done at Luxembourg, 10 June 1985.

*For the Council*

*The President*

M. FIORET

Official Journal of the European Communities No L 223/ 21. 8. 85

## COUNCIL RECOMMENDATION

### of 10 June 1985

### concerning holders of a diploma in architecture awarded in a third country

(85/386/EEC)

THE COUNCIL OF THE EUROPEAN COMMUNITIES,

In adopting Council Directive 85/384/EEC of 10 June 1985 on the mutual recognition of diplomas, certificates and other evidence of formal qualifications in architecture, including measures to facilitate the effective exercise of the right of establishment and freedom to provide services [1];

Noting that the said Directive refers only to diplomas, certificates and other evidence of formal qualifications awarded to nationals of Member States by other Member States;

Anxious, however, to take account of the special position of nationals of Member States who have studied in a third country and who hold a diploma in architecture recognized under the legislation of a Member State,

HEREBY

recommends the Governments of the Member States to facilitate the taking up and pursuit of activities in the field of architecture within the Community by persons referred to above by recognizing these diplomas in their territories.

Done at Luxembourg, 10 June 1985.

*For the Council*

*The President*

M. FIORET

(1) OJ No L 223, 21. 8. 1985, p. 15.

Official Journal of the European Communities No C 210/ 21. 8. 85

I

*(Information)*

# COUNCIL

## STATEMENT

**by the Representatives of the Governments of the Member States of the European Communities, meeting within the Council, on the subject of Greek-speaking citizens of third countries who are of Greek origin (ομογενείς)**

(85/C 210/01)

THE REPRESENTATIVES OF THE GOVERNMENTS OF THE MEMBER STATES OF THE EUROPEAN COMMUNITIES, MEETING WITHIN THE COUNCIL,

Noting that the Council has approved Directive 85/384/EEC on the mutual recognition of diplomas, certificates and other evidence of formal qualifications in architecture, including measures to facilitate the effective exercise of the right of establishment and freedom [1] to provide services,

Noting that this Directive refers only to diplomas, certificates and other evidence of formal qualifications awarded to nationals of Member States by other Member States;

Anxious to take account of the special situation of certain Greek-speaking persons of Greek origin who are nationals of third countries conterminous with Greece (ομογενείς), and who have studied architecture in a Member State, hold diplomas in architecture recognized under Greek law, and have been authorized, in accordance with Greek law, to register with the Technical Chamber of Greece,

HEREBY STATE THAT:

the taking up and pursuit in their territories of an activity covered by Directive 85/384/EEC by the persons referred to above must be given especially favourable consideration in order that the persons concerned might enjoy the most favourable treatment possible in their territories.

(1) OJ No L 223, 21. 8. 1985.

Official Journal of the European Communities No C 210/ 21. 8. 85

## STATEMENT

**by the Representatives of the Governments of the Member States of the European Communities, meeting within the Council, concerning refugees**

(85/C 210/02)

THE REPRESENTATIVES OF THE GOVERNMENTS OF THE MEMBER STATES OF THE EUROPEAN COMMUNITIES, MEETING WITHIN THE COUNCIL,

Having regard to the statement on refugees made at the 128th meeting of the Council, held in Brussels on 25 March 1964, at which the Council adopted the Regulation on freedom of movement for workers within the Community and the Directive on the abolition of restrictions on movement and residence within the Community for workers from Member States and their families,

Anxious to take account of the special situation of refugees in the spirit of the international instruments in force; having regard also to the wishes expressed by the Executive Committee of the Programme of the United Nations High Commissioner for Refugees;

Whereas, by virtue of the abovementioned statement, refugees employed in the activities referred to in the Directive 85/384/EEC [1] are to enjoy the most favourable treatment possible;

Anxious to grant to refugees resident in a Member State and pursuing an activity on a self-employed basis the same treatment as that granted to those pursuing this activity as employed persons;

Noting that the situation of refugees cannot be dealt with under the provisions of the Treaty concerning the right of establishment and freedom to provide services,

HEREBY STATE THAT:

the taking up and pursuit in their territories of an activity as a self-employed person covered by Directive 85/384/EEC, in respect of establishment or the provision of services, by refugees recognized as such within the meaning of the Convention of 1951 and established in the territory of another Member State, must be given especially favourable consideration, in particular in order to accord such refugees the most favourable treatment possible in their territories.

---

(1) OJ No L 223, 21. 8. 1985.

# 10. Pharmacists

Official Journal of the European Communities No L 253/24. 9. 85

II

*(Acts whose publication is not obligatory)*

# COUNCIL

## COUNCIL DIRECTIVE

**of 16 September 1985**

**concerning the coordination of provisions laid down by law, regulation or administrative action in respect of certain activities in the field of pharmacy**

(85/432/EEC)

THE COUNCIL OF THE EUROPEAN COMMUNITIES,

Having regard to the Treaty establishing the European Economic Community, and in particular Articles 49 and 57 thereof,

Having regard to the proposal from the Commission [1],

Having regard to the opinion of the European Parliament [2],

Having regard to the opinion of the Economic and Social Committee [3],

Whereas persons who hold a diploma, certificate or other formal qualification in pharmacy are for that reason specialists in the field of medicinal products and, in principle, must have access in all the Member States to a minimum range of activities in that field; whereas, in defining that minimum range, this Directive does not have the effect of limiting the activities accessible in the Member States to pharmacists, in particular with regard to medical biology analyses, and does not give them any monopoly, since the creation of a monopoly continues to be a matter for the Member States alone;

Whereas, moreover, this Directive does not ensure coordination of all conditions of access to and pursuit of activities in the field of pharmacy; whereas, in particular, the geographical distribution of pharmacies and the monopoly of the supply of medicinal products continue to be matters for the Member States;

Whereas, with a view to achieving mutual recognition of diplomas, certificates and other evidence of formal qualifications in pharmacy, as required by Council Directive 85/433/EEC of 16 September 1985 concerning the mutual recognition of diplomas, certificates and other evidence of formal qualifications in pharmacy, including measures to facilitate the effective exercise of the right of establishment relating to certain activities in the field of pharmacy [4], the broad comparability of training courses in the Member States enables coordination in this field to be confined to the requirement that minimum standards be observed, thus leaving the Member States freedom of organization as regards teaching;

Whereas this Directive does not prevent the Member States from requiring supplementary conditions of training for access to activities not included in the coordinated minimum range of activities; whereas for this reason a host Member State which lays down such conditions may subject thereto nationals of Member States who hold one of the diplomas referred to in Article 4 of Directive 85/433/EEC;

Whereas the coordination provided for by this Directive covers professional qualifications; whereas, as regards such qualifications, most Member States do not at present distinguish between professional persons who pursue their activities as employed persons and those who are self-employed; whereas, for this reason, it appears necessary to extend the application of this Directive to employed professional persons;

[1] OJ No C 35, 18. 2. 1981, p. 3.
[2] OJ No C 277, 17. 10. 1983, p. 160.
[3] OJ No C 230, 10. 9. 1981, p. 10.
[4] OJ No L 253, 24.9.1985, p.37.

Whereas further training is being developed in the Member States in certain aspects of pharmacy which is intended to extend certain areas of knowledge acquired during the training of pharmacists ; whereas, therefore, with a view to mutual recognition of diplomas, certificates and other evidence of formal qualifications in pharmacy specialities and in order to put all members of the profession who are nationals of the Member States on an equal footing within the Community, some coordination of the requirements for training in pharmacy specialities is necessary where there are specialized forms of training common to several Member States which can entitle a person to use a specialist title, without such training being a condition of access to the activities included in the coordinated minimum range of activities ; whereas such coordination does not seem possible at this stage, but constitutes an objective to be attained as soon as possible together with the relevant mutual recognition,

HAS ADOPTED THIS DIRECTIVE :

*Article 1*

1. Member States shall ensure that holders of a diploma, certificate or other university or equivalent qualification in pharmacy which meets the conditions laid down in Article 2 shall be entitled at least to access to the activities mentioned in paragraph 2 and to pursue such activities subject, where appropriate, to the requirement of additional professional experience.

2. The activities referred to in paragraph 1 are :

— the preparation of the pharmaceutical form of medicinal products,

— the manufacture and testing of medicinal products,

— the testing of medicinal products in a laboratory for the of medicinal of medicinal products,

— the storage, preservation and distribution of medicinal products at the wholesale stage,

— the preparation, testing, storage and supply of medicinal products in pharmacies open to the public,

— the preparation, testing, storage and dispensing of medicinal products in hospitals,

— the provisions of information and advice on medicinal products.

3. Where at the time of adoption of this Directive a system of competition based on tests exists in a Member State for the purpose of selecting from among the holders referred to in paragraph 1 those to be appointed to control the new pharmacies to be set up under a national geographical distribution system, that

Member State may, by way of derogation from paragraph 1, retain this competition system and may oblige nationals of the Member States holding the diplomas, certificates and other formal qualifications in pharmacy referred to in Article 2 (1) and Article 6 of Directive 85/433/EEC to take part in such a competition.

*Article 2*

Member States shall subordinate the award of the diplomas, certificates and other formal qualifications referred to in Article 1 to the following minimum conditions :

1. Training leading to the award of the diploma, certificate or other formal qualification shall ensure :

   (a) adequate knowledge of medicines and the substances used in the manufacture of medicines ;

   (b) adequate knowledge of pharmaceutical technology and the physical, chemical, biological and microbiological testing of medicinal products ;

   (c) adequate knowledge of the metabolism and the effects of medicinal products and of the action of toxic substances, and of the use of medicinal products ;

   (d) adequate knowledge to evaluate scientific data concerning medicines in order to be able to supply appropriate information on the basis of this knowledge ;

   (e) adequate knowledge of the legal and other requirements associated with the practice of pharmacy.

2. In order to be accepted for such training, the candidate must have a diploma or a certificate which entitles him to be admitted for the course of study concerned to the universities of a Member State or to higher education institutions recognized as having equivalent status.

3. The diploma, certificate or other formal qualification shall testify to the completion of a course of training covering a period of at least five years and comprising:

   — at least four years of full-time theoretical and practical training in a university, in a higher education institution of a level recognized as having equivalent status, or under the supervision of a university,

   — at least six months of in-service training in a pharmacy open to the public or in a hospital under the supervision of the pharamaceutical department of that hospital.

4. By way of derogation from point 3:

   (a) if at the time of the adoption of this Directive two courses of training coexist in a Member State, one of which lasts five years and the other four years, the diploma, certificate or other formal qualification testifying to the completion of the four-year course of training, shall be considered to fulfil the condition concerning duration referred to in point 3 provided that the diplomas, certificates or other formal qualifications testifying to the completion of the two courses of training are recognized as equivalent by that State;

   (b) if, because, there are insufficient places in pharmacies open to the public and in hospitals near training establishments, a Member State is unable to provide six months of in-service training, it may, for a period of five years following the expiry of the time limit laid down in Article 5, make provision for no more than half of that training period to involve activities as a pharmacist in an undertaking which manufactures medicinal products.

5. The course of training referred to in point 3 shall comprise as a minimum theoretical and practical training in the following subjects:

   — Plant and animal biology,
   — Physics,
   — General and inorganic chemistry,
   — Organic chemistry,
   — Analytical chemistry,
   — Pharmaceutical chemistry, including analysis of medicinal products,
   — General and applied biochemistry (medical),
   — Anatomy and physiology; medical terminology,
   — Microbiology,
   — Pharmacology and pharmacotherapy,
   — Pharmaceutical technology,
   — Toxicology,
   — Pharmacognosy,
   — Legislation and, where appropriate, professional ethics.

The balance between theoretical and practical training shall, in respect of each subject, give sufficient importance to theory to maintain the university character of the training.

*Article 3*

Not more than three years after the expiry of the time limit laid down in Article 5, the Commission shall submit to the Council appropriate proposals on specializations in pharmacy and in particular hospital pharmacy. The Council shall examine these proposals within one year.

*Article 4*

This Directive shall also apply to nationals of Member States who, in accordance with Council Regulation (EEC) No 1612/68 of 15 October 1968 on freedom of movement for workers within the Community [1], are pursuing or will pursue, as employed persons, one of the activities referred to in Article 1 of Directive 85/433/EEC.

*Article 5*

1. Member States shall take the measures necessary to comply with this Directive before 1 October 1987. They shall forthwith inform the Commission thereof.

2. Member States shall communicate to the Commission the texts of the main provisions of national law which they adopt in the field covered by this Directive.

[1] OJ No L 257, 19. 10. 1968, p. 2.

*Article 6*

Where a Member State encounters major difficulties in certain fields when applying this Directive, the Commission shall examine these difficulties in conjunction with that State and shall request the opinion of the Pharmaceutical Committee set up by Council Decision 75/320/EEC([1]).

Where necessary, the Commission shall submit appropriate proposals to the Council.

*Article 7*

This Directive is addressed to the Member States.

Done at Luxembourg, 16 September 1985.

*For the Council*

*The President*

M. FISCHBACH

([1]) OJ No L 147, 9. 6. 1975, p. 23.

Official Journal of the European Communities No L 253/24. 9. 85

# COUNCIL DIRECTIVE

## of 16 September 1985

## concerning the mutual recognition of diplomas, certificates and other evidence of formal qualifications in pharmacy, including measures to facilitate the effective exercise of the right of establishment relating to certain activities in the field of pharmacy (*)

(85/433/EEC)

THE COUNCIL OF THE EUROPEAN COMMUNITIES,

Having regard to the Treaty establishing the European Economic Community, and in particular Articles 49 and 57 thereof,

Having regard to the proposal from the Commission [1],

Having regard to the opinion of the European Parliament [2],

Having regard to the opinion of the Economic and Social Committee [3],

Whereas, pursuant to the Treaty, all discriminatory treatment based on nationality with regard to establishment and provision of services is prohibited as from the end of the transitional period; whereas the principle of such treatment based on nationality applies, in particular, to the grant of any authorization required for the practice of certain activities, and also to registration with or membership of professional organizations or bodies;

Whereas it nevertheless seems desirable that certain provisions be introduced to facilitate the effective exercise of the right of establishment;

Whereas, pursuant to Article 54 (3) (h) of the Treaty, the Member States are required not to grant any form of aid likely to distort the conditions of establishment;

Whereas Article 57 (1) of the Treaty provides that Directives be adopted for mutual recognition of diplomas, certificates and other evidence of formal qualifications;

Whereas, in view of the present disparities in training in pharmacy given in the Member States, it is necessary to lay down certain coordinating provisions to enable the Member States to introduce mutual recognition of diplomas, certificates and other evidence of formal qualifications; whereas such coordination has been established by Council Directive 85/432/EEC of 16 September 1985, concerning the coordination of provisions laid down by law, regulation or administrative action in respect of certain activities in the field of pharmacy [4];

Whereas in certain Member States access to certain activities in the field of pharmacy is, apart from the award of the relevant diploma, certificate or other formal qualification, subject to the requirement of additional professional experience; whereas, since there is as yet no convergence of views among the Member States on this point, it is advisable, in order to obviate any difficulties, to recognize as a sufficient condition appropriate practical experience of equal duration acquired in another Member State;

Whereas, under their national policies in the sphere of public health, which seek *inter alia* to ensure the satisfactory dispensing of medicinal products over their entire territories, certain Member States restrict the number of new pharmacies that may be established, while others have adopted no such provisions; whereas in these circumstances it is premature to provide that the effects of the recognition of diplomas, certificates and other evidence of formal qualifications in pharmacy must also extend to the pursuit of the activities of pharmacist as the controller of a pharmacy open to the public for less than three years; whereas this problem must be re-examined by the Commission and the Council within a certain period;

Whereas, with regard to the possession of a formal certificate of training, since a Directive on the mutual recognition of diplomas does not necessarily imply equivalence in the training covered by such diplomas, the use of such qualifications should be authorized only in the language of the Member State of origin or of the Member State from which the foreign national comes;

Whereas, to facilitate the application of this Directive by the national authorities, Member States may prescribe that, in addition to formal certificates of training,

(*) Text as amended by Directive 85/584/EEC of 20 December 1985 (OJ No L 372, 31.12.1985).

[1] OJ No C 35, 18. 2. 1981, p. 6 and OJ No C 40, 18. 2. 1984, p. 4.
[2] OJ No C 277, 17. 10. 1983, p. 160.
[3] OJ No C 230, 10. 9. 1981, p. 10.
[4] OJ No L 253, 24.9.1985, p.34.

the person who satisfies the conditions of training required by this Directive must provide a certificate from the competent authorities of his country of origin or of the country from which he comes stating that these certificates of training are those covered by the Directive ;

Whereas this Directive does not affect the provisions laid down by law, regulation or administrative action in the Member States which prohibit companies from practising certain activities or impose on them certain conditions for such practice ;

Whereas it is difficult to assess the extent to which rules aimed at facilitating freedom of pharmacists to provide services could at present be appropriate ; whereas, in these circumstances, it is not advisable to adopt such rules for the time being ;

Whereas, with regard to good character and good repute, a distinction should be drawn between the requirements to be satisfied on first taking up the profession and those to be satisfied in order to practise it ;

Whereas, as far as the activities of employed persons are concerned, Council Regulation (EEC) No 1612/68 of 15 October 1968 on freedom of movement for workers within the Community [1] lays down no specific provisions relating to good character or good repute, professional discipline or use of title for the professions covered ; whereas, depending on the individual Member State, such rules are or may be applicable both to employed and self-employed persons ; whereas the activities subject in the Member States to possession of a diploma, certificate or other evidence of formal qualification in pharmacy are pursued by both employed and self-employed persons, or by the same persons in both capacities in the course of their professional career ; whereas, in order to encourage as far as possible the free movement of those professional persons within the Community, it therefore appears necessary to extend the application of this Directive to employed persons.

HAS ADOPTED THIS DIRECTIVE :

## CHAPTER I

### Scope

*Article 1*

This Directive applies to activities, the access to and pursuit of which is subject to conditions of professional qualification in one or more Member States, and which are open to holders of one of the diplomas, certificates or other formal qualifications in pharmacy referred to in Article 4.

## CHAPTER II

### Diplomas, certificates and other evidence of formal qualifications in pharmacy

*Article 2*

1. Each Member State shall recognize the diplomas, certificates and other formal qualifications listed in Article 4 awarded to nationals of Member States by other Member States in accordance with Article 2 of Directive 85/432/EEC by giving such qualifications, as regards the right of access to and pursuit of the activities referred to in Article 1, the same effect in its territory as those diplomas, certificates and other formal qualifications, listed in Article 4, which it itself awards.

2. However, Member States need not give effect to the diplomas, certificates and other formal certificates referred to in paragraph 1 with respect to the establishment of new pharmacies open to the public. For the purposes of applying this Directive, pharmacies which have been in operation for less than three years shall also be regarded as new.

Five years after the date stipulated in Article 19 (1), the Commission shall submit a report to the Council on the way in which Member States have implemented the preceding subparagraph and on the possibility of extending the effects of mutual recognition of the diplomas, certificates and other formal certificates referred to in paragraph 1. It shall make any appropriate proposals.

[1] OJ No L 257, 19. 10. 1968, p. 2.

*Article 3*

1. By way of derogation from Article 2 and without prejudice to Article 45 of the 1979 Act of Accession, the Hellenic Republic shall not be required to give effect as laid down in Article 2 to the diplomas, certificates and other formal qualifications awarded by other Member States except in the case of the pursuit as an employed person in accordance with Regulation (EEC) No 1612/68 of the activities referred to in Article 1.

As long as the Hellenic Republic makes use of this derogation and without prejudice to Article 45 of the 1979 Act of Accession, the other Member States shall not be required to give effect as provided for in Article 2 to the certificates referred to in Article 4 (d) except in the case of the pursuit as an employed person in accordance with Regulation (EEC) No 1612/68 of the activities referred to in Article 1.

2. Ten years after the date stipulated in Article 19, the Commission shall submit to the Council appropriate proposals in order to extend the effects of mutual recognition of diplomas, certificates and other formal qualifications with a view to facilitating the effective exercise of the right of establishment between the Hellenic Republic and the other Member States. The Council shall act on these proposals in accordance with the procedure laid down in the EEC Treaty.

*Article 4*

The diplomas, certificates and other evidence of formal qualifications referred to in Article 2 are the following :

(a) *in Belgium :*

*Le diplôme légal de pharmacien/het wettelijk diploma van apoteker* (the legal diploma in pharmacy) awarded by the faculties of medicine and pharmacy of the Universities, by the Central examining board or by the State examining boards for university education ;

(b) *in Denmark :*

*Bevis for bestået farmaceutisk kandidateksamen* (the university pharmacy certificate) ;

(c) *in the Federal Republic of Germany :*

(1) *Zeugnis über die staatliche Pharmazeutische Prüfung* (the State examination certificate in pharmacy) awarded by the competent authorities ;

(2) Certificates from the competent authorities the Federal Republic of Germany stating that the diplomas awarded after 8 May 1945 by the competent authorities of the German Democratic Republic are recognized as equivalent to those referred to in point 1 above ;

(d) *in Greece :*

Πιατοποιητικό των αρμοδίων αρχών, ικανότητας άσκησης της φαρμακευτικής, χορηγούμενο μετά κρατική εξέταση (the certificate attesting competence to pursue the activity of a pharmacist) issued by the competent authorities following a State examination ;

(e) *in France :*

The State diploma in pharmacy awarded by the universities or the State diploma of Doctor in Pharmacy awarded by the universities ;

(f) *in Ireland :*

The certificate of *Registered Pharmaceutical Chemist ;*

(g) *in Italy :*

The diploma or certificate giving the right to practise pharmacy, obtained by passing a State examination ;

(h) *in Luxembourg :*

The State pharmacy diploma awarded by the State Examining Board and signed by the National Minister of Education ;

(i) *in the Netherlands :*

*Het getuigschrift van met goed gevolg afgelegd apothekersexamen* (the university pharmacy certificate) ;

(j) *in the United Kingdom :*

The certificate of *Registered Pharmaceutical Chemist*;

(k) *in Spain:*

título de licenciado en farmacia (university degree in pharmacy awarded by the Ministry of Education and Science or by the universities); (*)

(l) *in Portugal:*

Carta de curso de licenciatura em Ciências Farmacêuticas (the certificate in pharmaceutical sciences awarded by the universities). (*)

(*) Text as amended by Directive 85/584/EEC.

*Article 5*

Where, in a Member State, access to or pursuit of one of the activities referred to in Article 1 is subject not only to the possession of a diploma, certificate or other formal qualification mentioned in Article 4 but also to the requirement of additional professional experience, that State shall accept as sufficient evidence in this respect a certificate issued by the competent authorities of the person's Member State of origin or of the Member State from which he comes, attesting that he has pursued the said activities for an equivalent period in his Member State of origin or in the Member State from which he comes.

However, such recognition shall not apply with regard to the two-year period of professional experience required by the Grand Duchy of Luxembourg for the grant of a State public pharmacy concession.

CHAPTER III

## Established rights

*Article 6*

Diplomas, certificates and other university or equivalent qualifications in pharmacy which were awarded to nationals of Member States by Member States and which do not satisfy all the minimum training requirements laid down in Article 2 of Directive 85/432/EEC shall be treated as diplomas satisfying these requirements if:

— they are evidence of training which was completed before the implementation of the said Directive,

or

— they are evidence of training which was completed after but which was commenced before the implementation of the said Directive,

and, in each case, if:

— they are accompanied by a certificate stating that their holders have been effectively and lawfully engaged in one of the activities referred to in Article 1 (2) of Directive 85/432/EEC in a Member State for at least three consecutive years during the five years preceding the award of the certificate, provided that this activity is regulated in that State.

CHAPTER IV

## Use of academic title

*Article 7*

1. Without prejudice to Article 14, host Member States shall ensure that nationals of Member States who fulfil the conditions laid down in Articles 2, 5 and 6 have the right to use the lawful academic title and, where appropriate, the abbreviation thereof, of their Member State of origin or of the Member State from which they come, in the language of that State. Host Member States may require this title to be followed by the name and location of the establishment or examining board which awarded it.

2. If the academic title used in the Member State of origin, or in the Member State from which a foreign national comes, can be confused in the host Member State with a title requiring in that State additional training which the person concerned has not undergone, the host Member State may require such a person to use the title employed in the Member State of origin or the Member State from which he comes in suitable wording to be indicated by the host Member State.

CHAPTER V

## Provisions to facilitate the effective exercise of the right of establishment

*Article 8*

1. A host Member State which requires of its nationals proof of good character or good repute when they take up for the first time any of the activities referred to in Article 1 shall accept as sufficient evidence, in respect of nationals of other Member States, a certificate issued by a competent authority in the Member State of origin or in the Member State from which the foreign national comes, attesting that the requirements of the Member State as to good character or good repute for taking up the activity in question have been met.

2. Where the Member State of origin or the Member State from which the foreign national comes does not require proof of good character or good repute of persons wishing to take up the activity in question for the first time, the host Member State may require of nationals of the Member State of origin or of the Member State from which the foreign national comes an extract from the judicial record or, failing this, an equivalent document issued by a competent authority in the Member State of origin or the Member State from which the foreign national comes.

3. If the host Member State has detailed knowledge of a serious matter which, prior to the establishment in that State of the person in question, has occurred outside its territory and is likely to affect the taking up within its territory of the activity concerned, it may inform the Member State of origin or the Member State from which the foreign national comes.

The Member State of origin or the Member State from which the foreign national comes shall verify the accuracy of the facts if they are likely to affect the taking up of the activity in question in that Member State. The authorities in that State shall decide on the nature and extent of the investigations to be made and shall inform the host Member State of any consequential action which they take with regard to the certificates or documents they have issued.

4. Member States shall ensure the confidentiality of the information which is forwarded.

*Article 9*

1. Where, in a host Member State, provisions laid down by law, regulation or adminsitrative action are in force laying down requirements as to good character or good repute, including provisions for disciplinary action in respect of serious professional misconduct or conviction for criminal offences and relating to the pursuit of any of the activities referred to in Article 1, the Member State of origin or the Member State from which the foreign national comes shall forward to the host Member State all necessary information regarding measures or disciplinary action of a professional or administrative nature taken in respect of the person concerned, or criminal penalties imposed on him when pursuing his profession in the Member State of origin or in the Member State from which he came.

2. If the host Member State has detailed knowledge of a serious matter which, prior to the establishment in that State of the person in question, has occurred outside its territory and is likely to affect the pursuit within its territory of the activity concerned, it may inform the Member State of origin or the Member State from which the foreign national comes.

The Member State of origin or the Member State from which the foreign national comes shall verify the accuracy of the facts if they are likely to affect in that Member State the pursuit of the activity in question. The authorities in that State shall decide on the nature and extent of the investigations to be made and shall inform the host Member State of any consequential action which they take with regard to the information they have forwarded in accordance with paragraph 1.

3. Member States shall ensure the confidentiality of the information which is forwarded.

*Article 10*

Where a host Member State requires of its own nationals wishing to take up or pursue any of the activities referred to in Article 1, a certificate of physical or mental health, that State shall accept as sufficient evidence thereof the presentation of the document required in the Member State of origin or in the Member State from which the foreign national comes.

Where the Member State of origin or the Member State from which the foreign national comes does not impose any requirements of this nature on those wishing to take up or pursue the activity in question, the host Member State shall accept from such nationals a certificate issued by a competent authority in that State corresponding to the certificates issued in the host Member State.

*Article 11*

The documents referred to in Articles 8, 9 and 10 may not be presented more than three months after their date of issue.

*Article 12*

1. The procedure for authorizing the person concerned to take up any of the activities referred to in Article 1, pursuant to Articles 8, 9 and 10, must be completed as soon as possible and not later than three months after submission of all the documents relating to such person, without prejudice to delays resulting from any appeal that may be made upon the completion of this procedure.

2. In the cases referred to in Articles 8 (3) and 9 (2), a request for re-examination shall suspend the period stipulated in paragraph 1.

When consulted, the Member State of origin or the Member State from which the foreign national comes shall give its reply within three months.

On receipt of the reply or at the end of that period, the host Member State shall continue with the procedure referred to in paragraph 1.

*Article 13*

Where a host Member State requires its own nationals wishing to take up or pursue one of the activities referred to in Article 1 to take an oath or make a solemn declaration and where the form of such oath or declaration cannot be used by nationals of other Member States, that Member State shall ensure that an appropriate and equivalent form of oath or declaration is offered to the persons concerned.

*Article 14*

Where in a host Member State, the use of the professional title relating to one of the activities referred to in Article 1 is regulated, nationals of Member States who fulfil the conditions of professional qualification laid down in Articles 2, 5 and 6 shall be entitled to the professional title of the host Member State which in that State corresponds to those conditions, and shall use the abbreviation thereof.

*Article 15*

1. Member States shall take the necessary measures to enable the persons concerned to obtain information on the health and social security laws and, where applicable, on the professional ethics of the host Member State.

For this purpose, Member States may set up information centres from which such persons may obtain the necessary information. The host Member States may require the persons concerned to contact these centres.

2. Member States may set up the centres referred to in paragraph 1 under the aegis of the competent authorities and bodies which they shall designate within the period laid down in Article 19 (1).

3. Member States shall see to it that, where appropriate, the persons concerned acquire, in their own interest and in that of their customers, the linguistic knowledge necessary for the practice of their profession in the host Member State.

CHAPTER VI

**Final provisions**

*Article 16*

In the event of justified doubts, the host Member State may require of the competent authorities of another Member State confirmation of the authenticity of the diplomas, certificates and other formal qualifications issued in that other Member State and referred to in Chapters II and III, and also confirmation of the fact that the person concerned has fulfilled all the training requirements laid down in Directive 85/432/EEC.

*Article 17*

Within the time limit laid down inArticle 19 (1), Member States shall designate the authorities and bodies competent to issue or receive the diplomas, certificates and other formal qualifications as well as the documents and information referred to in this Directive and shall forthwith inform the other Member States and the Commission thereof.

*Article 18*

This Directive shall also apply to nationals of Member States who, in accordance with Regulation (EEC) No 1612/68, are pursuing or will pursue as employed persons one of the activities referred to in Article 1.

*Article 19*

1. Member States shall bring into force the measures necessary to comply with this Directive before 1 October 1987. They shall forthwith inform the Commission thereof.

2. Member States shall communicate to the Commission the texts of the main provisions of national law which they adopt in the field covered by this Directive.

*Article 20*

Where a Member State encounters major difficulties in certain fields when applying this Directive, the Commission shall examine these difficulties in conjunction with that State and shall request the opinion of the Pharmaceutical Committee set up under Decision 75/320/EEC [1].

Where necessary, the Commission shall submit appropriate proposals to the Council.

*Article 21*

This Directive is addressed to the Member States.

Done at Luxembourg, 16 September 1985.

*For the Council*

*The President*

M. FISCHBACH

[1] OJ No L 147, 9. 6. 1975, p. 23.

Official Journal of the European Communities No L 253/ 24. 9. 85

# COUNCIL RECOMMENDATION

## of 16 September 1985

## concerning nationals of the Grand Duchy of Luxembourg who hold a diploma in pharmacy conferred in a third State

(85/435/EEC)

THE COUNCIL OF THE EUROPEAN COMMUNITIES,

Approving Directive No 85/433/EEC of 16 September 1985 concerning the mutual recognition of diplomas, certificates and other evidence of formal qualifications in pharmacy, including measures to facilitate the effective exercise of the right of establishment relating to certain activities in the field of pharmacy (1);

Noting that this Directive refers only to diplomas, certificates and other evidence of formal qualifications conferred in a Member State;

Anxious, however, to take account of the special position of nationals of the Grand Duchy of Luxembourg who, since there is no complete university training in the Grand Duchy itself, have studies in a third State;

HEREBY RECOMMENDS that the Governments of the other Member States should allow nationals of the Grand Duchy of Luxembourg who hold a diploma conferring a degree in pharmacy awarded in a third State and which has obtained the official recognition of the Minister for Education, in accordance with the Law of 18 June 1969 on higher education and the recognition of foreign degrees and diplomas in higher education, to take up and pursue activities as pharmacists within the Community, by recognizing these diplomas in their territories.

Done at Luxembourg, 16 September 1985.

*For the Council*

*The President*

M. FISCHBACH

(1) OJ No L 253, 24.9.1985, p.37.

# 11. Transporters

Official Journal of the European Communities No L 308/19. 11. 74

II

*(Acts whose publication is not obligatory)*

# COUNCIL

## COUNCIL DIRECTIVE

### of 12 November 1974

### on admission to the occupation of road haulage operator in national and international transport operations (*)

(74/561/EEC)

THE COUNCIL OF THE EUROPEAN COMMUNITIES,

Having regard to the Treaty establishing the European Economic Community, and in particular Article 75 thereof;

Having regard to the proposal from the Commission;

Having regard to the Opinion of the European Parliament (1);

Having regard to the Opinion of the Economic and Social Committee (2);

Whereas the organization of the transport market is one of the essential factors in the implementation of the common transport policy provided for in the Treaty;

Whereas the adoption of measures aimed at coordinating the conditions of admission to the occupation of haulage operator is likely to favour effective exercise of the right of establishment;

Whereas it is necessary to provide for the introduction of common rules for admission to the occupation of road haulage operator in national and international transport operations in order to ensure that road haulage operators are better qualified, thus contributing to rationalization of the market, improvement in the quality of the service provided, in the interests of users, operators and the economy as a whole, and to greater road safety;

Whereas, therefore, the rules for admission to the occupation of road haulage operator should cover the good repute, financial standing and professional competence of operators;

Whereas, however, it is not necessary to include in these common rules certain kinds of transport which are of limited economic importance;

Whereas transitional measures must be introduced to enable Member States to adapt their national rules to those of the Community;

Whereas the harmonization of conditions for applying these common rules requires that provision be made for a Community consultation procedure as regards the appropriate national measures to be taken,

HAS ADOPTED THIS DIRECTIVE:

*Article 1*

1. Admission to the occupation of road haulage operator shall be governed by the provisions adopted by the Member States in accordance with the common rules contained in this Directive.

2. For the purposes of this Directive, 'the occupation of road haulage operator' means the activity of any natural person or any undertaking transporting goods for hire or reward by means of either a self-contained motor vehicle or a combination of coupled vehicles.

(*) Text as amended by:
- Directive 80/1178/EEC of 4 December 1980 (Official Journal of the European Communities No L 350, 23.12.1980, p.41).
- Directive 85/578/EEC of 20 December 1985 (Official Journal of the European Communities No L 372, 31.12.1985, p.34).

(1) OJ No C 72, 19. 7. 1968, p. 53.
(2) OJ No C 49, 17. 5. 1968, p. 2.

For the purposes of this Directive, 'undertaking' means any association or group of persons with or without legal personality, whether profit-making or not, or any official body whether having its own legal personality or being dependent upon an authority having such personality.

*Article 2*

1. This Directive shall not apply to natural persons or undertakings engaging in the occupation of road haulage operator by means of vehicles the permissible payload of which does not exceed 3·5 metric tons or the permissible total laden weight of which does not exceed six metric tons. Member States may, however, lower the said limits for all or some categories of transport operations.

2. Member States may, after consulting the Commission, exempt from the application of all or some of the provisions of this Directive natural persons or undertakings engaged exclusively in national transport operations having only a minor impact on the transport market because of :

— the nature of the goods carried, or

— the short distance involved.

*Article 3*

1. Natural persons or undertakings wishing to engage in the occupation of road haulage operator shall :

(a) be of good repute ;

(b) be of appropriate financial standing ;

(c) satisfy the condition as to professional competence.

Where the applicant is a natural person and does not satisfy provision (c), the competent authorities may nevertheless permit him to engage in the occupation of road haulage operator provided that he designates to the said authorities another person, satisfying provisions (a) and (c) above, who shall continuously and effectively manage the transport operations of the undertaking.

Where the applicant is an undertaking, provisions (a) and (c) above must be satisfied by one of the natural persons who will continuously and effectively manage the transport operations of the undertaking. Member States may also require that other persons in the undertaking satisfy provision (a) above.

2. Pending coordination at a later date, each Member State shall determine the provisions relating to good repute which must be satisfied by the applicant and, where appropriate, by the natural persons referred to in paragraph 1.

3. Appropriate financial standing shall consist in having available sufficient resources to ensure the launching and proper administration of the undertaking. Pending coordination at a later date, each Member State shall determine what provisions and what methods of furnishing proof may be adopted for this purpose.

4. The condition as to professional competence shall consist in the possession of skills in the subjects listed in the Annex and recognized by the authority or body designated for that purpose by each Member State. The necessary knowledge shall be acquired by attending courses, by practical experience in a transport undertaking or by a combination of both. Member States may exempt from the application of these provisions the holders of certain advanced diplomas or technical diplomas implying sound knowledge of the subjects listed in the Annex.

The production of a certificate issued by the authority or body referred to in the preceding subparagraph shall constitute proof of professional competence.

*Article 4*

1. Member States shall determine the circumstances in which a road haulage undertaking may, by way of derogation from Article 3 (1), be operated on a temporary basis for a maximum period of one year, with extension for a maximum period of six months, in duly justified special cases in the event of the death or physical or legal incapacity of the natural person engaged in the occupation of transport operator or of the natural person who satisfies the provisions of Article 3 (1) (a) and (c).

2. However, the competent authorities in the Member States may, by way of exception and in certain special cases, definitively authorize a person not fulfilling the condition of professional competence referred to in Article 3 (1) (c) to operate the transport undertaking provided that such person possesses at least three years' practical experience in the day-to-day management of the undertaking.

*Article 5*

1. Natural persons and undertakings furnishing proof that, before 1 January 1978, they were authorized under national regulations in a Member State to engage in the occupation of road haulage operator in

national and/or international road transport operations shall be exempt from the requirement to furnish proof that they satisfy the provisions laid down in Article 3.

2. However, those natural persons who, after 31 December 1974 and before 1 January 1978, were:

— authorized to engage in the occupation of road haulage operator without having furnished proof, under national regulations, of their professional competence, or

— designated continuously and effectively to manage the transport operations of the undertaking,

must satisfy, before 1 January 1980, the condition of professional competence referred to in Article 3 (4).

The same requirement shall apply in the case referred to in the third subparagraph of Article 3 (1).

3. With regard to Greece, the dates in paragraphs 1 and 2 shall be replaced as follows:

— in paragraph 1, "1 January 1978" shall be replaced by "1 January 1984";

— in paragraph 2, "31 December 1974", "1 January 1978" and "1 January 1980" shall be replaced by "31 December 1980", "1 January 1984" and "1 January 1986" respectively.(*)

4. With regard to Spain and Portugal, the dates in paragraphs 1 and 2 shall be replaced as follows:

— in paragraph 1, "1 January 1978" shall be replaced by "1 January 1986";

— in paragraph 2, "31 December 1974", "1 January 1978" and "1 January 1980" shall be replaced by "31 December 1982", "1 January 1986" and "1 January 1988" respectively. (**)

*Article 6*

1. Decisions taken by the competent authorities of the Member States pursuant to the measures adopted on the basis of this Directive and entailing the rejection of an application for admission to the occupation of road haulage operator shall state the grounds on which they are based.

2. Member States shall ensure that the competent authorities withdraw the authorization to pursue the occupation of haulage operator if they establish that the provisions of Article 3 (1) (a), (b) or (c) are no longer satisfied. In this case, however, they shall allow sufficient time for a substitute to be appointed.

3. With regard to the decisions referred to in paragraphs 1 and 2, Member States shall ensure that the natural persons or undertakings covered by this Directive are able to defend their interests by appropriate means.

*Article 7*

1. Member States shall, after consulting the Commission and before 1 January 1977, adopt the measures necessary for the implementation of this Directive, in particular Article 3 (4) thereof.

2. Member States shall ensure that the procedure for official verification of the skills mentioned in Article 3 (4) shall become operative for the first time before 1 January 1978.

*Article 8*

This Directive is addressed to the Member States.

Done at Brussels, 12 November 1974.

*For the Council*

*The President*

J. SAUVAGNARGUES

(*) Paragraph as added by Directive 80/1178/EEC.
(**) Paragraph as added by Directive 85/578/EEC.

*ANNEX*

## LIST OF SUBJECTS REFERRED TO IN ARTICLE 3 (4)

The knowledge to be taken into consideration for the official recognition of professional competence must cover at least the subjects listed below. These must be described in full detail and have been worked out or approved by the competent national authorities. They must be so designed as to be within the grasp of those persons whose education corresponds to the level normally reached at school-leaving age.

### A. SUBJECTS OF WHICH KNOWLEDGE IS REQUIRED FOR TRANSPORT OPERATORS INTENDING TO ENGAGE EXCLUSIVELY IN NATIONAL TRANSPORT OPERATIONS

1. **Law**

Elements of civil, commercial, social and fiscal law, as necessary for engaging in the occupation, with particular emphasis on :

— general contracts ;

— transport contracts, with particular reference to the responsibility of the haulage operator (nature and limits) ;

— commercial companies ;

— ledgers ;

— regulations governing labour, social security ;

— taxation systems.

2. **Business and financial management of an undertaking**

— methods of payment and financing ;

— costing ;

— pricing and haulage terms ;

— business accounts ;

— insurance ;

— invoicing ;

— transport agents.

3. **Access to the market**

— provisions relating to the taking up and pursuit of the occupation ;

— transport documents.

4. **Technical standards and aspects of operation**

— weight and dimensions of vehicles ;

— vehicle selection ;

— type-approval and registration ;

— vehicle maintenance standards ;

— loading and unloading of vehicles.

5. **Road safety**

— laws, regulations and administrative provisions applicable to traffic ;

— traffic safety ;

— accident prevention and procedure in the event of an accident.

B. SUBJECTS OF WHICH KNOWLEDGE IS REQUIRED FOR HAULAGE OPERATORS INTENDING TO ENGAGE IN INTERNATIONAL TRANSPORT

— subjects listed under A ;

— provisions applicable to the transport of goods by road between Member States and between the Community and non-member countries arising out of national laws, Community standards, international conventions and agreements ;

— customs practice and formalities ;

— main traffic regulations in the Member States.

Official Journal of the European Communities No L 308/23 19. 11. 74

# COUNCIL DIRECTIVE

## of 12 November 1974

## on admission to the occupation of road passenger transport operator in national and international transport operations (*)

(74/562/EEC)

THE COUNCIL OF THE EUROPEAN COMMUNITIES,

Having regard to the Treaty establishing the European Economic Community, and in particular Article 75 thereof;

Having regard to the proposal from the Commission;

Having regard to the Opinion of the European Parliament (1);

Having regard to the Opinion of the Economic and Social Committee (2);

Whereas the organization of the transport market is one of the essential factors in the implementation of the common transport policy provided for in the Treaty;

Whereas the adoption of measures aimed at coordinating the conditions of admission to the occupation of road passenger transport operator is likely to favour effective exercise of the right of establishment;

Whereas it is necessary to provide for the introduction of common rules for admission to the occupation of road passenger transport operator in national and international transport operations in order to ensure that road passenger transport operators are better qualified, thus contributing to rationalization of the market, improvement in the quality of the service provided in the interests of users, transport operators and the economy as a whole, and to greater road safety;

Whereas, therefore, the rules for admission to the occupation of road passenger transport operator should cover the good repute, financial standing and professional competence of operators;

Whereas, however, it is not necessary to include in these common rules certain kinds of transport which are of limited economic importance;

Whereas transitional measures must be introduced to enable Member States to adapt their national rules to those of the Community;

Whereas the harmonization of conditions for applying these common rules requires that provision be made for a Community consultation procedure as regards the appropriate national measures to be taken,

HAS ADOPTED THIS DIRECTIVE:

*Article 1*

1. Admission to the occupation of road passenger transport operator shall be governed by the provisions adopted by the Member States in accordance with the common rules contained in this Directive.

2. For the purpose of this Directive, 'the occupation of road passenger transport operator' means the activity of any natural person or any undertaking operating by means of motor vehicles so constructed and equipped as to be suitable for carrying more than nine persons — including the driver — and intended for that purpose, passenger transport services for the public or for specific categories of users against payment by the person transported or by the transport organizer.

For the purposes of this Directive, 'undertaking' means any association or group of persons with or without legal personality, whether profit-making or not, or any official body, whether having its own legal personality or being dependent upon an authority having such personality.

3. Member States may, after consulting the Commission, exempt from the application of all or some of the provisions of this Directive natural persons or undertakings engaged exclusively in road passenger transport services for non-commercial purposes or having a main occupation other than that of road passenger transport operator, in so far as their transport operations have only a minor impact on the transport market.

(*) Text as amended by:
- Directive 80/1179/EEC of 4 December 1980 (Official Journal of the European Communities No L 350, 23.12.1980, p.42).
- Directive 85/579/EEC of 20 December 1985 (Official Journal of the European Communities No L 372, 31.12.1985, p.35).

(1) OJ No C 17, 12. 2. 1969, p. 6.
(2) OJ No C 26, 28. 2. 1969, p. 8.

*Article 2*

1. Natural persons or undertakings wishing to engage in the occupation of road passenger transport operator shall :

(a) be of good repute ;

(b) be of appropriate financial standing ;

(c) satisfy the condition as to professional competence.

Where the applicant is a natural person and does not satisfy provision (c), the competent authorities may nevertheless permit him to engage in the occupation of road passenger transport operator provided that he designates to the said authorities another person, satisfying provisions (a) and (c) above, who shall continuously and effectively manage the transport operations of the undertaking.

Where the applicant is an undertaking, provisions (a) and (c) above must be satisfied by one of the natural persons who will continuously and effectively manage the transport operations of the undertaking. Member States may also require that other persons in the undertaking satisfy provision (a) above.

2. Pending coordination at a later date, each Member State shall determine the provisions relating to good repute which must be satisfied by the applicant and, where appropriate, the natural persons referred to in paragraph 1.

3. Appropriate financial standing shall consist in having available sufficient financial resources to ensure the launching and proper administration of the undertaking. Pending coordination at a later date, each Member State shall determine what provisions and what methods of furnishing proof may be adopted for this purpose.

4. The condition as to professional competence shall consist in the possession of skills in the subjects listed in the Annex and recognized by the authority or body designated for that purpose by each Member State. The necessary knowledge shall be acquired by attending courses, by practical experience in a transport undertaking or by a combination of both. The Member States may exempt from the application of these provisions the holders of certain advanced diplomas or technical diplomas implying sound knowledge of the subjects listed in the Annex.

The production of a certificate issued by the authority or body referred to in the preceding subparagraph shall constitute proof of professional competence.

*Article 3*

1. Member States shall determine the circumstances in which operation of a road passenger transport undertaking may, by way of derogation from the provisions of Article 2 (1), be continued on a temporary basis for a maximum period of one year, with extension for a maximum period of six months, in duly justified special cases, in the event of the death or physical or legal incapacity of the natural person engaged in the occupation of transport operator or of the natural person who satisfies the provisions of Article 2 (1) (a) and (c).

2. However, the competent authorities in the Member States may, by way of exception and in certain special cases, definitively authorize a person not fulfilling the condition as to professional competence referred to in Article 2 (1) (c) to continue to operate the transport undertaking provided that such person possesses at least three years' practical experience in the day-to-day management of the undertaking.

*Article 4*

1. Natural persons and undertakings furnishing proof that before 1 January 1978, they were authorized under national regulations in a Member State to engage in the occupation of road passenger transport operator in national and/or international transport operations shall be exempt from the requirement to furnish proof that they satisfy the provisions laid down in Article 2.

2. However, those natural persons who, after 31 December 1974 and before 1 January 1978, were :

— authorized to engage in the occupation of road passenger transport operator without having furnished proof, under national regulations, of their professional competence, or

— designated continuously and effectively to manage the transport operations of the undertaking,

must satisfy, before 1 January 1980 the condition of professional competence referred to in Article 2 (4).

The same requirement shall apply in the case referred to in the third subparagraph of Article 2 (1).

3. With regard to Greece, the dates in paragraphs 1 and 2 shall be replaced as follows:

— in paragraph 1, "1 January 1978" shall be replaced by "1 January 1984";

— in paragraph 2, "31 December 1974", "1 January 1978" and "1 January 1980" shall be replaced by "31 December 1980", "1 January 1984" and "1 January 1986" respectively. (*)

4. With regard to Spain and Portugal, the dates in paragraphs 1 and 2 shall be replaced as follows:

— in paragraph 1, "1 January 1978" shall be replaced by "1 January 1986",

— in paragraph 2, "31 December 1974", "1 January 1978" and "1 January 1980" shall be replaced by "31 December 1982", "1 January 1986" and "1 January 1988" respectively. (**)

*Article 5*

1. Decisions taken by the competent authorities of Member States pursuant to the measures adopted on the basis of this Directive and entailing the rejection of an application for admission to the occupation of road passenger transport operator shall state the grounds on which they are based.

2. Member States shall ensure that the competent authorities withdraw the authorization to pursue the occupation of passenger transport operator if they establish that the provisions of Article 2 (1) (a), (b) or (c) are no longer satisfied. In this case, however, they shall allow sufficient time for a substitute to be appointed.

3. With regard to the decisions referred to in paragraphs 1 and 2, Member States shall ensure that the natural persons or undertakings covered by this Directive are able to defend their interests by appropriate means.

*Article 6*

1. Member States shall, after consulting the Commission and before 1 January 1977, adopt the measures necessary for the implementation of this Directive, in particular Article 2 (4) thereof.

2. Member States shall ensure that the procedure for official verfication of the skills mentioned in Article 2 (4) shall become operative for the first time before 1 January 1978.

*Article 7*

This Directive is addressed to the Member States.

Done at Brussels, 12 November 1974.

*For the Council*

*The President*

J. SAUVAGNARGUES

(*) Paragraph as added by Directive 80/1179/EEC.
(**) Paragraph as added by Directive 85/579/EEC.

*ANNEX*

## LIST OF SUBJECTS REFERRED TO IN ARTICLE 2 (4)

The knowledge to be taken into consideration for the official recognition of professional competence must cover at least the subjects listed below. These must be described in full detail and have been worked out or approved by the competent national authorities. They must be so designed as to be within the grasp of those persons whose education corresponds to the level normally reached at school-leaving age.

### A. SUBJECTS OF WHICH KNOWLEDGE IS REQUIRED FOR TRANSPORT OPERATORS INTENDING TO ENGAGE EXCLUSIVELY IN NATIONAL TRANSPORT OPERATIONS

1. **Law**

Elements of civil, commercial, social and fiscal law, as necessary for engaging in the occupation, with particular emphasis on :

— general contracts ;

— transport contracts, with particular reference to the responsibility of the transport operator (nature and limits) ;

— commercial companies ;

— ledgers ;

— regulations governing labour, social security ;

— taxation systems.

2. **Business and financial management of an undertaking**

— methods of payment and financing ;

— costing ;

— system of fares, prices and conditions of transport ;

— business accounts ;

— insurance ;

— invoices ;

— travel agencies.

3. **Regulation of road passenger services**

— institution of transport services and transport plans ;

— conditions of fulfilment of passenger services ;

— provisions relating to admission to and pursuit of the occupation ;

— transport documents.

4. **Technical standards and aspects of operation**

— vehicle selection ;

— type-approval and registration ;

— vehicle maintenance standards.

5. **Road safety**

— laws, regulations and administrative provisions applicable to traffic ;
— traffic safety ;
— geographical knowledge of routes ;
— accident prevention and procedure in the event of an accident.

B. SUBJECTS OF WHICH KNOWLEDGE IS REQUIRED FOR TRANSPORT OPERATORS INTENDING TO ENGAGE IN INTERNATIONAL TRANSPORT

— subjects listed under A ;
— provisions applicable to passenger transport by road between Member States and between the Community and non-member countries, arising out of national laws, Community standards, international conventions and agreements ;
— practice and formalities connected with border-crossings ;
— main traffic regulations in the Member States.

Official Journal of the European Communities No L 334/ 24. 12. 77

# COUNCIL DIRECTIVE

of 12 December 1977

**aiming at the mutual recognition of diplomas, certificates and other evidence of formal qualifications for goods haulage operators and road passenger transport operators, including measures intended to encourage these operators effectively to exercise their right to freedom of establishment (*)**

(77/796/EEC)

THE COUNCIL OF THE EUROPEAN COMMUNITIES,

Having regard to the Treaty establishing the European Economic Community, and in particular Articles 49, 57 and 235 thereof,

Having regard to the proposal from the Commission,

Having regard to the opinion of the European Parliament (1),

Having regard to the opinion of the Economic and Social Committee (2),

Whereas, in its Directives 74/561/EEC (3) and 74/562/EEC (4), the Council imposed certain conditions for admission to the occupation of goods haulage operator and road passenger transport operator in national and international transport and whereas it is appropriate to ensure the mutual recognition of diplomas, certificates and other evidence of formal qualifications in respect of the activities covered by these Directives; whereas this Directive does not concern those undertakings referred to in the abovementioned Directives unless they are companies or firms within the meaning of Article 58 of the Treaty;

Whereas, in respect of good repute and financial standing, it would be appropriate to acknowledge [relevant] documents issued by a competent authority in the transport operator's country of origin or the country whence he comes as sufficient proof for admission to the activities concerned in a host Member State;

Whereas, in respect of professional competence, the certificates issued pursuant to the Community provisions on admission to the occupation of transport operator, must be recognized as sufficient proof by the host Member State;

Whereas to the extent that Member States also make admission to, or the carrying out of, the activities covered by this Directive by employees subject to the possession of skills and professional competence, this Directive must also apply to that category of person; whereas it would therefore also be appropriate to apply to employees the provisions on proof of good repute and of no previous bankruptcy,

HAS ADOPTED THIS DIRECTIVE:

*Article 1*

1. Member States shall, in respect of the activities referred to in Article 2, take the measures defined in this Directive concerning the establishment in their territories of the natural persons and undertakings referred to in Title I of the General Programme for the abolition of restrictions on freedom of establishment.

2. This Directive shall also apply to nationals of Member States who, pursuant to Council Regulation (EEC) No 1612/68 of 15 October 1968 on freedom of movement for workers within the Community (5), carry on the activities referred to in Article 2 in the capacity of employees.

*Article 2*

This Directive shall apply to activities covered by Council Directives 74/561/EEC and 74/562/EEC.

*Article 3*

1. Without prejudice to paragraphs 2 and 3 below, a host Member State shall, for the purpose of admission to any of the activities referred to in Article 2, accept as

(*) Text as amended by Directive 80/1180/EEC of 4 December 1980 (OJ No L 350/80, p.43).

(1) OJ No C 125, 8. 6. 1976, p. 54.
(2) OJ No C 197, 23. 8. 1976, p. 35.
(3) OJ No L 308, 19. 11. 1974, p. 18.
(4) OJ No L 308, 19. 11. 1974, p. 23.

(5) OJ No L 257, 19. 10. 1968, p. 2.

sufficient proof of good repute or of no previous bankruptcy an extract from a judicial record or, failing that, an equivalent document issued by a competent judicial or administrative authority in the transport operator's country of origin or the country whence he comes, showing that these requirements have been met.

2. Where the host Member State imposes on its own nationals certain requirements as to good repute and proof that such requirements are satisfied cannot be obtained from the document referred to in paragraph 1, that State shall accept as sufficient evidence in respect of nationals of other Member States a certificate issued by a competent judicial or administrative authority in the country of origin or in the country whence the foreign national comes stating that the requirements in question have been met. Such certificates shall relate to the specific facts regarded as relevant by the host country.

3. Where the country of origin or country whence the foreign national comes does not issue the document required in accordance with paragraphs 1 and 2, such document may be replaced by a declaration on oath or by a solemn declaration — made by the person concerned before a competent judicial or administrative authority or, where appropriate, a notary in that person's country of origin or the country whence he comes; such authority or notary shall issue a certificate attesting the authenticity of the declaration on oath or solemn declaration. The declaration in respect of no previous bankrupty may also be made before a competent professional body in the same country.

4. Documents issued in accordance with paragraphs 1 and 2 shall not be accepted if produced more than three months after their date of issue. This condition shall apply also to declarations made in accordance with paragraph 3.

*Article 4*

1. Where in a host Member State a certificate is required as proof of financial standing, that State shall regard corresponding certificates issued by banks in the country of origin or in the country whence the foreign national comes or by other financial bodies designated by that country, as equivalent to certificates issued in its own territory.

2. Where a Member State imposes on its own nationals certain requirements as to financial standing and where proof that such requirements are satisfied cannot be obtained from the document referred to in paragraph 1, that State shall accept as sufficient evidence, in respect of nationals of other Member States, a certificate issued by a competent administrative authority in the country of origin or in the country whence the foreign national comes, stating that the requirements in question have been met. Such certificate shall relate to the specific facts regarded as relevant by the host country.

*Article 5*

1. Member States shall recognize the certificates referred to in the second subparagraph of Article 3 (4) of Directive 74/561/EEC and the second subparagraph of Article 2 (4) of Directive 74/562/EEC and issued by another Member State as sufficient proof of professional competence if they are based on an examination passed by the applicant or on three years' practical experience.

2. With regard to natural persons and undertakings authorized, before 1 January 1975, under national regulations in a Member State to engage in the occupation of goods haulage operator or passenger transport operator in national and/or international road transport and in so far as the undertakings concerned are companies or firms within the meaning of Article 58 of the Treaty, Member States shall accept as sufficient proof of professional competence certificates stating that the activity concerned has actually been carried on in a Member State for a period of three years. This activity must not have ceased more than five years before the date of submission of the certificate.

In the case of an undertaking, the certificate stating that the activity has actually been carried on shall be issued in respect of one of the natural persons actually in charge of the transport activities of the undertaking.

3. With regard to Greece, the date "1 January 1975" in paragraph 2 shall be replaced by "1 January 1981". (*)

(*) Paragraph as added by Directive 80/1180/EEC.

*Article 6*

Member States shall, within the time limit laid down in Article 7, designate the authorities and bodies competent to issue the documents referred to in Articles 3 and 4 and the certificate referred to in Article 5 (2). They shall immediately inform the other Member States and the Commission thereof.

*Article 7*

1. Member States shall bring into force the measures necessary to comply with this Directive before 1 January 1979 and shall immediately inform the Commission thereof.

2. Member States shall forward to the Commission the text of the main provisions of national law which they adopt in the field covered by this Directive.

*Article 8*

This Directive is addressed to the Member States.

Done at Brussels, 12 December 1977.

*For the Council*

*The President*

L. DHOORE

Official Journal of the European Communities No L 322/12. 11. 87

II

*(Acts whose publication is not obligatory)*

# COUNCIL

## COUNCIL DIRECTIVE

### of 9 November 1987

### on access to the occupation of carrier of goods by waterway in national and international transport and on the mutual recognition of diplomas, certificates and other evidence of formal qualifications for this occupation (*)

(87/540/EEC)

THE COUNCIL OF THE EUROPEAN COMMUNITIES,

Having regard to the Treaty establishing the European Economic Community, and in particular Article 75 thereof,

Having regard to the proposal from the Commission ([1]),

Having regard to the opinion of the European Parliament ([2]),

Having regard to the opinion of the Economic and Social Committee ([3]),

Whereas the organization of the transport market is one of the necessary preconditions for the implementation of the common transport policy which is provided for in the Treaty;

Whereas the adoption of measures designed to coordinate the conditions for access to the occupation of carrier is likely to encourage the achievement of freedom to provide services and the effective exercise of the right of establishment;

Whereas provision must be made for the introduction of common rules governing access to the occupation of carrier of goods by waterway in national and international transport in order to improve the level of qualifications of carriers; whereas such improvement is likely to help towards putting the market on a sounder footing, eliminating structural excess capacities and improving the quality of the service provided, in the interests of users, carriers and the economy as a whole;

Whereas satisfactory results have been obtained through the implementation of Council Directive 74/561/EEC of 12 November 1974 on admission to the occupation of road haulage operator in national and international transport operations ([4]) and Council Directive 77/796/EEC of 12 December 1977 aiming at the mutual recognition of diplomas, certificates and other evidence of formal qualifications for goods haulage operators and road passenger transport operators, including measures intended to encourage these operators effectively to exercise their right to freedom of establishment ([5]);

Whereas the rules governing access to the occupation of carrier of goods by waterway should therefore cover at least the professional competence of the carrier; whereas Member States may also maintain or lay down rules governing the good repute and financial standing of the carrier;

Whereas, however, there is no need to include in the common rules laid down by this Directive certain transport activities with a minor economic impact and whereas transport on own account is by definition excluded from these rules; whereas it also seems appropriate to provide for the possible exclusion from the scope of this Directive of carriers operating exclusively on navigable waterways within their territory not linked to the waterway network of another Member State;

Whereas there is a need for mutual recognition of diplomas, certificates and other evidence of formal qualifications for the activities covered by this Directive, in order to promote the effective exercise of the right of establishment;

(*) Corrigendum published in OJ No L 344, 8.12.1987, p. 14.

([1]) OJ No C 351, 24. 12. 1983, p. 5.
([2]) OJ No C 172, 2. 7. 1984, p. 8.
([3]) OJ No C 248, 17. 9. 1984, p. 40.

([4]) OJ No L 308, 19. 11. 1974, p. 18.
([5]) OJ No L 334, 24. 12. 1977, p. 37.

Whereas the certificate of professional competence issued pursuant to the provisions of this Directive regarding access to the occupation of carrier must be recognized as sufficient proof by the host Member State;

Whereas Member States which impose on their own nationals certain requirements as to good repute and financial standing must recognize the productinon of appropriate documents issued by a competent authority in the carrier's State of origin or prior establishment as sufficient evidence in respect of nationals of other Member States;

Whereas, further, this Directive must also apply to employed persons covered by Council Regulation (EEC) No 1612/68 of 15 October 1968 on freedom of movement for workers within the Community [1], if the Member States make access to the occupation covered by this Directive or the exercise thereof by such persons conditional on the possession of professional knowledge and skills,

HAS ADOPTED THIS DIRECTIVE:

CHAPTER I

## Definitions and scope

*Article 1*

1. Access to the occupation of carrier of goods by waterway in national and international transport shall be governed by the provisions adopted by the Member States pursuant to the common rules laid down in this Directive.

2. For the purposes of this Directive:

— 'occupation of carrier of goods by waterway vessel' means the activities engaged in by any natural person or any undertaking carrying goods by inland waterway for hire or reward, even if this occupation is not exercised on a regular basis,

— 'undertaking' means companies or firms within the meaning of Article 58 of the Treaty and groups or cooperatives of operators whose purpose is to obtain business from shipping agents for distribution among their members, irrespective of whether such groups or cooperatives possess legal personality.

*Article 2*

This Directive shall not apply to natural persons or undertakings pursuing the occupation of carrier of goods by waterway using vessels with a deadweight capacity at maximum draft not exceeding 200 tonnes.

Member States may lower this limit for all or some transport operations or certain categories of transport.

This Directive shall likewise not apply to natural persons or undertakings operating ferries.

CHAPTER II

## Access to the occupation

*Article 3*

1. Natural persons or undertakings wishing to pursue the occupation of carrier of goods by waterway must satisfy the condition of professional competence, even if they are members of a group or cooperative of operators within the meaning of Article 1 (2) or exercise their occupation exclusively for a specific period of time as subcontractors to another waterway transport undertaking.

If the applicant is a natural person who does not satisfy that condition, the competent authorities may nevertheless authorize him to pursue the occupation of carrier of goods by waterway provided that he indicates to them another person satisfying the condition who in actual fact manages the transport operations on a permanent basis.

If the applicant is an undertaking within the meaning of Article 1 (2) one of the natural persons who in actual fact manage the undertaking's transport operations on a permanent basis must meet the condition of professional competence.

2. The condition of professional competence shall consist in the possession of the standard of competence accepted by the authority or body appointed for this purpose by each Member State in the subjects listed in the Annex. The necessary knowledge shall be acquired either by attending courses or by practical experience in a waterway transport undertaking, or by a combination of the two. Member States may exempt the holders of certain diplomas from providing evidence of their knowledge of the subjects listed in the Annex which are covered by the said diplomas.

[1] OJ No L 257, 19. 10. 1968, p. 2.

After verifying possession of the knowledge concerned, the authority or body referred to in the first subparagraph shall issue a certificate.

3. A Member State may, after consulting the Commission, exempt from application of this Directive carriers operating exclusively on navigable waterways within their territory not linked to the waterway network of another Member State. Practical experience gained in a transport undertaking exempted from application of these conditions shall not give entitlement to the certificate referred to in paragraph 2.

*Article 4*

1. Member States shall lay down the terms on which a transport undertaking may, by way of derogation from Article 3 (1), operate on a provisional basis for a maximum of one year, which period may be extended by not more than six months in special duly justified cases, in the event of the death or physical or legal incapacity of the natural person pursuing the occupation of carrier or the natural person complying with the provisions of Article 3.

2. However, the competent authorities of the Member States may, by way of exception, permanently authorize in certain special cases the operation of an undertaking by a person who does not meet the condition of professional competence referred to in Article 3, but who has had at least three years' practical experience in the everyday management of the undertaking concerned.

*Article 5*

Natural persons who provide proof that before 1 July 1990 they legally pursued in a Member State the occupation of carrier of goods by waterway in national or international transport shall, for the purposes of obtaining the certificate referred to in Article 3 (2), be exempt from the obligation to prove that they meet the conditions laid down therein.

*Article 6*

1. Reasons must be given for any decision rejecting an application for access to the occupation of carrier of goods by waterway taken by the competent authorities of the Member States pursuant to the measures adopted on the basis of this Directive.

2. Member States shall ensure that the competent authorities withdraw an authorization to pursue the occupation of carrier of goods by waterway if they find that the conditions laid down in Article 3 are no longer met, subject to allowing, where appropriate, sufficient time for the recruitment of a replacement.

3. Member States shall ensure that the natural persons and undertakings referred to in this Directive have the opportunity to defend their interests by appropriate means with regard to the decisions referred to in paragraphs 1 and 2.

CHAPTER III

**Mutual recognition of diplomas, certificates and other evidence of formal qualifications**

*Article 7*

Member States shall recognize the certificates referred to in the second subparagraph of Article 3 (2) which have been issued by another Member State as sufficient proof of professional competence.

*Article 8*

1. Where a Member State imposes on its own nationals certain requirements as to good repute or absence of bankruptcy, that State shall accept as sufficient evidence in respect of nationals of other Member States, without prejudice to paragraphs 2 and 3, an extract from a judicial record or, failing that, an equivalent document issued by a competent judicial or administrative authority in the carrier's country of origin or prior establishment showing that these conditions have been met.

2. Where a Member State imposes on its own nationals certain requirements as to good repute, and proof that such requirements are met cannot be furnished by means of the document referred to in paragraph 1, that State shall accept as sufficient evidence in respect of nationals of other Member States a certificate issued by a competent judicial or administrative authority in the State of origin or prior establishment stating that the requirements in question have been met. Such certificates shall relate to the specific facts regarded as relevant by the host State.

3. Where the document required in accordance with paragraphs 1 and 2 is not issued by the State of origin or prior establishment, such document may be replaced by a declaration on oath or by a solemn declaration made by the person concerned before a competent judicial or administrative authority or, where appropriate, a notary in that person's State of origin or prior establishment; such authority or notary shall issue a certificate attesting the

authenticity of the declaration on oath or solemn declaration. The declaration in respect of bankruptcy may likewise be made before a competent professional body in the same State.

4. Documents issued in accordance with paragraphs 1 and 2 must not, when produced, have been issued more than three months earlier. This condition shall also apply to declarations made in accordance with paragraph 3.

*Article 9*

1. Where a Member State imposes certain requirements as to financial standing on its own nationals and where a certificate is required as proof, that State shall regard corresponding certificates issued by banks in the State of origin or prior establishment, or by other bodies designated by that State, as equivalent to certificates issued within its own territory.

2. Where a Member States imposes certain requirements as to financial standing on its own nationals and where proof that such requirements are satisfied cannot be furnished by means of the document referred to in paragraph 1, that State shall accept as sufficient evidence in respect of nationals of other Member States a certificate issued by a competent administrative authority in the State of origin or prior establishment stating that the requirements in question have been met. Such certificates shall relate to the specific facts regarded as relevant by the host State.

*Article 10*

Articles 7, 8 and 9 shall also apply to nationals of Member States who, pursuant to Regulation (EEC) No 1612/68, are required to engage as employed persons in the activities referred to in Article 1 of this Directive.

CHAPTER IV

**Final provisions**

*Article 11*

1. Member States shall bring into force the measures necessary to comply with this Directive by 30 June 1988. They shall forthwith inform the Commission thereof.

They shall ensure that the initial verification of the standards of competence referred to in Article 3 takes place before 1 July 1990.

2. Member States shall forward to the Commission the texts of the main provisions of national law which they adopt in the fields governed by this Directive.

*Article 12*

This Directive is addressed to the Member States.

Done at Brussels, 9 November 1987.

*For the Council*

*The President*

B. HAAKONSEN

*ANNEX*

## LIST OF THE SUBJECTS REFERRED TO IN ARTICLE 3 (2) FOR WHICH PROOF OF PROFESIONAL COMPETENCE MUST BE PROVIDED

The knowledge to be taken into consideration for recognition of professional competence must relate to at least the subjects listed below. The latter must be described in detail and be defined or approved by the competent national authorities. The subject matter must be such that it can be assimilated by persons whose educational level is equivalent to that attained at the end of compulsory schooling.

**A. Subjects of which a satisfactory knowledge is required in the case of carriers intending to engage solely in national transport operations**

1. *Law*

Rudiments of civil law and commercial, social and tax legislation of which knowledge is necessary for the pursuit of the occupation, particularly as regards :

— contracts in general,
— haulage contracts, in particular the liability of the carrier (nature and limits),
— commercial companies,
— business accounts,
— labour and social security regulations,
— the tax system.

2. *The commercial and financial management of an undertaking*

— methods of payment and financing,
— calculation of cost prices,
— system of prices and terms of carriage,
— commercial accounting,
— insurance,
— invoices,
— transport agents.

3. *Access to the market*

— the provisions relating to the taking up and pursuit of the occupation,
— chartering systems,
— transport documents.

4. *Technical standards and technical aspects of operation*

— the technical features of vessels,
— the choice of vessels,
— registration,
— lay days and demurrage.

5. *Safety*

— the provisions laid down by law, regulation or administrative action concerning waterway traffic,
— accident prevention and measures to be taken in the event of accident.

B. **Subjects of which a knowledge is required in the case of carriers intending to engage in international transport operations**

— subjects listed under A,

— provisions applicable to waterway transport between the Member States and between the Community and non-member countries which are derived from national law, Community standards and international conventions and agreements, particularly with regard to chartering and prices and terms of carriage,

— customs practices and formalities,

— principal traffic regulations in the Member States.

# 12. Lawyers

Official Journal of the European Communities No L 78/26. 3. 77

# COUNCIL DIRECTIVE

## of 22 March 1977

## to facilitate the effective exercise by lawyers of freedom to provide services (*)

(77/249/EEC)

THE COUNCIL OF THE EUROPEAN COMMUNITIES,

Having regard to the Treaty establishing the European Economic Community, and in particular Articles 57 and 66 thereof,

Having regard to the proposal from the Commission,

Having regard to the opinion of the European Parliament ([1]),

Having regard to the opinion of the Economic and Social Committee ([2]),

Whereas, pursuant to the Treaty, any restriction on the provision of services which is based on nationality or on conditions of residence has been prohibited since the end of the transitional period ;

Whereas this Directive deals only with measures to facilitate the effective pursuit of the activities of lawyers by way of provision of services ; whereas more detailed measures will be necessary to facilitate the effective exercise of the right of establishment ;

Whereas if lawyers are to exercise effectively the freedom to provide services host Member States must recognize as lawyers those persons practising the profession in the various Member States ;

Whereas, since this Directive solely concerns provision of services and does not contain provisions on the mutual recognition of diplomas, a person to whom the Directive applies must adopt the professional title used in the Member State in which he is established, hereinafter referred to as 'the Member State from which he comes',

HAS ADOPTED THIS DIRECTIVE :

*Article 1*

1. This Directive shall apply, within the limits and under the conditions laid down herein, to the activities of lawyers pursued by way of provision of services.

Notwithstanding anything contained in this Directive, Member States may reserve to prescribed categories of lawyers the preparation of formal documents for obtaining title to administer estates of deceased persons, and the drafting of formal documents creating or transferring interests in land.

2. 'Lawyer' means any person entitled to pursue his professional activities under one of the following designations :

| | |
|---|---|
| *Belgium :* | Avocat — Advocaat |
| *Denmark :* | Advokat |
| *Germany :* | Rechtsanwalt |
| *France :* | Avocat |
| *Ireland :* | Barrister<br>Solicitor |
| *Italy :* | Avvocato |
| *Luxembourg :* | Avocat-avoué |
| *Netherlands :* | Advocaat |
| *United Kingdom :* | Advocate<br>Barrister<br>Solicitor |
| Greece: | δικηγόρος (**) |
| *Spain:* | Abogado (***) |
| *Portugal:* | Advogado. (***) |

*Article 2*

Each Member State shall recognize as a lawyer for the purpose of pursuing the activities specified in Article 1 (1) any person listed in paragraph 2 of that Article.

*Article 3*

A person referred to in Article 1 shall adopt the professional title used in the Member State from which he comes, expressed in the language or one of the languages, of that State, with an indication of the professional organization by which he is authorized to

(*) Text as amended by:
– the Act of Accession for Greece (OJ No L 291, 19.11.1979, p.91).
– the Act of Accession for Spain and Portugal (OJ No L 302, 15.11.1987, p.160).
(**) Text as amended by the Act of Accession for Greece.
(***) Text as amended by the Act of Accession for Spain and Portugal.

([1]) OJ No C 103, 5. 10. 1972, p. 19 and OJ No C 53, 8. 3. 1976, p. 33.
([2]) OJ No C 36, 28. 3. 1970, p. 37 and OJ No C 50, 4. 3. 1976, p. 17.

practise or the court of law before which he is entitled to practise pursuant to the laws of that State.

*Article 4*

1. Activities relating to the representation of a client in legal proceedings or before public authorities shall be pursued in each host Member State under the conditions laid down for lawyers established in that State, with the exception of any conditions requiring residence, or registration with a professional organization, in that State.

2. A lawyer pursuing these activities shall observe the rules of professional conduct of the host Member State, without prejudice to his obligations in the Member State from which he comes.

3. When these activities are pursued in the United Kingdom, 'rules of professional conduct of the host Member State' means the rules of professional conduct applicable to solicitors, where such activities are not reserved for barristers and advocates. Otherwise the rules of professional conduct applicable to the latter shall apply. However, barristers from Ireland shall always be subject to the rules of professional conduct applicable in the United Kingdom to barristers and advocates.

When these activities are pursued in Ireland 'rules of professional conduct of the host Member State' means, in so far as they govern the oral presentation of a case in court, the rules of professional conduct applicable to barristers. In all other cases the rules of professional conduct applicable to solicitors shall apply. However, barristers and advocates from the United Kingdom shall always be subject to the rules of professional conduct applicable in Ireland to barristers.

4. A lawyer pursuing activities other than those referred to in paragraph 1 shall remain subject to the conditions and rules of professional conduct of the Member State from which he comes without prejudice to respect for the rules, whatever their source, which govern the profession in the host Member State, especially those concerning the incompatibility of the exercise of the activities of a lawyer with the exercise of other activities in that State, professional secrecy, relations with other lawyers, the prohibition on the same lawyer acting for parties with mutually conflicting interests, and publicity. The latter rules are applicable only if they are capable of being observed by a lawyer who is not established in the host Member State and to the extent to which their observance is objectively justified to ensure, in that State, the proper exercise of a lawyer's activities, the standing of the profession and respect for the rules concerning incompatibility.

*Article 5*

For the pursuit of activities relating to the representation of a client in legal proceedings, a Member State may require lawyers to whom Article 1 applies :

— to be introduced, in accordance with local rules or customs, to the presiding judge and, where appropriate, to the President of the relevant Bar in the host Member State ;
— to work in conjunction with a lawyer who practises before the judicial authority in question and who would, where necessary, be answerable to that authority, or with an 'avoué' or 'procuratore' practising before it.

*Article 6*

Any Member State may exclude lawyers who are in the salaried employment of a public or private undertaking from pursuing activities relating to the representation of that undertaking in legal proceedings in so far as lawyers established in that State are not permitted to pursue those activities.

*Article 7*

1. The competent authority of the host Member State may request the person providing the services to establish his qualifications as a lawyer.

2. In the event of non-compliance with the obligations referred to in Article 4 and in force in the host Member State, the competent authority of the latter shall determine in accordance with its own rules and procedures the consequences of such non-compliance, and to this end may obtain any appropriate professional information concerning the person providing services. It shall notify the competent authority of the Member State from which the person comes of any decision taken. Such exchanges shall not affect the confidential nature of the information supplied.

*Article 8*

1. Member States shall bring into force the measures necessary to comply with this Directive within two years of its notification and shall forthwith inform the Commission thereof.

2. Member States shall communicate to the Commission the texts of the main provisions of national law which they adopt in the field covered by this Directive.

*Article 9*

This Directive is addressed to the Member States.

Done at Brussels, 22 March 1977.

*For the Council*

*The President*

Judith HART

# 13. Insurance agents and brokers

Official Journal of the European Communities No L 26/ 31. 1. 77

# COUNCIL DIRECTIVE

## of 13 December 1976

## on measures to facilitate the effective exercise of freedom of establishment and freedom to provide services in respect of the activities of insurance agents and brokers (ex ISIC Group 630) and, in particular, transitional measures in respect of those activities (*)

(77/92/EEC)

THE COUNCIL OF THE EUROPEAN COMMUNITIES,

Having regard to the Treaty establishing the European Economic Community, and in particular Articles 49, 57, 66 and 235 thereof,

Having regard to the proposal from the Commission,

Having regard to the opinion of the European Parliament (1),

Having regard to the opinion of the Economic and Social Committee (2),

Whereas, pursuant to the Treaty, all discriminatory treatment based on nationality with regard to establishment and to the provision of services is prohibited from the end of the transitional period; whereas the principle of such national treatment applies in particular to the right to join professional organizations where the professional activities of the person concerned necessarily involve the exercise of this right;

Whereas not all Member States impose conditions for the taking up and pursuit of activities of insurance agent and broker; whereas in some cases there is freedom to take up and pursue such activities but in other cases there are strict provisions making access to the profession conditional upon possession of formal evidence of qualifications;

Whereas, in view of the differences between Member States as regards the scope of activities of insurance agent and broker, it is desirable to define as clearly as possible the activities to which this Directive is to apply;

Whereas, moreover, Article 57 of the Treaty provides that, in order to make it easier for persons to take up and pursue activities as self-employed persons, Directives are to be issued for the mutual recognition of diplomas, certificates and other evidence of formal qualifications and for the coordination of the provisions laid down by law, regulation or administrative action in Member States;

Whereas, in the absence of mutual recognition of diplomas or of immediate coordination, it nevertheless appears desirable to facilitate the effective exercise of freedom of establishment and freedom to provide services for the activities in question, in particular by the adoption of transitional measures of the kind envisaged in the General Programmes (3) in order to avoid undue constraint on the nationals of Member States in which the taking up of such activities is not subject to any conditions;

Whereas, in order to prevent such difficulties arising, the object of the transitional measures should be to allow, as sufficient qualification for taking up the activities in question in host Member States which have rules governing the taking up of such activities, the fact that the activity has been pursued in the Member State whence the foreign national comes for a reasonable and sufficiently recent period of time, in cases where previous training is not required, to ensure that the person concerned possesses professional knowledge equivalent to that required of the host Member State's own nationals;

Whereas, in view of the situation in the Netherlands, where insurance brokers are, depending on their professional knowledge, divided up into several categories, an equivalent system should be provided for in respect of nationals of other Member States who wish to take up an activity in one or other of the categories concerned; whereas the most appropriate and objective criterion for this purpose is the number of employees whom the person concerned has or has had working under him;

Whereas, where the activity of agent includes the exercise of a permanent authority from one or more insurance undertakings empowering the beneficiary, in respect of certain or all transactions falling within the normal scope of the business of the undertaking

(1) OJ No C 78, 2. 8. 1971, p. 13.
(2) OJ No C 113, 9. 11. 1971, p. 6.
(3) OJ No 2, 15. 1. 1962, pp. 32/62 and 36/62.

(*) Text as amended by:
- the Act of Accession for Greece (OJ No L 291, 19.11.1979, p.90).
- the Act of Accession for Spain and Portugal (OJ No L 302, 15.11.1987, p.156).

or undertakings concerned, to enter in the name of such undertaking or undertakings into commitments binding upon it or them, the person concerned must be able to take up the activity of broker in the host Member State;

Whereas the purpose of this Directive will disappear once the coordination of conditions for the taking up and pursuit of the activities in question and the mutual recognition of diplomas, certificates and other formal qualifications have been achieved;

Whereas, in so far as in Member States the taking up or pursuit of the activities referred to in this Directive is also dependent in the case of paid employees on the possession of professional knowledge and ability, this Directive should also apply to this category of persons in order to remove an obstacle to the free movement of workers and thereby to supplement the measures adopted in Council Regulation (EEC) No 1612/68 of 15 October 1968 on freedom of movement for workers within the Community ([1]), as amended by Regulation (EEC) No 312/76 ([2]);

Whereas, for the same reason, the provisions laid down in respect of proof of good repute and proof of no previous bankruptcy should also be applicable to paid employees,

HAS ADOPTED THIS DIRECTIVE:

*Article 1*

1. Member States shall adopt the measures defined in this Directive in respect of establishment or provision of services in their territories by natural persons and companies or firms covered by Title I of the General Programmes (hereinafter referred to as 'beneficiaries') wishing to pursue in a self-employed capacity the activities referred to in Article 2.

2. This Directive shall also apply to nationals of Member States who, as provided in Regulation (EEC) No 1612/68, wish to pursue as paid employees the activities referred to in Article 2.

*Article 2*

1. This Directive shall apply to the following activities falling within ex ISIC Group 630 in Annex III to the General Programme for the abolition of restrictions on freedom of establishment:

(a) professional activities of persons who, acting with complete freedom as to their choice of undertaking, bring together, with a view to the insurance or reinsurance of risks, persons seeking insurance or reinsurance and insurance or reinsurance undertakings, carry out work preparatory to the conclusion of contracts of insurance or reinsurance and, where appropriate, assist in the administration and performance of such contracts, in particular in the event of a claim;

(b) professional activities of persons instructed under one or more contracts or empowered to act in the name and on behalf of, or solely on behalf of, one or more insurance undertakings in introducing, proposing and carrying out work preparatory to the conclusion of, or in concluding, contracts of insurance, or in assisting in the administration and performance of such contracts, in particular in the event of a claim;

(c) activities of persons other than those referred to in (a) and (b) who, acting on behalf of such persons, among other things carry out introductory work, introduce insurance contracts or collect premiums, provided that no insurance commitments towards or on the part of the public are given as part of these operations.

2. This Directive shall apply in particular to activities customarily described in the Member States as follows:

(a) activities referred to in paragraph 1 (a):

— *in Belgium:*

— Courtier d'assurance
Verzekeringsmakelaar,

— Courtier de réassurance
Herverzekeringsmakelaar;

— *in Denmark:*

— Juridiske og fysiske personer, som driver selvstændig virksomhed som formidler ved afsætning af forsikringskontrakter;

— *in Germany:*

— Versicherungsmakler,

— Rückversicherungsmakler;

([1]) OJ No L 257, 19. 10. 1968, p. 2.
([2]) OJ No L 39, 14. 2. 1976, p. 2.

— *in France:*

— Courtier d'assurance,

— Courtier d'assurance maritime,

— Courtier de réassurance;

— *in Ireland:*

— Insurance broker,

— Reinsurance broker;

— *in Italy:*

— Mediatore di assicurazioni,

— Mediatore di riassicurazioni;

— *in the Netherlands:*

— Makelaar,

— Assurantiebezorger,

— Erkend assurantieagent,

— Verzekeringsagent;

— *in the United Kingdom:*

— Insurance broker;

— *in Spain:* (*)

— Agentes libres de seguros,

— Corredores de reaseguro;

— *in Portugal:* (*)

— Corretor de seguros,

— Corretor de resseguros;

(b) activities referred to in paragraph 1 (b):

— *in Belgium:*

— Agent d'assurance
Verzekeringsagent;

— *in Denmark:*

— Forsikringsagent;

— *in Germany:*

— Versicherungsvertreter;

— *in France:*

— Agent général d'assurance;

— *in Ireland:*

— Agent;

— *in Italy:*

— Agente di assicurazioni;

— *in Luxembourg:*

— Agent principal d'assurance,

— Agent d'assurance;

— *in the Netherlands:*

— Gevolmachtigd agent,

— Verzekeringsagent;

— *in the United Kingdom:*

— Agent;

— in Greece: (**)
Γενικόςπράκτωρ
Πράκτωρ;

— *in Spain:* (*)

— Agentes afectos de seguros (representantes y no representantes);

— *in Portugal:* (*)

— Agente de seguros;

(c) activities referred to in paragraph 1 (c):

— *in Belgium:*

— Sous-agent
Sub-agent;

— *in Denmark:*

— Underagent;

— *in Germany:*

— Gelegenheitsvermittler,

— Inkassant;

— *in France:*

— Mandataire,

— Intermédiaire,

— Sous-agent;

(*) Indent as added by the Act of Accession for Spain and Portugal.
(**) Indent as added by the Act of Accession for Greece.

— *in Ireland:*

— Sub-agent;

— *in Italy:*

— Subagente;

— *in Luxembourg:*

— Sous-agent;

— *in the Netherlands:*

— Sub-agent;

— *in the United Kingdom:*

— Sub-agent;

— *in Spain:* (*)

— Subagentes de seguros;

— *in Portugal:* (*)

— Submediador.

*Article 3*

Member States in which the taking up or pursuit of any activity referred to in Article 2 is subject to the fulfilment of certain qualifying conditions shall ensure that any beneficiary who applies therefor be provided, before he establishes himself or before he begins to pursue any activity on a temporary basis, with information as to the rules governing the profession which he proposes to pursue.

*Article 4*

Where in a Member State the taking up or pursuit of any activity referred to in Article 2 (1) (a) and (b) is subject to possession of general, commercial or professional knowledge and ability, that Member State shall accept as sufficient evidence of such knowledge and ability the fact that one of the activities in question has been pursued in another Member State for any of the following periods:

(a) four consecutive years in an independent capacity or in a managerial capacity; or

(b) two consecutive years in an independent capacity or in a managerial capacity, where the beneficiary proves that he has worked for at least three years with one or more insurance agents or brokers or with one or more insurance undertakings; or

(c) one year in an independent capacity or in a managerial capacity, where the beneficiary proves that for the activity in question he has received previous training attested by a certificate recognized by the State or regarded by a competent professional body as fully satisfying its requirements.

*Article 5*

1. If a Member State makes the taking up or pursuit of any activity referred to in Article 2 (1) (a) dependent on more stringent requirements than those which it lays down in respect of the activities referred to in Article 2 (1) (b), it may in the case of the taking up or pursuit of the first-mentioned activity require this to have been pursued in another Member State in the branch of the profession referred to in Article 2 (1) (a) for:

(a) four consecutive years in an independent capacity or in a managerial capacity; or

(b) two consecutive years in an independent capacity or in a managerial capacity, where the beneficiary proves that he has worked for at least three years with one or more insurance agents or brokers or with one or more insurance undertakings; or

(c) one year in an independent capacity or in a managerial capacity, where the beneficiary proves that for the activity in question he has received previous training attested by a certificate recognized by the State or regarded by a competent professional body as fully satisfying its requirements.

An activity pursued by the beneficiary in accordance with Article 2 (1) (b), where it includes the exercise of a permanent authority from one or more insurance undertakings empowering the person concerned, in respect of certain or all transactions falling within the normal scope of the business of the undertaking or undertakings concerned, to enter in the name of such undertaking or undertakings into commitments

(*) Indent as added by the Act of Accession for Spain and Portugal.

binding upon it or them, shall be regarded as equivalent to the activity referred to in Article 2 (1) (a).

2. However, in the Netherlands, the taking up or pursuit of the activities referred to in Article 2 (1) (a) shall in addition be subject to the following conditions:

— where the beneficiary wishes to work as a 'makelaar', he must have carried on the activities concerned in a business where he was in charge of at least 10 employees,

— where the beneficiary wishes to work as an 'assurantiebezorger', he must have carried on the activities concerned in a business where he was in charge of at least five employees,

— where the beneficiary wishes to work as an 'erkend assurantieagent', he must have carried on the activities concerned in a business where he was in charge of at least two employees.

*Article 6*

1. Where in a Member State the taking up or pursuit of an activity referred to in Article 2 (1) (c) is dependent on the possession of general, commercial or professional knowledge and ability, that Member State shall accept as sufficient evidence of such knowledge and ability the fact that the activity in question has been pursued in another Member State for either of the following periods:

(a) two consecutive years either in an independent capacity or working with one or more insurance agents or brokers or with one or more insurance undertakings; or

(b) one year under the conditions specified under paragraph (a), where the beneficiary proves that for the activity in question he has received previous training attested by a certificate recognized by the State or regarded by a competent professional body as fully satisfying its requirements.

2. The pursuit for at least one year of one of the activities referred to in Article 2 (1) (a) or (b) and receipt of the relevant training shall be regarded as satisfying the requirements laid down in paragraph 1.

*Article 7*

In the cases referred to in Articles 4, 5 and 6, pursuit of the activity in question shall not have ceased more than 10 years before the date when the application provided for in Article 9 (1) is made. However, where a shorter period is laid down in a Member State for its own nationals, that period must also be applied in respect of beneficiaries.

*Article 8*

1. A person shall be regarded as having pursued an activity in a managerial capacity within the meaning of Articles 4 and 5 (1) where he has pursued the corresponding activity:

(a) as manager of an undertaking or manager of a branch of an undertaking; or

(b) as deputy to the manager of an undertaking or as its authorized representative, where such post involved responsibility equivalent to that of the manager represented.

2. A person shall also be regarded as having pursued an activity in a managerial capacity within the meaning of Article 4 where his duties in an insurance undertaking have involved the management of agents or the supervision of their work.

3. The work referred to in Articles 4 (b) and 5 (1) (b) must have entailed responsibility in respect of the acquisition, administration and performance of contracts of insurance.

*Article 9*

1. Proof that the conditions laid down in Articles 4, 5, 6 and 7 are satisfied shall be established by a certificate, issued by the competent authority or body in the Member State of origin or Member State whence the person concerned comes, which the latter shall submit in support of his application to pursue one of the activities in question in the host Member State.

2. Member States shall, within the time limit laid down in Article 13, designate the authorities and

bodies competent to issue the certificate referred to in paragraph 1 and shall forthwith inform the other Member States and the Commission thereof.

3. Within the time limit laid down in Article 13 every Member State shall also inform the other Member States and the Commission of the authorities and bodies to which an application to pursue in the host Member State an activity referred to in Article 2 and the documents in support thereof are to be submitted.

*Article 10*

1. Where a host Member State requires of its own nationals wishing to take up or pursue any activity referred to in Article 2 proof of good repute and proof that they have not previously been declared bankrupt, or proof of either one of these, it shall accept as sufficient evidence in respect of nationals of other Member States the production of an extract from the 'judicial record' or, failing this, of an equivalent document issued by a competent judicial or administrative authority in the Member State of origin or the Member State whence the foreign national comes showing that these requirements have been met.

2. Where the Member State of origin or the Member State whence the foreign national concerned comes does not issue the document referred to in paragraph 1 it may be replaced by a declaration on oath, — or, in States where there is no provision for declaration on oath, by a solemn declaration — made by the person concerned before a competent judicial or administrative authority or, where appropriate, a notary in the Member State of origin or the Member State whence that person comes; such authority or notary shall issue a certificate attesting the authenticity of the declaration on oath or solemn declaration. The declaration in respect of no previous bankruptcy may also be made before a competent professional body in the said country.

3. Documents issued in accordance with paragraphs 1 and 2 must not be produced more than three months after their date of issue.

4. Member States shall, within the time limit laid down in Article 13, designate the authorities and bodies competent to issue the documents referred to in paragraphs 1 and 2 of this Article and shall forthwith inform the other Member States and the Commission thereof.

Within the time limit laid down in Article 13, each Member State shall also inform the other Member States and the Commission of the authorities or bodies to which the documents referred to in this Article are to be submitted in support of an application to carry on in the host Member State an activity referred to in Article 2.

5. Where in the host Member State proof of financial standing is required, that State shall regard certificates issued by banks in the Member State of origin or the Member State whence the foreign national concerned comes as equivalent to certificates issued in its own territory.

*Article 11*

A host Member State, where it requires its own nationals wishing to take up or pursue one of the activities referred to in Article 2 to take an oath or make a solemn declaration, and where the form of such oath or declaration cannot be used by nationals of other Member States, shall ensure that an appropriate and equivalent form of oath or declaration is offered to the persons concerned.

*Article 12*

This Directive shall remain applicable until the entry into force of provisions relating to the coordination of national rules concerning the taking up and pursuit of the activities in question.

*Article 13*

Member States shall bring into force the measures necessary to comply with this Directive within 18 months of its notification and shall forthwith inform the Commission thereof.

*Article 14*

Member States shall communicate to the Commission the texts of the main provisions of national law which they adopt in the field covered by this Directive.

*Article 15*

This Directive is addressed to the Member States.

Done at Brussels, 13 December 1976.

*For the Council*

*The President*

M. van der STOEL

Official Journal of the European Communities No C 136/ 5. 6. 81

**Communication from the Commission concerning the proofs, declarations and certificates laid down in the Council Directive of 13 December 1976 on measures to facilitate the effective exercise of freedom of establishment and freedom to provide services in respect of the activities of insurance agents and brokers (ex ISIC 630) and, in particular, transitional measures in respect of those activities (77/92/EEC) (¹)**

1. According to the communications from the Member States and pursuant to Article 9 (2) of the Directive, the following authorities and bodies are competent to *issue* the certificates referred to in Article 9 (1):

*Germany*

The Chambers of Commerce and Industry (Industrie- und Handelskammern).

*Belgium*

Ministère des Affaires économiques
Administration du Commerce
à l'attention du Service de la Réglementation Commerciale
Rue de Mot, 24-26
1040 Bruxelles.

World Trade Center,
tour II, 19e étage,
Boulevard Émile Jacqmain 162, boîte 54,
1000 Bruxelles. (*)

The latter is competent in respect of small and medium-sized commercial firms and crafts firms which employ, respectively, no more than twenty or fifty workers. The Minister for Economic Affairs is competent in respect of other firms.

*Denmark*

Forsikringsrådet (Insurance Council)
Hammerichsgade, 14
DK-1611 København V.

*France*

The Syndicat national des courtiers d'assurances et de réassurances (National union of insurance agents and brokers), for brokers and the partners or other persons with administrative powers in an insurance brokerage, and for their employees and representatives.

The Fédération française des sociétés d'assurances (Federation of insurance companies), for insurance agents.

The Fédération nationale des syndicats d'agents généraux d'assurances (Federation of insurance agents' unions), for the employees and representatives of insurance agents.

*Ireland*

Insurance (Agents and Brokers)
Certification Committee of Ireland
18 Fitzwilliam Square
Dublin 2.

*Italy*

Ministero dell'Industria
d.g. assicurazioni private e di interesse privato.

*Luxembourg*

Service de contrôle des entreprises d'assurances
3, rue de la Congrégation
Luxembourg.

*Netherlands*

Sociaal-Economische Raad
Afdeling Uitvoering Wet Assurantiebemiddeling
Bezuidenhoutseweg, 60
2594 AW 's-Gravenhage.

(¹) The competent authorities and bodies in Greece will be published later.

(*) Corrigendum published in OJ No C 238, 17.9.1981, p.32.

*United Kingdom*

— In England, Scotland and Wales:
The Department of Trade
Certificates of Experience Unit
1 Victoria Street
London SW 1H 0ET.

— In Northern Ireland:
The Department of Commerce
Chichester House
43-47 Chichester Street
Belfast BT 1 4JX.

2. According to the communications from the Member States and pursuant to *Article 9 (3)* of the Directive, the following are the competent authorities and bodies to which applications to pursue in the host Member State an activity referred to in Article 2 and the documents in support thereof must *be submitted.*

*Germany*

Not applicable.

*Belgium*

The Secretary of the Chamber of Trade and Commerce for each province.

*Denmark*

Forsikringsrådet (Insurance Council)
Hammerichsgade 14
DK-1611 København V.

*France*

Ministère de l'économie.

*Ireland*

Insurance (Agents and Brokers)
Certification Committee of Ireland
18 Fitzwilliam Square
Dublin 2.

*Italy*

Ministero dell'Industria
d.g. assicurazioni private e di interesse privato.

*Luxembourg*

Service de contrôle des entreprises d'assurances
3, rue de la Congrégation
Luxembourg.

*Netherlands*

Sociaal-Economische Raad
Afdeling Uitvoering Wet Assurantiebemiddeling
Bezuidenhoutseweg 60
2594 AW 's-Gravenhage.

*United Kingdom*

— In England, Scotland and Wales:
The Department of Trade
Certificates of Experience Unit
1 Victoria Street
London SW 1H 0ET.

— In Northern Ireland:
The Department of Commerce
Chichester House
43-47 Chichester Street
Belfast BT 1 4JX.

3. According to the communication from the Member States and pursuant to the *first paragraph of Article 10 (4)* of the Directive, the following authorities and bodies are competent to *issue* the documents referred to in Article 10 (1) and (2):

*Germany*

The Generalbundesanwalt-Bundeszentralregister in Berlin. Notaries, and consuls within their own district, before whom equivalent declarations on oath may be made.

*Belgium*

The Service du Casier judiciaire central. A declaration on oath made before a notary may constitute proof of no previous bankruptcy.

*Denmark*

— The extract from the judicial record is issued by the chief of police of the district in which the person concerned was born, or, in Copenhagen, by the registry of the City Court,

If the person concerned was born abroad, the extract is issued by the registry of the Copenhagen City Court.

— A solemn declaration made before a notary is sufficient proof that the person concerned has not previously been declared bankrupt.

*France*

Proof of good repute is evidenced by the production of an extract from the judicial record issued as follows:

— for persons born in Paris, by the registry of the Paris Regional Court;

— for persons born in the departments, including the overseas departments, by the registry of the court in the place of birth;

— for persons born in the overseas territories, by the registry of the court or of the justices of the peace having extended jurisdiction in the place of birth or, in cases of emergency or difficulty, by the public prosecutor's office in the place of birth;

— for persons born abroad or who do not possess a valid birth certificate, by the Ministry of Justice (Casier judiciaire central).

*Ireland*

The declaration must be authenticated by a notary.

*Italy*

Ministero dell'Industria
Via Campania 59
Roma.

*Luxembourg*

Service du Casier judiciaire
Rue du Palais de Justice
Luxembourg.

*Netherlands*

— The mayor is the competent authority to issue proof of good repute.

— Proof of no previous bankruptcy may be replaced by a copy, issued by a notary, of a notarial act.

*United Kingdom*

— In England, Scotland and Wales:
Commissioners for oaths, justices of the peace and notaries public;

— In Northern Ireland:
Justices of the peace and, for solemn declarations only, notaries public.

4. According to the communications from the Member States and pursuant to the second paragraph of *Article 10 (4)*, the following are the competent authorities or bodies to which the documents referred to in Article 10 must *be submitted* in support of an application to carry on in the host Member State an activity referred to in Article 2:

*Germany*

Not applicable.

*Belgium*

The Secretary of the Chamber of Trade and Commerce for each province.

*Denmark*

Forsikringsrådet
Hammerichsgade 14
DK-1611 København V.

*France*

Ministère de l'Économie.

*Ireland*

Not applicable.

*Italy*

Ministero dell'Industria
Via Campania 59
Roma.

*Luxembourg*

Tribunal de Commerce
Palais de Justice
Case postale 15
Luxembourg.

*Netherlands*

Sociaal-Economische Raad
Afdeling Uitvoering Wet Assurantiebemiddeling
Bezuidenhoutseweg 60
2594 AW 's-Gravenhage.

*United Kingdom*

The Insurance Brokers Registration Council
15 St Helen's Place
London EC 3A 6DS.

# 14. Hairdressers

Official Journal of the European Communities No L 218/ 27. 7. 82

II

*(Acts whose publication is not obligatory)*

# COUNCIL

## COUNCIL DIRECTIVE
### of 19 July 1982
### laying down measures to facilitate the effective exercise of the right of establishment and freedom to provide services in hairdressing

(82/489/EEC)

THE COUNCIL OF THE EUROPEAN COMMUNITIES,

Having regard to the Treaty establishing the European Economic Community, and in particular Articles 49, 57 and 66 thereof,

Having regard to the proposal from the Commission [1],

Having regard to the opinion of the European Parliament [2],

Having regard to the opinion of the Economic and Social Committee [3],

Whereas, pursuant to the Treaty, all discriminatory treatment based on nationality with regard to establishment and provision of services is prohibited as from the end of the transitional period ; whereas the principle of such treatment based on nationality applies in particular to the grant of any authorization required to practise as a hairdresser and also to the registration with or membership of professional organizations or bodies ;

Whereas it nevertheless seems desirable that certain provisions be introduced to facilitate the effective exercise of the right of establishment and freedom to provide services in hairdressing ;

Whereas conditions of qualification for the taking up or pursuit of the activity of hairdresser are not imposed in all Member States ; whereas some Member States have special provisions making the taking up or pursuit of hairdressing subject to possession of formal qualifications ;

Whereas, it does not appear possible to proceed at this stage with coordination in this matter ; whereas such coordination is, however, an objective which it is desirable to attain as rapidly as possible ;

Whereas, pending such coordination, it is nonetheless desirable and possible to facilitate the mobility of hairdressers within the Community, by recognizing as sufficient qualification for taking up the activities in question in host Member States which have rules governing the taking up of such activities, the fact that the activity has been pursued in a self-employed capacity or as manager of an undertaking in the Member State whence the foreign national comes for a reasonable and sufficiently recent period of time to ensure that the person concerned possesses professional knowledge equivalent to that required in the host Member State ;

Whereas, in so far as in Member States the taking up or pursuit of the activities of hairdressers is also dependent in the case of paid employees on the possession

(1) OJ No C 106, 23. 10. 1971, p. 6.
(2) OJ No C 103, 5. 10. 1972, p. 14.
(3) OJ No C 89, 28. 8. 1972, p. 9.

of professional knowledge and ability, this Directive should also apply to this category of persons in order to remove an obstacle to the free movement of workers and thereby to supplement the measures adopted in Council Regulation (EEC) No 1612/68 of 15 October 1968 on freedom of movement for workers within the Community([1]);

Whereas the activity in question must have been pursued and any vocational training received in the same branch of trade as that in which the beneficiary wishes to establish himself in the host Member State, where the latter imposes this requirement in its own territory,

HAS ADOPTED THIS DIRECTIVE:

*Article 1*

This Directive shall apply, amongst the activities of group ISIC 855, to the activities of hairdressers.

*Article 2*

1. Where in a Member State the taking up or pursuit of the activities referred to in Article 1 is subject to possession of general, commercial and professional knowledge and ability, that Member State shall accept as sufficient evidence of such knowledge and ability the fact that the activities in question have been pursued lawfully in another Member State for any of the following periods:

(a) six consecutive years either in a self-employed capacity or as a person responsible for managing an undertaking; or

(b) three consecutive years either in a self-employed capacity or as a person responsible for managing an undertaking, where the beneficiary can prove that for the occupation in question he has received at least three years' previous training, attested by a certificate recognized by the State, or regarded by a competent professional body as fully satisfying its requirements; or

(c) three consecutive years in a self-employed capacity, where the beneficiary can prove that he has pursued the occupation in question for at least five years in the capacity of employee.

The host Member State, in so far as it lays down different conditions of qualification for the activities of men's and women's hairdressing, may require of nationals of other Member States that the activity in question has been pursued and vocational training received, in the same branch as that in which the beneficiary wishes to establish himself in the host Member State.

2. In the cases referred to in paragraph 1 (a) and (c), pursuit of the activity in question shall not have ceased more than 10 years before the date on which the application provided for in Article 3 is made. Activities in a self-employed capacity or as a person responsible for managing an undertaking as referred to in subparagraphs 1 (a) and (c) must have been pursued after the age of 20.

*Article 3*

Proof that the conditions laid down in Article 2 are satisfied shall be established by a certificate issued by the competent authority or body in the Member State of origin or Member State whence the person concerned comes, which the latter shall submit in support of his application for authorization to pursue the activity or activities in question in the host Member State.

*Article 4*

1. Where a host Member State requires of its own nationals wishing to take up the activities referred to in Article 1 proof of good repute and proof that they have not previously been declared bankrupt, or proof of either one of these, that State shall accept as sufficient evidence, in respect of nationals of other Member States, the production of an extract from the 'judicial record' or, failing this, of an equivalent document issued by a competent judicial or administrative authority in the Member State of origin or the Member State whence the foreign national comes showing that these requirements have been met.

2. Where the country of origin or the country whence the foreign national comes does not issue the document referred to in paragraph 1, furnishing proof of good repute or proof of no previous bankruptcy, such proof may be replaced by a declaration on oath — or, in States where there is no provision for declaration on oath, by a solemn declaration — made by the person concerned before a competent judicial or administrative authority, or where appropriate a notary, in the country of origin or the country whence that person comes; such authority or notary will issue a certificate attesting the authenticity of the declaration on oath or solemn declaration. The declaration in respect of no previous bankruptcy may also be made before a competent professional or trade body in the said country.

([1]) OJ No L 257, 19. 10. 1968, p. 2.

3. Where in the host Member State proof of financial standing is required, that State shall regard certificates issued by banks in other Member States as equivalent to certificates issued in its own territory.

4. Documents issued in accordance with paragraphs 1, 2 and 3 may not be produced more than three months after their date of issue.

*Article 5*

Member States shall, within the time limit laid down in Article 8, designate the authorities and bodies competent to issue or receive the declarations, applications and documents referred to in this Directive and shall forthwith inform the other Member States and the Commission thereof.

*Article 6*

No later than three years after the expiry of the period laid down in Article 8, the Commission shall submit appropriate proposals to the Council for achieving coordinated conditions of training for hairdressers. The Council shall examine these proposals within a year.

*Article 7*

This Directive shall also apply to nationals of Member States who, in accordance with Regulation (EEC) No 1612/68, are pursuing or will pursue as employed persons the activities referred to in Article 1.

*Article 8*

Member States shall bring into force the measures necessary to comply with this Directive within 18 months following its notification and shall forthwith inform the Commission thereof.

*Article 9*

Member States shall communicate to the Commission the texts of the main provisions of national law which they adopt in the field covered by this Directive.

*Article 10*

This Directive is addressed to the Member States.

Done at Brussels, 19 July 1982.

*For the Council*

*The President*

K. OLESEN

# 15. Self-employed commercial agents

15.

Official Journal of the European Communities No L 382/ 31. 12. 86

# COUNCIL DIRECTIVE

## of 18 December 1986

## on the coordination of the laws of the Member States relating to self-employed commercial agents

(86/653/EEC)

THE COUNCIL OF THE EUROPEAN COMMUNITIES,

Having regard to the Treaty establishing the European Economic Community, and in particular Articles 57 (2) and 100 thereof,

Having regard to the proposal from the Commission ([1]),

Having regard to the opinion of the European Parliament ([2]),

Having regard to the opinion of the Economic and Social Committee ([3]),

Whereas the restrictions on the freedom of establishment and the freedom to provide services in respect of activities of intermediaries in commerce, industry and small craft industries were abolished by Directive 64/224/EEC ([4]);

Whereas the differences in national laws concerning commercial representation substantially affect the conditions of competition and the carrying-on of that activity within the Community and are detrimental both to the protection available to commercial agents *vis-à-vis* their principals and to the security of commercial transactions; whereas moreover those differences are such as to inhibit substantially the conclusion and operation of commercial representation contracts where principal and commercial agent are established in different Member States;

Whereas trade in goods between Member States should be carried on under conditions which are similar to those of a single market, and this necessitates approximation of the legal systems of the Member States to the extent required for the proper functioning of the common market; whereas in this regard the rules concerning conflict of laws do not, in the matter of commercial representation, remove the inconsistencies referred to above, nor would they even if they were made uniform, and accordingly the proposed harmonization is necessary notwithstanding the existence of those rules;

Whereas in this regard the legal relationship between commercial agent and principal must be given priority;

Whereas it is appropriate to be guided by the principles of Article 117 of the Treaty and to maintain improvements already made, when harmonizing the laws of the Member States relating to commercial agents;

Whereas additional transitional periods should be allowed for certain Member States which have to make a particular effort to adapt their regulations, especially those concerning indemnity for termination of contract between the principal and the commercial agent, to the requirements of this Directive,

HAS ADOPTED THIS DIRECTIVE:

### CHAPTER I

### Scope

*Article 1*

1. The harmonization measures prescribed by this Directive shall apply to the laws, regulations and administrative provisions of the Member States governing the relations between commercial agents and their principals.

2. For the purposes of this Directive, 'commercial agent' shall mean a self-employed intermediary who has continuing authority to negotiate the sale or the purchase of goods on behalf of another person, hereinafter called the 'principal', or to negotiate and conclude such transactions on behalf of and in the name of that principal.

3. A commercial agent shall be understood within the meaning of this Directive as not including in particular:

— a person who, in his capacity as an officer, is empowered to enter into commitments binding on a company or association,

— a partner who is lawfully authorized to enter into commitments binding on his partners,

([1]) OJ No C 13, 18. 1. 1977, p. 2; OJ No C 56, 2. 3. 1979, p. 5.
([2]) OJ No C 239, 9. 10. 1978, p. 17.
([3]) OJ No C 59, 8. 3. 1978, p. 31.
([4]) OJ No 56, 4. 4. 1964, p. 869/64.

— a receiver, a receiver and manager, a liquidator or a trustee in bankruptcy.

*Article 2*

1. This Directive shall not apply to:

— commercial agents whose activities are unpaid,

— commercial agents when they operate on commodity exchanges or in the commodity market, or

— the body known as the Crown Agents for Overseas Governments and Administrations, as set up under the Crown Agents Act 1979 in the United Kingdom, or its subsidiaries.

2. Each of the Member States shall have the right to provide that the Directive shall not apply to those persons whose activities as commercial agents are considered secondary by the law of that Member State.

CHAPTER II

**Rights and obligations**

*Article 3*

1. In performing has activities a commercial agent must look after his principal's interests and act dutifully and in good faith.

2. In particular, a commercial agent must:

(a) make proper efforts to negotiate and, where appropriate, conclude the transactions he is instructed to take care of;

(b) communicate to his principal all the necessary information available to him;

(c) comply with reasonable instructions given by his principal.

*Article 4*

1. In his relations with his commercial agent a principal must act dutifully and in good faith.

2. A principal must in particular:

(a) provide his commercial agent with the necessary documentation relating to the goods concerned;

(b) obtain for his commercial agent the information necessary for the performance of the agency contract, and in particular notify the commercial agent within a reasonable period once he anticipates that the volume of commercial transactions will be significantly lower than that which the commercial agent could normally have expected.

3. A principal must, in addition, inform the commercial agent within a reasonable period of his acceptance, refusal, and of any non-execution of a commercial transaction which the commercial agent has procured for the principal.

*Article 5*

The parties may not derogate from the provisions of Articles 3 and 4.

CHAPTER III

**Remuneration**

*Article 6*

1. In the absence of any agreement on this matter between the parties, and without prejudice to the application of the compulsory provisions of the Member States concerning the level of remuneration, a commercial agent shall be entitled to the remuneration that commercial agents appointed for the goods forming the subject of his agency contract are customarily allowed in the place where he carries on his activities. If there is no such customary practice a commercial agent shall be entitled to reasonable remuneration taking into account all the aspects of the transaction.

2. Any part of the remuneration which varies with the number or value of business transactions shall be deemed to be commission within the meaning of this Directive.

3. Articles 7 to 12 shall not apply if the commercial agent is not remunerated wholly or in part by commission.

*Article 7*

1. A commercial agent shall be entitled to commission on commercial transactions concluded during the period covered by the agency contract:

(a) where the transaction has been concluded as a result of his action; or

(b) where the transaction is concluded with a third party whom he has previously acquired as a customer for transactions of the same kind.

2. A commercial agent shall also be entitled to commission on transactions concluded during the period covered by the agency contract:

— either where he is entrusted with a specific geographical area or group of customers,

— or where he has an exclusive right to a specific geographical area or group of customers,

and where the transaction has been entered into with a customer belonging to that area or group.

Member States shall include in their legislation one of the possibilities referred to in the above two indents.

*Article 8*

A commercial agent shall be entitled to commission on commercial transactions concluded after the agency contract has terminated:

(a) if the transaction is mainly attributable to the commercial agent's efforts during the period covered by the agency contract and if the transaction was entered into within a reasonable period after that contract terminated; or

(b) if, in accordance with the conditions mentioned in Article 7, the order of the third party reached the principal or the commercial agent before the agency contract terminated.

*Article 9*

A commercial agent shall not be entitled to the commission referred to in Article 7, if that commission is payable, pursuant to Article 8, to the previous commercial agent, unless it is equitable because of the circumstances for the commission to be shared between the commercial agents.

*Article 10*

1. The commission shall become due as soon as and to the extent that one of the following circumstances obtains:

(a) the principal has executed the transaction; or

(b) the principal should, according to his agreement with the third party, have executed the transaction; or

(c) the third party has executed the transaction.

2. The commission shall become due at the latest when the third party has executed his part of the transaction or should have done so if the principal had executed his part of the transaction, as he should have.

3. The commission shall be paid not later than on the last day of the month following the quarter in which it became due.

4. Agreements to derogate from paragraphs 2 and 3 to the detriment of the commercial agent shall not be permitted.

*Article 11*

1. The right to commission can be extinguished only if and to the extent that:

— it is established that the contract between the third party and the principal will not be executed, and

— that face is due to a reason for which the principal is not to blame.

2. Any commission which the commercial agent has already received shall be refunded if the right to it is extinguished.

3. Agreements to derogate from paragraph 1 to the detriment of the commercial agent shall not be permitted.

*Article 12*

1. The principal shall supply his commercial agent with a statement of the commission due, not later than the last day of the month following the quarter in which the commission has become due. This statement shall set out the main components used in calculating the amount of commission.

2. A commercial agent shall be entitled to demand that he be provided with all the information, and in particular an extract from the books, which is available to his principal and which he needs in order to check the amount of the commission due to him.

3. Agreements to derogate from paragraphs 1 and 2 to the detriment of the commercial agent shall not be permitted.

4. This Directive shall not conflict with the internal provisions of Member States which recognize the right of a commercial agent to inspect a principal's books.

CHAPTER IV

## Conclusion and termination of the agency contract

*Article 13*

1. Each party shall be entitled to receive from the other on request a signed written document setting out the terms of the agency contract including any terms subsequently agreed. Waiver of this right shall not be permitted.

2. Notwithstanding paragraph 1 a Member State may provide that an agency contract shall not be valid unless evidenced in writing.

*Article 14*

An agency contract for a fixed period which continues to be performed by both parties after that period has expired shall be deemed to be converted into an agency contract for an indefinite period.

*Article 15*

1. Where an agency contract is concluded for an indefinite period either party may terminate it by notice.

2. The period of notice shall be one month for the first year of the contract, two months for the second year commenced, and three months for the third year commenced and subsequent years. The parties may not agree on shorter periods of notice.

3. Member States may fix the period of notice at four months for the fourth year of the contract, five months for the fifth year and six months for the sixth and subsequent years. They may decide that the parties may not agree to shorter periods.

4. If the parties agree on longer periods than those laid down in paragraphs 2 and 3, the period of notice to be observed by the principal must not be shorter than that to be observed by the commercial agent.

5. Unless otherwise agreed by the parties, the end of the period of notice must coincide with the end of a calendar month.

6. The provisions of this Article shall apply to an agency contract for a fixed period where it is converted under Article 14 into an agency contract for an indefinite period, subject to the proviso that the earlier fixed period must be taken into account in the calculation of the period of notice.

*Article 16*

Nothing in this Directive shall affect the application of the law of the Member States where the latter provides for the immediate termination of the agency contract:

(a) because of the failure of one party to carry out all or part of his obligations;

(b) where exceptional circumstances arise.

*Article 17*

1. Member States shall take the measures necessary to ensure that the commercial agent is, after termination of the agency contract, indemnified in accordance with paragraph 2 or compensated for damage in accordance with paragraph 3.

2. (a) The commercial agent shall be entitled to an indemnity if and to the extent that:

— he has brought the principal new customers or has significantly increased the volume of business with existing customers and the principal continues to derive substantial benefits from the business with such customers, and

— the payment of this indemnity is equitable having regard to all the circumstances and, in particular, the commission lost by the commercial agent on the business transacted with such customers. Member States may provide for such circumstances also to include the application or otherwise of a restraint of trade clause, within the meaning of Article 20;

(b) The amount of the indemnity may not exceed a figure equivalent to an indemnity for one year calculated from the commercial agent's average annual remuneration over the preceding five years and if the contract goes back less than five years the indemnity shall be calculated on the average for the period in question;

(c) The grant of such an indemnity shall not prevent the commercial agent from seeking damages.

3. The commercial agent shall be entitled to compensation for the damage he suffers as a result of the termination of his relations with the principal.

Such damage shall be deemed to occur particularly when the termination takes place in circumstances:

— depriving the commercial agent of the commission which proper performance of the agency contract would have procured him whilst providing the principal with substantial benefits linked to the commercial agent's activities,

— and/or which have not enabled the commercial agent to amortize the costs and expenses that he had incurred for the performance of the agency contract on the principal's advice.

4. Entitlement to the indemnity as provided for in paragraph 2 or to compensation for damage as provided for under paragraph 3, shall also arise where the agency contract is terminated as a result of the commercial agent's death.

5. The commercial agent shall lose his entitlement to the indemnity in the instances provided for in paragraph 2 or to compensation for damage in the instances provided for in paragraph 3, if within one year following termination of the contract he has not notified the principal that he intends pursuing his entitlement.

6. The Commission shall submit to the Council, within eight years following the date of notification of this Directive, a report on the implementation of this Article, and shall if necessary submit to it proposals for amendments.

*Article 18*

The indemnity or compensation referred to in Article 17 shall not be payable:

(a) where the principal has terminated the agency contract because of default attributable to the commercial agent which would justify immediate termination of the agency contract under national law;

(b) where the commercial agent has terminated the agency contract, unless such termination is justified by circumstances attributable to the principal or on grounds of age, infirmity or illness of the commercial agent in consequence of which he cannot reasonably be required to continue his activities;

(c) where, with the agreement of the principal, the commercial agent assigns his rights and duties under the agency contract to another person.

*Article 19*

The parties may not derogate from Articles 17 and 18 to the detriment of the commercial agent before the agency contract expires.

*Article 20*

1. For the purposes of this Directive, an agreement restricting the business activities of a commercial agent following termination of the agency contract is hereinafter referred to as a restraint of trade clause.

2. A restraint of trade clause shall be valid only if and to the extent that:

(a) it is concluded in writing; and

(b) it relates to the geographical area or the group of customers and the geographical area entrusted to the commercial agent and to the kind of goods covered by his agency under the contract.

3. A restraint of trade clause shall be valid for not more than two years after termination of the agency contract.

4. This Article shall not affect provisions of national law which impose other restrictions on the validity or enforceability of restraint of trade clauses or which enable the courts to reduce the obligations on the parties resulting from such an agreement.

CHAPTER V

## General and final provisions

*Article 21*

Nothing in this Directive shall require a Member State to provide for the disclosure of information where such disclosure would be contrary to public policy.

*Article 22*

1. Member States shall bring into force the provisions necessary to comply with this Directive before 1 January 1990. They shall forthwith inform the Commission thereof. Such provisions shall apply at least to contracts concluded after their entry into force. They shall apply to contracts in operation by 1 January 1994 at the latest.

2. As from the notification of this Directive, Member States shall communicate to the Commission the main laws, regulations and administrative provisions which they adopt in the field governed by this Directive.

3. However, with regard to Ireland and the United Kingdom, 1 January 1990 referred to in paragraph 1 shall be replaced by 1 January 1994.

With regard to Italy, 1 January 1990 shall be replaced by 1 January 1993 in the case of the obligations deriving from Article 17.

*Article 23*

This Directive is addressed to the Member States.

Done at Brussels, 18 December 1986.

*For the Council*

*The President*

M. JOPLING

# LIST OF JUDGMENTS BY THE COURT OF JUSTICE ON THE RIGHT OF ESTABLISHMENT AND FREEDOM TO PROVIDE SERVICES

- 15.7.1964 (Costa v. Enel 6/64), ECR 1964, p.585; direct applicability of Article 53 EEC; prohibition on the introduction of new restrictions.
- 21.6.1974 (Reyners 2/74), ECR 1974, p.631; direct applicability of Article 52 EEC; Article 55, direct and specific connection with the exercise of official authority; lawyers.
- 12.12.1974 (Van Binsbergen 33/74), ECR 1974, p.1299; direct applicability of Article 59; applications of rules justified by the general good.
- 3.12.1974 (Walrave 36/74), ECR 1974, p.1405; application of Community law to the practice of sport; extension of the scope of Article 59 to cover acts not emanating from public authorities.
- 26.11.1975 (Coenen 39/75), ECR 1975, p.1547; requirement of residence in the host country.
- 28.4.1977 (Thieffry 71/76), ECR 1977, p.765; disguised discrimination; lawyers.
- 28.6.1977 (Patrick 11/77), ECR 1977, p.1199; equivalence of diplomas; architects.
- 24.10.1978 (Koestler 15/78), ECR 1978, p.1971; forward stock exchange transactions; concept of services; provision of services by a person established in a Member State other than that of the person for whom the services are intended.
- 18.1.1979 (Van Wesemael 110/111/78), ECR 1979, p.35; fee-charging employment agencies for entertainers; comparability of legislation between the Member State in which the person providing services is established and the State in which the service is provided.
- 7.2.1979 (Knoors 115/78), ECR 1979, p.399; transactional measures Directive; application to nationals of the host country.
- 7.2.1979 (Auer 136/78), ECR 1979, p.437; non-application of Article 52 to nationals of the host country; reverse discrimination.
- 25.10.1979 (Commission v. Italy 159/78), ECR 1979, p.3247; customs agents.
- 6.10.1981 (Broekmeulen 246/80), ECR 1981, p.2311; doctors.
- 18.3.1980 (Debauve 52/79), ECR 1980, p.833; transmission of signals by cable diffusion of television; application of national legislation prohibiting advertisements.
- 18.3.1980 (Coditel 62/79), ECR 1980, p.881; application of national laws on the protection of copyrights.
- 17.12.1981 (Webb 279/80), ECR 1981, p.3305; undertaking hiring out staff; restrictions justified by the general good.
- 3.2.1982 (Seco 62 and 63/81), ECR 1982, p.223; social security contributions.
- 10.2.1982 (Transporoute 76/81), ECR 1982, p.417; public works contracts Directive (71/305).
- 15.12.1982 (Commission v. Netherlands 160/82), ECR 1982, p.4637; failure to transpose Directive 73/239 on direct insurance.
- 1.3.1983 (Commission v. Italy and Belgium 300/81 and 301/81), ECR 1983, p.449; failure to transpose Directive 77/780 on banking.
- 22.9.1983 (Auer 271/82), ECR 1983, p.2727; consequences of failure to transpose the Directives on veterinary surgeons.

- 15.12.1983 (Rienks 5/83), ECR 1983, p.4233; consequences of failure to transpose the Directives on veterinary surgeons.
- 31.1.1984 (Luisi and Carbone 286/82 and 26/83), ECR 1984, p.377; tourists; recipients of services.
- 12.7.1984 (Klopp 107/83), ECR 1984, p.2971; right of establishment for lawyers; more than one place of work.
- 18.9.1984 (Commission v. Italy 221/83), ECR 1984, p.3249; failure to implement Directive 78/1026 (veterinary surgeons) and incomplete implementation of Directive 78/1027 (veterinary surgeons).
- 6.11.1984 (Fearon 182/83), ECR 1984, p.3677; Member States' right to establish a system of compulsary land acquisition by public bodies, even vis-à-vis non-resident nationals of other Member States.
- 13.2.1985 (Gravier 293/83), ECR 1985, p.593; acces to voccational training (foreign student's fee).
- 28.3.1985 (Commission v. Italy 274/83), ECR 1985, p.873; infringement of the public works contracts Directive (71/305).
- 22.4.1985 (European Parliament v. Council 13/83), ECR 1985, p.1513; failure to act with regard to a common transport policy.
- 18.6.1985 (Steinhauser 197/84), ECR 1985, p.1819; renting of commercial premises.
- 11.12.1985 (Hillegom v. Hillenius 110/84); interpretation of the Directive on banking (77/780); professional secrecy. Not yet published in the Court Repports.
- 28.1.1986 (Commission v. France 270/83); freedom of establishment for insurance companies; company taxes and taxable assets. Not yet published in the Court Reports.
- 30.4.1986 (Commission v. France 96/85); more than one place of work, doctors, dentists; infringement of Articles 48, 52 and 59. Not yet published in the Court Reports.
- 12.6.1986 (Bertini and others 98/85, 162/85 en 258/85); restrictions on admission to medical faculties. Not yet published in the Court Reports.
- 10.7.1986 (Segers 79/85); discrimination between workers according to whether they are employed by a company constituted under national law or one constituted under the law of another Member State. Indirect discrimination. Not yet published in the Court Reports.
- 15.10.1986 (Commission v. Italy 168/85); acces to certain activities (activities associated with tourism, journalism, pharmacy); condition of reciprocity or nationality. Not yet published in the Court Reports.
- 4.12.1986 (Commission v. France 252/83; Commission v. FRG 205/84; Commission v. Ireland 206/84); insurance, co-insurance. Not yet published in the Court Reports.
- 12.2.1987 (Commission v. Belgium 306/84); failure to implement the Directives on doctors (75/362 and 75/363. Not yet published in the Court Reports.
- 12.2.1987 (Commission v. Belgium 221/85); health insurance reimbursement for clinical biology services; rejection. Not yet published in the Court Reports.
- 10.3.1987 (Commission v. Italy 199/85); infringement of the public works contracts Directive (71/305); failure to publish a notice in the Official Journal of the European Communities. Not yet published in the Court Reports.
- 9.7.1987 (CEI and others v. Fonds des Routes and others 27, 28 and 29/86); interpretation of the public works contracts Directive (71/305); conditions for access, economic and financial strength of tenderers. Not yet published in the Court Reports.
- 15.10.1987 (Heylens 222/86); equivalence of diplomas; sports trainer. Not yet published in the Court Reports.

# LIST OF DIRECTIVES ON THE RECOGNITION OF QUALIFICATIONS BASED ON WORK EXPERIENCE

| | |
|---|---|
| *Wholesale trade and intermediaries in commerce, industry and small craft industries* | |
| Directive laying down detailed provisions concerning transitional measures in respect of activities in wholesale trade and activities of intermediaries in commerce, industry and small craft industries | Directive 64/222/EEC of 25 February 1964 (OJ 56, 4.4.1964) |
| *Industry and small craft industries* | |
| Directive laying down detailed provisions concerning transitional measures in respect of activities of self-employed persons in manufacturing and processing industries falling within ISIC Major Groups 23-40 (industry and small craft industries)<br>Amended by Directive 69/77/EEC of 4 March 1969 (OJ L 59, 10.3.1969). | Directive 64/427/EEC of 7 July 1964 (OJ 117, 23.7.1964) |
| *Retail trade* | |
| Directive laying down detailed provisions concerning transitional measures in respect of activities of self-employed persons in retail trade (ISIC ex Group 612) | Directive 68/364/EEC of 15 October 1968 (OJ L 260, 22.10.1968) |
| *Personal service* | |
| Directive laying down detailed provisions concerning transitional measures in respect of activities of self-employed persons in the personal services sector (ISIC ex Major Group 85):<br>1. Restaurants, cafes, taverns and other drinking and eating places (ISIC Group 852);<br>2. Hotel, rooming houses, camps and other lodging places (ISIC Group 853) | Directive 68/368/EEC of 15 October 1968 (OJ L 260, 22.10.1968) |
| *Food manufacturing and beverage industries* | |
| Directive laying down detailed provisions concerning transitional measures in respect of activities of self-employed persons in the food manufacturing and beverage industries (ISIC Major Groups 20 and 21) | Directive 68/366/EEC of 15 October 1968 (OJ L 260, 22.10.1968) |
| *Wholesale coal trade* | |
| Directive laying down detailed provisions concerning transitional measures in respect of activities of self-employed persons in the wholesale coal trade and in respect of activities of intermediaries in the coal trade (ISIC ex Group 6112) | Directive 70/523/EEC of 30 November 1970 (OJ L 267, 10.12.1970) |

*Various activities*

| | |
|---|---|
| Directive on measures to facilitate the effective exercise of freedom of establishment and freedom to provide services in respect of various activities (ex ISIC Divisions 0.1 to 85) and, in particular, transitional measures in respect of those activities | Directive 75/368/EEC of 16 June 1975 (OJ L 167, 30.6.1975) |

*Itinerant activities*

| | |
|---|---|
| Directive on measures to facilitate the effective exercise of freedom of establishment and freedom to provide services in respect of itinerant activities and, in particular, transitional measures in respect of those activities | Directive 75/369/EEC of 16 June 1975 (OJ L 167, 30.6.1975) |

*Insurance agents and brokers*

| | |
|---|---|
| Directive on measures to facilitate the effective exercise of freedom of establishment and freedom to provide services in respect of insurance agents and brokers (ex ISIC Group 630) and, in particular, transitional measures in respect of those activities | Directive 77/92/EEC of 13 December 1976 (OJ L 26, 31.1.1977) |

*Services incidental to transport*

| | |
|---|---|
| Directive on measures to facilitate the effective exercise of freedom of establishment and freedom to provide services in respect of activities of self-employed persons in certain services incidental to transport and travel agencies (ISIC Group 718) and in storage and warehousing (ISIC Group 720) | Directive 82/470/EEC of 29 June 1982 (OJ L 213, 21.7.1982) |

*Hairdressing*

| | |
|---|---|
| Directive laying down measures to facilitate the effective exercise of the right of establishment and freedom to provide services in hairdressing | Directive 82/489/EEC of 19 July 1982 (OJ L 218, 27.7.1982) |

# LIST OF ADVISORY COMMITTEES ON TRAINING

- Advisory Committee on Medical Training (established by Council Decision 75/364/EEC of 16 June 1975 – OJ No L 167, 30.6.1975).
- Advisory Committee on Training in Nursing (established by Council Decision 77/454/EEC of 27 June 1977 – OJ No L 176, 15.7.1977).
- Advisory Committee on the Training of Dental Practitioners (established by Council Decision 78/688/EEC of 25 July 1978 – OJ No L 233, 21.8.1978).
- Advisory Committee on Veterinary Training (established by Council Decision 78/1028/EEC of 18 December 1978 – OJ No L 362, 23.12.1978).
- Advisory Committee on the Training of Midwives (established by Council Decision 80/156/EEC of 21 January 1980 – OJ No L 33, 11.2.1980).
- Advisory Committee on Education and Training in the field of Architecture (established by Council Decision 85/385/EEC of 10 June 1985 – OJ No L 223, 21.8.1985).
- Advisory Committee on Pharmaceutical Training (established by Council Decision 85/434/EEC of 16 September 1985 – OJ No L 253, 24.9.1985).